How We Became Human

The Library of Object Relations
Series Editors: David E. Scharff and Jill Savege Scharff

The Library of Object Relations provides an expanding body of theory for understanding individual development and pathology, human interaction, and new avenues of treatment. They apply to realms of experience from the internal world of the individual to the human community, from the clinical situation to everyday life, and from individual psychoanalysis and psychotherapy, to group therapy, couple and family therapy, and to social policy.

Titles in the Series

The Autonomous Self: The Work of John D. Sutherland, edited by Jill Savege Scharff

From Instinct to Self, Volumes I & II: Selected Papers of W. R. D. Fairbairn, edited by David E. Scharff and Ellinor Fairbairn Birtles

Refinding the Object and Reclaiming the Self, by David E. Scharff

Projective and Introjective Identification and the Use of the Therapist's Self, by Jill Savege Scharff

Object Relations Family Therapy, by David E. Scharff and Jill Savege Scharff

How We Became Human

A Challenge to Psychoanalysis

Julio Moreno

ROWMAN & LITTLEFIELD
Lanham • Boulder • New York • Toronto • Plymouth, UK

Translated by Judith Filc

Originally published in Spanish as *Ser humano: la inconsistencia, los vínculos, la crianza*, 2002. This English edition is published with the permission of Libros del Zorzal de Malkok.

Published by Rowman & Littlefield
4501 Forbes Boulevard, Suite 200, Lanham, Maryland 20706
www.rowman.com

10 Thornbury Road, Plymouth PL6 7PP, United Kingdom

British Library Cataloguing in Publication Information Available

Library of Congress Cataloging-in-Publication Data

Moreno, Julio, 1944- author.
[Ser humano. English]
How we became human : a challenge to psychoanalysis / by Julio Moreno ; translated by Judith Filc.
p. ; cm. -- (Library of object relations)
Translation of: Ser humano.
Includes bibliographical references and index.
ISBN 978-1-4422-2885-6 (cloth : alk. paper) -- ISBN 978-1-4422-2886-3 (electronic)
I. Title. II. Series: Library of object relations.
[DNLM: 1. Anthropology. 2. Psychoanalytic Interpretation. 3. Child Psychology. 4. Psychoanalysis. WM 460.7]
RC504
616.89'17--dc23
2013046441

♾ ™ The paper used in this publication meets the minimum requirements of American National Standard for Information Sciences Permanence of Paper for Printed Library Materials, ANSI/NISO Z39.48-1992.

Printed in the United States of America

Contents

Acknowledgments

I would like to note that this first English edition has been possible thanks to the critical help I received from Rowman & Littlefield, from Associate Acquisitions Editor Amy King, and especially from the editors of the series, David and Jill Scharff. In addition, I would like to thank Judith Filc for her excellent translating and editing work (more than once I found that her translation was clearer and more precise than the original). I am also grateful to my wife, Virginia Ungar, and my sons, Nicolás and Manuel, who supported me during the writing of this book and the vicissitudes of the English publication. My gratitude goes to them and to many others whose names I am not including here.

Preface

Like everything else, this book starts with a story that, like all stories, is, to some extent, a fabrication. I would like to tell it and, in the telling, express my gratitude to some of those who have supported me over the years.

I grew up in the provinces. When I came to the capital city to study at Buenos Aires University (UBA), I enrolled in two programs—psychology and medicine.[1]

Back then I believed that this twofold interest would lead me toward a kind of unifying plan forged in my mind. Today I think it had to do with my ambivalence between the humanities and the sciences, which I still feel and whose traces can be easily detected in this book.

After two years of this dual focus, I dropped out of the school of psychology, probably because in medical school I met my first mentor, Hersch Gerschenfeld. Gerschenfeld allowed me to work in his prestigious neurophysiology lab, along with Enrico Steffani and Dante Chiarandini. I spent three happy and highly productive years there until the advent of the "night of long sticks," when the military brutally attacked student demonstrations and provoked a wave of emigration of intellectuals. Gerschenfeld, Steffani, and Chiarandini left the country. I was in my next-to-last year of medical school and had already decided I wanted to be a researcher.

As soon as I graduated I became a fellow at Argentina's Scientific and Technological Research Council (CONICET), where I conducted research in the fields of physiology and biophysics under Marcelino Cereijido's direction. Cereijido was my dissertation advisor, and he trained and supported me for three memorable years. Psychology had apparently been set aside; science had triumphed.

In 1970 I received a fellowship from the NIH and started working with Jared Diamond. Diamond's intelligence and interests left an indelible mark in me. Back then he was a physiology professor at UCLA and a well-known naturalist. After four years of intense and fruitful work in the basic sciences under Diamond's environmentalist influence, I went back to Argentina as a CONICET researcher. I had published a good number of papers in renowned scientific journals, and the doors of many international research centers were apparently open for me.

We do not know why it is that at certain moments in our lives we decide to change course. I have been able to find some explanations—difficult years, my old vocation, a glimpse of the decline of scientific romanticism. Yet I still do not know why I made a crucial shift in my career; shortly after my return from the United States I started a residency in psychopathology at Lanús Hospital, in Greater Buenos Aires. Not long after that I began my psychoanalytic training.

Nonetheless, two distinct influences continued to shape my training, namely, basic sciences on the one hand, and psychiatry, psychoanalysis, and the knowledge of the soul on the other. These pages perhaps illustrate my efforts (of which I have recently become aware) to reach rather than a synthesis, a work in parallel—a productive counterpoint between my biophysics and neurobiology training, and my analytic practice. I believe this book is a testament to such efforts.

NOTE

1. In Argentina, medicine is a six-year undergraduate degree. (T.N.)

Chapter One

Human-ness

WHAT IS HUMAN ABOUT HUMANS?

Against all appearances, this is not a trivial question. To begin with, any answer we might attempt should consider the hominid *Homo sapiens*. *Homo sapiens* is just another animal species that appeared around 200,000 years ago in Africa but, at the same time, it is the unprecedentedly transformed species that has been relentlessly creating an ever-changing culture for the past 40,000 years and is changing the planet.[1]

We should divide the question into two. What is animal about humans? And, what is human about humans? The first one seems simpler. Our animalness probably renders us similar to all other animals, particularly to our closest relatives, the extinct hominids and to the primates that are still living (orangutans, gorillas, chimpanzees, and gibbons). Lately, however, students of animal behavior are increasingly claiming that much of what we call human about humans is actually part of our animal features; that we are animals to a much larger extent than we believe we are.

The typical approach to the second question (what is human about humans?) tends to highlight that the difference between us and the other living beings is an attribute—soul, intelligence, language, divine grace, and so on—that is only present in humans and renders us superior. Two aspects coexist in human beings that have always been conceived of in conjunction, namely, an organic life (the "animal within," the nude life), and a soul (a *logos*, a divine element). Although perhaps, following Agamben (2002), we should think of human beings precisely as the result of the disconnection between the two.

Based in part on this line of thought, this chapter discusses human-ness starting from the following hypothesis: what is human about humans is a failure of their animalness. Such failure has allowed our species to change its

1

habits constantly, to expand and "progress" endlessly beyond any form of homeostatic balance. Humans, therefore, do not fulfill a requirement that is essential for Darwin's laws (which have regulated life in our planet for billions of years) to work, namely, that each species only displays what is determined by its genomic or hereditary potential. Since this is a complex matter, we should go step by step.

HUMAN-NESS AND ANIMALNESS

If we called what is human in humans (what is present in us that monkeys will never achieve) "U" and what is animal in us "A," we might say that humans ("H") are the result of the sum of A and U (H=A+U). Undoubtedly, complex interactions must exist between this A and this U that cannot be represented by a simple addition. Moreover, the very existence of A and U is but the effect both of envisaging their difference and of a certain disconnection between them. This has been pointed out, in a way, by those who consider that human beings are the only animals capable of envisioning and getting to know themselves (Linnaeus, 1735; Hofstadter, 2007).

Even so, it might be valid to think that (persisting) animalness converges in humans with something different. This duality (thinking of something as the conjunction of, or difference between, two elements) is a fairly typical approach to baffling issues. Perhaps for this reason the boundary between A and U has been the cause of great debate. Generally speaking, some state that humans are basically A with greater neuronal complexity, while others assert that humans are fully U with some instinctive vestige that does not concern their being. Humans emerge, in my view, from this very difference.

WHAT IS ANIMAL IN HUMANS

Our close kinship with the other animals is so evident that it is quite intriguing that it took us so long to learn that we "descend" from them. From the simple fact of our material composition to our remarkable anatomical similarity with primates (have you ever seen an orangutan baby?) and the astonishing correspondences between so many different behaviors, everything points to a very close relationship. This relationship, however, remained concealed from our understanding for thousands of years. If there had been any doubt about our kinship, recent comparative nuclear and mitochondrial DNA studies have dispelled it. More than 98 percent of our genome (about 30,000 genes that determine our hereditary traits) is identical to that of chimpanzees, and more than 99.5 percent to that of our Neanderthal cousins.[2] With regard to genes, the indisputable determinants of our animalness, we are much more similar to primates and to the other hominids than we had ever believed.

The general theory or, if you will, the ideology that may be found in many of the works of socioethologists contends that contrary to what we think, we have not become independent from the laws of natural selection. Rather, the validity of Darwin's laws and/or the prevalence of simple forms that condition animal life can be shown in many if not all of our attitudes (Fodor and Piatelli-Palmarini, 2010). We can detect features that have always been considered human in gibbons, seagulls, dolphins, chimpanzees, and macaques. The evolutionists' insistent claim is, "Why do we resort to the non-animal aspects of humans to explain these features?"

Neither is it surprising that these ideas have clashed with—or at least seem to oppose—some psychoanalytic postulates on this matter that state that these very features, exclusive to humans, are irreducible to any form of animalness. Psychoanalysts thus take the Church's position in this controversy, albeit from a different perspective: what ethologists think of as A corresponds to a great extent, if not fully, to U. Ethologists and psychoanalysts see their ability to reconcile their views reduced by a not-at-all trivial fact. They both have a very particular interest in a specific aspect of human life—sexuality. The latter imposed itself upon Freud as incontrovertible evidence. Behind every conflict, every symptom, every thought Freud found unconscious motivations tied to it. Yet sexuality is also of great interest to ethologists since, as they claim, natural selection, a key step in the evolution of sexed living beings, operates above all in the field of sexual behavior. Not in the species vs. species game (either I kill you or you kill me), but in the game of what sexual feature makes it more likely that I will choose or be chosen so that my genes have a better chance of being transmitted than those of my peers.

For instance, evolutionists claim that humans have a sexual tendency that lies halfway between the strict monogamy of gibbons and the unabashed polygamy of chimpanzees. Naturally, this placement between hairy cousins makes psychoanalysts nervous—just as it makes biologists nervous to read entire books on the topic that do not mention the word gene. Yet evolutionists have their reasons. It is logical, they say, for human males to be adulterous and for females to demand faithfulness. From a Darwinian perspective, the only important thing is that genes survive. For this purpose, the technique of fertilizing and fleeing (that is, being unfaithful and a Don Juan) works for human males, who have a huge number of sperm cells, but not for females. The latter require assistance for the gestation and breeding of their single monthly egg, thence their preference for powerful males and their demand for faithfulness. At the same time, if men like females with generous breasts, wide, fleshy hips, maternal attitude, and angelic faces, it is because these are signs that the chosen mate will be a good, fertile mother; that she will take better care of the male's genes. If, in turn, women like strong, powerful males it is because, besides providing good genes for their children, these males can best take care of them and of their brood in the hard times awaiting them.

The problem is that psychoanalysts believe that these very signs show and even demonstrate the validity of the Oedipus complex. Men seek traces of their idealized mothers (breasts, hips, look) in every woman because they were marked by their childhood experiences with their first love—their mother. And in a more complex fashion that also ultimately refers to their Oedipus complex, women want to be loved and protected by a powerful, strong man who recalls the potent father they either had or imagined they had. In this way, by clinging to the power of the Freudian discovery of the unconscious determination of psychic acts, many psychoanalysts dismiss socioethologists' findings. At the same time, in the fervor provoked by verifying the validity of their discoveries, ethologists tend to believe that they have revealed the secret key to human-ness.

I think that ethology's incredibly interesting findings indeed show how much more animal we are than we believe we are, but say very little about why humans are human. Its conclusions about humans' animalness serve well to explain generalities expressed in statistical trends (men commit adultery and murder much more frequently than women; men are more likely to prefer beautiful women, and women, powerful men) but do not account for humans' uniqueness. Psychoanalysis, instead, specializes in singularities, but it ought to be said that it is not very good at postulating generalities or producing forecasts. I believe that both approaches are wrong in their extreme forms. It is not possible to reduce humans' exceptionality to instinctive formulae inscribed in genetic maps, as some biologists would like. Nonetheless, it is equally true that neither the Oedipus complex nor the human *logos* explains everything we are or captures every sense of the animal that inhabits us. Human-ness is such only in so far as it operates on a foundation that has supported living beings' behavior for some three billion years with broadly recurring patterns.

Like the detours that may be imposed upon the course of a river, what is human in humans can significantly change the flow of the current of our animal nature but cannot reverse its general direction. The list of undeniable genetic features of human behavior speaks of humans' animal or mechanical aspect, not of their human-ness. I would bet that *Homo neanderthalensis*, and even *Homo erectus*, very much resembled the animal aspect of humans but not what I am calling here what is human in humans which, even so, must have had these species' animalness as a condition for its emergence.

HOW HUMAN ARE ANIMALS?

Students of animal behavior have made progress on this issue by showing not only how animal humans are, but also how human animals are (another form of serious anthropomorphism in which we constantly engage). The favored ones in these studies are chimpanzees, but macaques, dolphins, and even certain birds are showcased as well. The idea is to demonstrate that many of the qualities that have always been considered human, such as political skills, Machiavellianism, intelligence, and the use and recognition of symbols when communicating complex messages are present in animals. Monkeys like Kanzi (Savage-Rumbaugh et al., 1998) became famous for learning how to add and how to recognize tens of symbols and use them to communicate with their patient researchers while in captivity. It is well known that chimpanzees and macaques are capable of discovering the use of rudimentary "tools" like sticks, stones, and straws, and of propagating their knowledge in their communities through imitation.

With regard to the topic we are discussing here, however, these findings lead us to a paradox. The more we demonstrate that animals have qualities erstwhile believed to be only human and the more similarities we find between us and our living and extinct cousins, the greater the power of the question of why, if animals have the capabilities described above, they did not develop any of these capabilities during millions of years of existence. Given their potential access to a system of signs and their intelligence, why couldn't primates change their way of life in ten million years while we are about to make the planet explode after only 40,000? What is strictly human about humans? Why, if we are so similar, have we become so different? The enigmatic leap taken by our species 40,000 years ago is not easy to elucidate.

Many answers have been attempted that have led to concepts such as soul, superior intelligence, divine grace, self-awareness, syntax, brain complexity, brain mutation, articulate language, and mirror neurons. All these answers, it ought to be said, agree on one fact that appears to be obvious only if we address this issue from the perspective of our superiority complex. The attribute that makes us different is one that humans have and animals lack. We cannot even imagine that it could be the other way around—that humans might lack an attribute that animals possessed. The persistent, untenable notion underlying this viewpoint is that we constitute the pinnacle of evolution toward which all living forms should unquestionably tend.

WHAT IS HUMAN ABOUT HUMANS

Our ability to ceaselessly introduce novelties—and their accumulation and "progress" (the reader will understand the quotation marks) within an informational pool that we broadly call *culture*—is what differentiates us from every other living species. I will hence suggest an alternative to the ideas previously discussed. We should start from the following hypothesis: What is specific about humans is their ability to vary. Culture, which regulates the relationship between humans and their surroundings and sanctions what we call reality in each case, is continually evolving across time and space. So much so that in order to know what we are talking about when we say "culture" we must qualify it with the name of the region and the approximate date we are discussing.

Jared Diamond (1992) illustrates this fact as follows. If somebody showed us chopsticks to eat with, a Guinness beer, and a bow and arrow and asked us to associate these objects with Ireland, Borneo, or China, we would have no trouble giving the right answer. Neither would it be hard to decide which of the following human objects is older than the others: an arrow, a blunderbuss, or a missile. Human-ness is characterized and distinguished by this incessant variation. Or to put it differently, humans change their surroundings. It is disquieting, moreover, that this change is leading to the deterioration of their natural resources.

Our ability to self-generate change, unique to us, is the essential reason for the supremacy that has led us, in the eyes of many, to be the superstar species of evolution. They see us as the owners of the planet where we appeared as yet another species of hominids barely a few hundreds of thousands of years ago (the blink of an eye in terms of evolutionary time). Contrariwise, many others claim that this distinctive desire for progress (in the sense not of an ascent but of a tendency toward complexity), which breaks the homeostatic balance with our environment, is not an honor in any way. It may actually condemn us to a speedy extinction.

Not only does human-ness vary. Humans' transforming novelties become obsolete more and more quickly, and are produced after increasingly shorter intervals. This vertiginous acceleration, which tends to infinity, is one of the issues that cause greatest concern.

NON-HUMAN LIVING BEINGS AND MACHINES DO NOT SELF-GENERATE CHANGES

The ability to self-generate change, which exceeds any explanation based on the notion of unfolded potential, is unique to humans. It is outside the scope of other living beings or manmade machines. When paleoanthropologists uncover the remains of *Homo erectus* or *Homo neanderthalensis*, very close relatives of ours, their discoveries are similar to the ones they make when they examine the vestiges of glyptodonts, mammoths, or any other living beings. There are no signs of essential variations in habits or customs throughout the existence of the species. Some remains may belong to a *Homo erectus* that lived 2,000,000 years ago in Kenya, and others to one that lived 700,000 years ago in Serbia. No matter. Their utensils, hunting techniques, and habits have not changed. This is typical of all biological species. As far as we know, present-day sharks and turtles have the same behavior and way of life they had hundreds of millions of years ago.

To the best of our knowledge, no revolutionary transformation suddenly occurred in prehistoric hominid societies or in those of present-day primates and dolphins (to name species that live in groups, have a complex communication system, and are considered smart) that may have radically transformed their "culture." If this did happen, if change took place, it must have been fleeting, for it left no after-effects. It did not accumulate, nor did it generate significant modifications in these species' lifestyle. Generally speaking, gorillas, chimpanzees, orangutans, and dolphins still live as they did millions of years ago, monotonously and effectively repeating the range of actions allowed by their genome—the potential inscribed in it. And were it not for the effects of humans' incursions into their territories, they would not have done too badly. Non-human animals live in a daze in a closed world where only some signs interest them, which Uexküll defined as "meaning carriers" (*Bedeutungsträger*) (Agamben, 2002). In the case of ticks, for instance, these signs consist of their preys' butyric acid smell, hairy tissue, and blood temperature. Our vision of this world is utterly different.

In this sense, non-human living beings resemble machines developed by humans. As far as I know, even the most sophisticated of these machines cannot take into account what they are not prepared to detect, and are unable to change by their own initiative unless they follow a planned program embedded in them. One of science fiction's favorite themes contradicts this postulate. A machine, typically a computer, suddenly becomes capable of self-generating change and is, therefore, able to avoid human control. The effect on us of such transformation is chilling and unanimous; the machine has become human. Yet although present-day computers can win a game of chess against the best human masters, they can do so only by repeating previously inscribed complex orders. It is not easy (for better or worse) to reproduce the unique event that made us human.

CHALLENGES TO THESE ASSERTIONS

What I would like to highlight here is that machines and animals resemble each other in what they differ from humans. It might seem that I believe that between living beings, the product of billions of years of evolution, and manmade machines there are no significant dissimilarities. That is not so. There are, and they are important. First, the complexity of animal systems is unparalleled within the known universe. Just to give an idea, the human brain cortex has ten billion neurons and 10^{15} neuronal connections or synapses. Edelman (1992) illustrates the scope of this last figure as follows: counting the synapses in a human brain one by one at the rate of one per second would take about 32 million years. I do not know the numbers for primate or hominid brains, but these numbers are likely to be similar.

Second, even if a brain bears resemblance to a network of electric connections, its formation differs from that of other natural network structures or of manmade ones. The network of brain neurons expands over the course of individual development (Kandel, 1998, 1999; Ansermet and Magistretti, 2004). Its connections are established as individuals grow. The brain is hence a system that self-organizes based on experience, to a certain extent. This is the main problem faced by those who attempt to see it as a computing system. These features are responsible for living beings' remarkable adaptive plasticity, which is immensely higher than that of any machine. Nonetheless, it remains true that the brain's potential unfolds within the boundaries of what had been previously inscribed. Machines and non-human living beings share this trait, which differentiates them from what is human about humans.

Two other relevant arguments could be made against the affirmation that self-generating changes are characteristically human. First, even without becoming others, animals and machines can strikingly modify their behavior. Animal trainers can make a lion, monkey, or dolphin do things that would be unimaginable in their natural habitat. Furthermore, even in their own environment animals are capable of changing their habits to some extent to adapt to new situations. Anyone who doubts this has only to compare my neighbor's Pekingese with a wild dog from the Argentine Pampas or an Australian dingo to be persuaded.

Sophisticated machines can also adapt to changing situations. Computers, for instance, can respond to users' commands in a myriad different ways. Second, machines and Earth life forms have constantly changed since times immemorial. To say that they have not is to overlook their incredible diversity, which is one of the most significant traits of both life and technology. We must then distinguish machines' and non-human living beings' variety and plasticity from what I have called the human-ness of humans.

FIRST OBJECTION: THE ARISTOTELIAN MACHINE OR THE JUKEBOX

Machines and animals have innate dispositions or options that are inscribed as dormant potentialities and emerge or become present when triggered by the right stimulus. The click on an icon on my computer screen or the sight of a flying eagle's profile immediately prompts specific, purposeful responses on the part of my PC and of the terrified hens that flee at the sign of the predator bird's proximity. That is why these responses lend themselves to be thought of as the outcome of a design, thus evoking the image of a designer.

Following Sir Medawar (1954), I refer to the mechanism supporting this adaptive plasticity as jukebox. The name alludes to the old music-playing machine. This machine consisted of a series of numbered buttons that must be pressed to activate a mechanism that led the machine to play the chosen song from one of its records. Based on this simple system of successive triggers, an organism can develop behaviors that become progressively more complex because the outcome of each reconfigures the conditions for the emergence of the subsequent ones. In this way, the end result—for instance, adult behavior—is highly adaptive, a true process of learning from experience. This phenomenon is reflected in the uniqueness of the behavior of any individual from a superior animal species (within the species' range of possibilities).

Something similar happens with computer applications and games, where new levels must be reached for certain paths to open. Or with hypertexts, which may lead to different prewritten story lines depending on the user's chosen itinerary. Nonetheless, the mechanism underlying all these possibilities is elective; we choose among several options that, like the songs the jukebox can play, are already recorded and waiting to be played out. The number of possibilities inscribed in organisms and machines may be huge but not infinite.

We might also call this consistent, self-sufficient functioning of machines, non-human living beings, and part of the human psyche (what is animal in humans) the Aristotelian machine in honor of Aristoteles's concept of potency. According to this notion, everything that is act was previously potency. Within this model the possible is what bears no logical opposition with the existent. It should be stressed that the responses of an Aristotelian machine elude both awareness of the system's inconsistencies in relation to its environment, and logical opposition to the existent. In Aristotelian systems, therefore, there is no potential for creation. What takes place, rather, is the unfolding of potencies inscribed in the system since its inception.

All interpretations of the human psyche that follow Aristotle, even moderate ones, contend that we are made of a series of unfolding potencies. These potencies are seen as engraved in the genes, imprinted in early childhood, forming an instinctive fabric, or woven into the structure of an Other. They thus imply the existence of a text that may be tremendously long and complex but is prewritten and determining. It is undeniable that the potential for change that characterizes and distinguishes humans is sustained by a jukebox functioning. Yet the ability that differentiates us is not elective, nor is it explained by the unfurling of dormant potencies.

SECOND OBJECTION: MACHINES
AND LIVING BEINGS CHANGE

To say, as I have done, that humans are unique in their capacity to generate change overlooks the obvious fact that machines and living beings change as well. From internal combustion engines to my dentist's drill, today's machines differ from yesterday's (Arthur, 1993). The field where technological transformations have been most striking is information technology. The most revolutionary machine created by humans, the computer, has changed so much in the last twenty years that for practical purposes a 2009 PC will be useless junk by 2015. The very jukebox that inspired Sir Medawar back in the 1950s is now a museum piece—MP3 and MP4 players store thousands or millions of digitized downloaded songs in a remarkably smaller space. Undoubtedly, machines change.

So do living beings. Since life appeared on Earth some 3.5 billion years ago, biological evolution has generated such incredible variety that nobody could tell how many species exist today, let alone how many existed in the past. It is not true, moreover, that only humans transform their surroundings through their production. Living beings typically modify their environment. For instance, oxygen, without which we could not survive even for one minute, was not in our atmosphere awaiting the arrival of our delicate lungs. The first life forms that appeared in the planet (or came from extraterrestrial space, we do not know) produced it. In a liquid environment, these forms "invented" photosynthesis, a process that generates a by-product that is highly toxic because it favors combustion: oxygen. The atmosphere thus increased its oxygen content, and the planet gradually changed. So much so that today many life forms considered superior, humans among them, could not exist without this gas. In other words, one feature of life is that it ceaselessly changes its forms and that its variations, in turn, alter the environment, reconfiguring starting conditions and promoting new transformations.

We must admit that changes have occurred both in machines and in living organisms, and that these changes have moved in a certain direction. Machines and organisms evolve in the direction that tends to increase the complexity and efficiency of their products. Does this not contradict my affirmation that non-human organisms do not change? This is a valid question that allows me to be more precise. The difference between human beings on one side, and machines and the other living beings on the other, lies in the fact that the latter are incapable of generating changes, I'd like to repeat and stress this, *by themselves*. For them to transform, someone or something must produce change from the outside. The most evident and simple case is that of machines. Personal devices are not at all concerned with progress and cannot modify their performance capacity by themselves in any way. Yet Microsoft or Apple programmers and users and the market can. That is why they endlessly generate increasingly effective and complex software and hardware.

Nonetheless, as far as I know, machines are utterly incapable of transforming themselves or self-generating changes, let alone of recording and transmitting these changes to their community. Transformations in machines are actually an effect of what is human about humans. The same is true for living organisms. If a living being cannot sufficiently modify its behavior to face an adverse situation, even by implementing its jukebox potential to the maximum, it will die. It cannot learn anything from this experience that it did not already have the potential to learn. Living organisms do not become aware of inconsistencies in their functioning; they develop their behavior just as they were programmed to do. They "live" within an *Umwelt*, a world-environment constituted by a set of marks or "meaning carriers" (Uexküll, 1934), and these are the only ones that interest them. If these marks are adequate animals live and reproduce; if these marks are insufficient they do not. That is all animals' contribution to the cause of change.

Still, this is no small contribution; it is critical to the operation of another machine, the Darwinian machine, which does not transform individuals but species. If despite having unfolded its inscribed potency an individual is unable to overcome adversity, it will die. Since adversity, however, has a different effect on individuals with different potencies inscribed in their genomes and there is a certain diversity among the genomes of a population (due in part to sexual reproduction), those individuals with the worst genes to face the new situation will reproduce statistically less. Once some generations have lived under these conditions, the species will change because the prevailing genes will differ from the ones that made up its genome originally; they will be the best with which to face the new situation. From the point of view of its potencies, as a jukebox this species has simply ceased to be what it was. What has changed thanks to the Darwinian machine is the species.

THE DARWINIAN MACHINE

While the work of the Darwinian machine radically differs from that of the Aristotelian machine, the former depends on the latter. Contrary to what was assumed in the past, the Darwinian machine does not unfold hidden potencies. Its actions have no predictable fate. The biology text drawings that often illustrate the evolution of one species into another one and of this one, in turn, into another one along a path that leads from an inferior to a superior form (typically, from a hunched monkey to an upright human) run counter, strictly speaking, to the very foundations of the Darwinian machine. The latter has no preestablished direction because it is powered by chance. With regard to evolution, God seems to play his dice carelessly. From this perspective, humans are but the result of a random throw. In any case, we are the successful result of a failure. We are neither the unfolding of an essence nor the product of an Aristotelian machine. Rather, we are the outcome of an event—the one that determined the Great Leap 40,000 years ago.[3] This is Darwin's dangerous idea (Dennet, 1995): there is no prewritten destiny, and neither is there any prewriting.

This idea is certainly hard to assimilate. It is more acceptable to think that there is an intelligent designer, or that animals themselves come up with ways to overcome the difficulties they face. A few seventeenth-century scientists were the first to posit that living species may be the product of natural evolution rather than sudden creation. They logically thought that evolution was the result of individuals' ability to overcome disadvantages. In this sense, they assumed that individuals could become aware of their drawbacks to a certain extent. Their awareness, in turn, would give rise to a transforming momentum that would allow them to correct their shortcomings, and they would be able to transmit this transformation to their descendants. In other words, when they came across animal evolution these scientists pondered its mechanism based on the model for human change. Hence the classic example of the giraffe that usually serves to illustrate Lamarck's views on evolution. The lack of adaptation of the giraffe's neck to the high treetops led to the extension of its neck, an acquisition that was then transmitted to its offspring.

This idea suffered its first decisive setback when it was discovered that living beings could not inherit acquired features. The second blow—less mentioned but equally final—is this: there is no way for animals to become aware of their inconsistencies or to transcend the field of the possible, which is demarcated by their genome. The drive behind evolution, therefore, is not awareness and the consequent overcoming of a drawback at the individual level. If the genetic potential with which animals have been endowed renders them unable to face adverse circumstances, they will never change beyond their potential; they will either die or not reproduce. As odd as it might seem, death may favor species change albeit through an indirect path—it constitutes a decisive step in the operation of the Darwinian machine.

In this way, if animals were capable of modifying the boundaries determined by their genetic potential without changing their genome, they would hinder the work of the Darwinian machine at its most critical stage, namely, that of natural selection. And this is precisely what humans do. Or rather, this is what is human about humans. Of course, one might say that our history and future were written in our genome as potency since our inception. Yet if we want to go beyond this extreme deterministic thought, the only thing left for us to do is affirm that humans have broken the general law of Aristotelian devices ("not to go beyond what potency—the genome—indicates"). This break, in turn, makes it impossible for the Darwinian machine to operate in the domain of the human function, thus challenging a hegemony that, we should recall here, has persisted for more than three billion years. The key human defect or virtue that led us to this situation is the ability to become aware of inconsistencies, which Aristotelian machines are utterly unable to do.

ANIMALS AND MACHINES DO NOT BECOME AWARE OF INCONSISTENCIES

The main idea of Darwinism is that the incredible variety that characterizes life in this planet was caused by something that lies beyond individuals' reach. This something is chance, which acts by way of genetic recombination and mutations in the chain of reproduction. The links in this chain—individuals—only play the transmission game by managing the potential given by their genome. The game poses a challenge: which genes are most effective when it comes to reproduction? It is not a game played by individuals but by genes. A gene is by definition the descendant of another gene that succeeded in being transmitted to future generations. How it did so does not really matter; probably thanks to individuals. Just as chess pawns do not play the checkmate game but are used by it, individuals do not play the evolution game but are used by it. The Darwinian machine plays the evolution game.

The human aspect of humans aims to break this legendary system. To continue with the allegory, humans aspire to be a piece *and* move pieces (and they achieve it to a certain extent). The variations we see unfurl among the world's living species are sparked by the Darwinian machine. These changes are not self-generated but produced by an external source.[4] Changes characteristic of human-ness, by contrast, cannot be attributed to external sources. In our short history as a species no noteworthy modifications to our genome have occurred. Consequently, the Darwinian machine cannot have operated on us, or at least not significantly. Changes typical of human-ness are not brought about by a transcendent entity. Rather, they are immanently self-generated.

If we consider, therefore, that a good animal is one that expressly and faithfully follows the orders of its genome, what is human about humans is an aberration of this animal law of obedience. The fundamental issue is that humans have been graced or disgraced with a very simple, exceptional gift—they are capable of incorporating chance into the discourse that organizes their behavior. And this is what makes all the difference.

HUMAN-NESS

Humans were not always human, at least according to the definition I am attempting here. For 160,000 years they were just another hominid species and not a very successful one, if truth be told. According to Stringer and McKie, they were close to extinction about 150,000 years ago. What may be assessed from available remains tells us that their culture did not change during this period, neither in time nor in space. From what we know about them we can say that they were not very different from *Homo neanderthalensis* or *Homo erectus*, with whom they coexisted for thousands of years.

Yet in the Upper Paleolithic, about 40,000 years ago, an astounding event took place. Without changing their genome, *Homo sapiens* hominids became human. This mysterious radical change, known as the creative explosion (Pfeiffer, 1982) or The Great Leap Forward (Diamond, 1992), is likely the most fascinating anthropological conundrum.[5] The truth is that since then, evidence of humans' passage through the world suggests exactly the reverse of what may be gleaned from non-human remains: an endless variation in habits, customs, tools, utensils, and devices. This variation traverses the space and time covered by humans and, as we mentioned earlier, cannot be explained by way of changes either to the genome or to any other physical feature.[6]

As it usually happens with events, while we cannot say how the great leap took place, we can infer its effect. Human beings acquired the ability to generate radical transformations in their exchange with their surroundings and to incorporate these transformations and transmit them to their community and their progeny. The consequence has been a ceaseless emergence of incorporated supplementations as irreversible steps in a non-genetic informational heritage that is transmitted through culture. An explosion that shook the balance of the planet, the great leap was probably the first event in the living world that was not managed by the genetic code, and therefore left no marks in the genome.

This process does not only characterize human experience as a whole; it may also be verified at the individual level. Psychoanalysts can see it up close. When they listen to a patient they can detect that the features that distinguish this person—the ways in which his or her life has evolved, the configuration of his or her internal world—are utterly unique and owe their singularity to the fact that they are the outcome of a chain of linking encounters. To put it differently, they are the product of changes that cannot be reduced to the display of dormant potencies. That is why, as we shall discuss in the following chapters, in this field deterministic theories see their explanatory power reduced.

Humans are incapable of transcribing information, of repeating it exactly. Each attempt to do so inscribes singularities that, like irreversible steps, condition the next stages. Is this a defect or a virtue? It depends. In any case, it is the species' distinctive trait. Humans are quite less capable of transcribing without errors than the machines they manufacture. When they try to represent, they introduce a variable that generates change by excess or defect, and this change falsifies the copy. It is hence valid to say that what is human about humans is a flaw in their animalness. This imperfection opens a gap through which they may come into contact with those aspects of their surroundings that their minds cannot connect causally.

PERCEIVING BEYOND ONE'S RESOURCES

We may attempt an answer to the question about humans' ability to vary, which distinguishes them from all other living beings: human subjects perceive beyond their resources. "Perceiving beyond one's resources" is another way of saying "coming into contact with those elements in one's surroundings in relation to which one is inconsistent." In this sense, in its most radical form, thinking (a feature that is exclusively human) means crossing the boundaries of coherence to penetrate the domain of what Aristotle called logical opposition. Neither the other animals nor machines (so far) can do so.

My thesis is that the key to this essential, unique human capacity to self-generate change is humans' ability to become aware of, and be affected by, what transcends the rationality outlined by their representations. This ability rests on an animal foundation, humans' mechanical or animal aspect, which is precisely the device whereby they perceive only what can be understood by way of their representational resources. On this foundation there developed what is strictly human about humans, that is, the capacity to perceive, be affected by, and incorporate as supplementary production what lies beyond their mechanical aspect—what they cannot understand about each situation because they lack the resources to do so. That is why the incomplete, the paradoxical, and the enigmatic are typically human. That is why their logic is open, even though humans (in actuality, what is animal in humans) keep trying to close it.

Still, we should ask ourselves, how can subjects be touched by something they neither understand nor have represented to themselves? According to the argument I develop in the following chapters, one pole of the psyche, which I call psychic counting or associative system,[7] bases its organization on the associative link that connects representations. In this way, this associative system views everything it perceives as a peculiarity of what it knows and what has not been represented as non-existent. The previous question is hence answered negatively.

Yet the thesis I advance in this book is that while they tirelessly struggle against it, subjects are affected by the unrepresented. We might call the undetermined and lacking representation a *trait*. A trait would thus be pure difference without representation, and it would become a mark only when granted meaning by an act. For instance, while this page is full of marks we call letters, there are also myriad irregularities that are not marks but traits. If readers look carefully, they may find an irregularity that would have gone unnoticed were it not for my comment. For a trait to become mark it must be transformed by a cultural sanction.

It is then a cultural sanction that separates the significant from the insignificant in each case. Since sanctions originate in a shared culture, this fact tends to be overlooked. Yet the significant/insignificant distinction stems in most cases from the logic that rules the observer's mind rather than from the properties of the observed object. If the overlooked (or in-significant) thing could produce effects within that logic—let us accept for now that it can— these effects would have no precedent and would be unthinkable. In this case, mental logic would be inconsistent if it considered that only what it had previously sanctioned as mark could be a possible cause of the perceived effects.

ARE THERE INDIVIDUALS THAT PERCEIVE WITHIN THE BOUNDARIES OF THEIR RESOURCES?

Perhaps it would be simpler to address this issue if we turned it around. A system that is unable to perceive beyond its own resources or is insensitive to what exceeds its understanding would never be capable of self-generating radical change. To put it differently, a system unable to transcend the closed circle of its potential cannot change. Unlike humans, other living beings, machines, and even the animal foundation of the human psyche are unable to perceive beyond their resources or to become concerned with the paradoxes and inconsistencies that their logics might produce. They thus avoid contact with inconsistencies that an external observer might notice.[8] This is another of the theses of this chapter.

For instance, despite being a highly sophisticated machine, the computer with which I am writing is utterly incapable of perceiving beyond its resources. The only data that tell its operational system something about the world around it are the pressing of a key and the clicking of the mouse. It is extremely accurate in determining which key has been pressed; it records the exact sequence of hits and never makes mistakes. With just this way of incorporating data and its innate wiring, my computer can perform specific tasks that are much more complex than the ones a person could do with pen and paper.

Nonetheless, if I happen to press the keys in a sequence it cannot grasp or load an application that exceeds its understanding (that is, if I expect it to perceive beyond its resources), a dialogue box will appear on the screen warning me that my computer will ignore the content of my contribution because I have exceeded its ability to understand. If I ask it to solve a problem that has no solution according to its logic (for instance, to divide any number by zero), it will answer with an absurdity or, in the best-case scenario, will display a dialogue box that announces that its logic has detected an error. Yet neither the absurdity nor the sign produces anything.

If more violent but equally incomprehensible stimuli attempted to penetrate its world (like the heat of fire, the interruption of the current powering it, or a blow with a hammer that smashed it), my computer would collapse. It only identifies something as information if this something belongs within the field of what it is able to perceive. For this reason, my good PC cannot produce change by itself. Neither can it broaden the range of its perceptions or solve a problem that exceeds the logic with which IBM brought it into the world. Unless, of course, a hand foreign to its domain changed its wiring or its software from the outside, or it had been programmed with the necessary information to effect such changes, just like a caterpillar is programmed to become a butterfly. In this case, however, change would not be self-generated. Rather, it would stem from the development of inscribed dispositions.

All machines and living systems operate in this way except for the human aspect of humans. Non-human living beings also register the world around them only in terms consistent with the system that organizes their behavior and functions. An observer may consider that a particular response of an animal to a stimulus is inconsistent. For example, when I see a butterfly insistently crashing against a burning light bulb I may think, "How inconsistent! Phototropism, which was probably designed to help this poor butterfly survive [I know it is not so, but I am human and tend to think that nature designs its creatures with a purpose], is leading it to such horrible martyrdom." Yet the stunned butterfly lets the light or the flame that attracted it burn it without ever coming into contact with anything similar to my thought about its inconsistent behavior. To the last minute, the light or the flame remains obstinately unknown to the insect, which simply behaves like a machine that got stuck.

Still, conceiving of animals as complete in themselves or seeing the logic of their behavior as free of inconsistencies is not easy. Our typical way of reasoning is that animals lack something we possess. I have heard people say that animal language is incomplete, unfinished; that it is missing this or that to be human. The same happens with animal intelligence. These arguments, however, are based on an anthropomorphism that reverses evolutionary logic. Animal behavior and communication would thus be the result of a language and intelligence minus something, that is, a deficient language and intelligence (Deacon, 1997). Adopting this perspective entails believing that humans have achieved the final goal of these mechanisms.

Animals' communication systems and the ways in which they process data provided by their perception are fully self-sufficient and consistent. What humans have is something different that is neither more nor less. It is something that allows them to become aware of the inconsistencies of the system whereby they understand the world. As we shall see, such awareness opens a window through which our species can set out on the road of no return that we call progress without needing to change its genetic heritage. This ability may be our glory or our misfortune, but it is not a pattern by which to identify alleged animal deficits.

Perfection and the homeostatic adjustment to the environment that stems from hundreds of millions of years of evolution belong in the animal, mechanical order; imperfect adjustment, which makes awareness of inconsistencies possible and allows chance to be incorporated into the system, belongs in the human order. It is humans then who are defective or incomplete animals. In the face of the right stimulus a worthy Aristotelian machine would, above all, unfold the potency with which it had been endowed. It would never invent unheard-of alternatives or perceive beyond its resources. This invention, which might favor an individual, would horribly cripple the operation of the Darwinian machine.

BECOMING AWARE OF INCONSISTENCIES?

Perhaps it would be advisable to approach this issue by way of examples from the history of mathematics. In this field it is possible to see with singular clarity both the obstacle posed to logical systems by their inconsistencies, and the inevitability of the transformation of these systems over time when such inconsistencies are taken into account and hence exert their influence. In the case of a system that only admits whole numbers and fractions [that is, the product of a division between whole numbers ($F = \{n$, such that $n = x/y\}$, where x and y are whole numbers)], real numbers such as π or $\sqrt{2}$ (which are not the result of a quotient) are inadmissible. Consequently, for system F the relationship between a circumference and its radius (number π) or the value of the diagonal of a unit square (number $\sqrt{2}$) is impossible. It is thus said that system F is inconsistent in the face of values such as π or $\sqrt{2}$.

Let us suppose that somebody says to a system F user, "I want you to tell me the exact relationship between the perimeter and the radius of a circumference" or, "I want you to tell me the exact relationship between a diagonal and the side of a unit square." If the user only knows system F, he or she could resort to two elegant solutions. One would be to say, "I can't, because the system F I use is incomplete and doesn't have the numbers you are requesting." The other would be to answer, "I can't respond to your question because the system F I use is inconsistent in the face of problems such as the one you have presented." The third option, more modest, would be to admit that he or she did not understand what the person was asking.

Humans have a hard time giving answers like the first two because these answers entail looking beyond the logic that supports our predicates. At the same time, our nature prevents us from giving the third answer, which would be equivalent to an animal's inexpressive look. We are trapped and intrigued by questions we cannot answer, but do not remain indifferent to them as the other animals would. To protect ourselves from this awkward situation, we usually convince ourselves that the limit of the universe is that of the system we uphold; or that the only things that exist are those in the face of which our logic is consistent.

To maintain this state of affairs, we must exclude inconsistencies. Yet history—and each individual history—exposes time and time again the failure of this effort due to the human aspect of humans. This is what happened to the ancient Greeks, fervent defenders of system F. Like Aristotle, Pythagoras believed that emptiness, the zero, and the infinite did not exist and that everything could be represented by ratios—the system F we discussed above. Fractions played a very special role. According to Pythagoras, the universe was organized on the basis of ratios, of fractions between numbers. That is why when members of the powerful Pythagorean sect in the island of Samos realized that there were natural relations that could not be expressed in terms of system F (that is, when they became aware of the inconsistency of their system), they probably felt the cold sweat that heralds catastrophes. Irrational numbers like π or $\sqrt{2}$ are not the result of a fraction, and it is well known that one single exception can crush the universe that excludes it.

These issues configured the main plot of a moving story involving Pythagoras himself (Strohmeier and Westbrook, 1999). As the story goes, the Pythagorean sect discovered the horrifying fact that the diagonal of a unit square was not the result of a fraction. Indeed, we know today that it is irrational number $\sqrt{2}$, as can be deduced from the famous Pythagoras theorem. The powerful sect banned their members from revealing this truth. Yet one of them, Hippasus of Metapontum, disclosed the secret and, they say, Pythagoras himself killed him for it. As history shows, it is not that easy to make room for the inconsistencies underlying thought. Nonetheless, history also shows that over time these inconsistencies may make their way through and shake people's beliefs.

WHAT IS AN INCONSISTENCY?

In logic, a system and its interpretation are inconsistent when at least two of its derivations or theorems contradict each other. If it allows us to deduce both that a = a and that a ≠ a, a system is logically inconsistent. Still, a theory can be inconsistent when the (physical, biological, social) reality it defines contradicts it. For instance, the theory that "there are animals that are not made up of cells" is inconsistent in terms of contemporary biological reality. The theory of sexual difference upheld by children during the phallic stage (Freud, 1923), "Every living being has a penis," becomes inconsistent based on the sight of a female sexual organ. I believe that castration theory, which according to Freud claims that "we all had a penis, but some of us were (or may be) castrated" and replaces children's phallic theory to prevail in every adult's unconscious, has become inconsistent in light of present-day theoretical developments concerning sex and gender.

Although it pains us to admit it, every system is inconsistent in the face of some issues. There are two reasons for this: a) the reality analyzed by any theory is irreducible to the system of representations used by this theory, however comprehensive and meticulous; and b) according to Gödel's incompleteness theorem, all sufficiently powerful systems are incomplete by virtue of their power (Hofstadter, 1979; Dawson, 1999). For the time being, they cannot define themselves.

Now, not only does Gödel's theorem unequivocally point out the limited power of symbolic systems; it can also answer the question of why becoming aware of inconsistencies can promote change in humans. In agreement with this theorem, contemporary scientists acknowledge that the proof of the consistency of any logical system cannot be formalized within that system. As a consequence, the proof of the consistency of a language must be expressed in a metalanguage that has logical means superior to those of that language. The only way to avoid collapse when becoming aware of the inconsistency of a system is hence to search for another system—a metasystem that may account for the inconsistencies of the first one. The new system, in turn, will inevitably show inconsistencies over time and will have to be replaced by a meta-metasystem... and so on and so forth. We can see why becoming aware of inconsistencies is a condition for change. Nowhere is it written that the succession of transformations or changes must have a certain direction, or that the new system must be richer or more powerful than the preceding one, but this is the general trend and that is why we speak about progress.

I said that what is human in humans constitutes a clear insubordination against the power of the machine that has regulated life forms in our planet for billions of years. At the height of our insolence, we are now trying to manipulate the genome directly. In other words, we are trying to modify the biological starting point with which we were launched into the world only 200,000 years ago. From the Darwinian point of view, therefore, it would not be outlandish to posit the extinction of our species. Let us hope it will not happen, but if it did, it would be the end of the history of a failure of the living world—what is human in humans.

Nonetheless, something of the Darwinian machine's mode of functioning has been preserved in the change that characterizes human-ness. In both cases we are dealing with the coupling of a structure and a chaotic system. The operation of the biological world lies in a particular articulation of an invariable—the fixed aspects of the genome and its expression—and the randomness of genetic recombination and mutations. In humans we find a similar kind of coupling between the homeostatic inertia that characterizes our animal aspect, and chance, which intrudes through our becoming aware of inconsistencies thanks to our human aspect.

NOTES

1. Chapter 9 provides more details on this matter.
2. See 9n8.
3. See chapter 9.
4. According to the Bible this someone was God. According to contemporary scientific thought, the Darwinian machine. Given that it does not assume an appealable creator, the second conception is the hardest one to accept for those who disbelieve chance, but in both views change is generated from the outside.
5. See chapter 9.
6. Our genetic heritage has scarcely changed since the arrival of our species some 200,000 years ago (see chapter 9).
7. See chapter 5, section 1.
8. This would be valid for a human observer, not for animals (or machines) that live in a daze within the limits traced by meaning-carrying marks that do not match what humans "see" or think they see.

Chapter Two

Virtual Reality

NEW REALITIES

At the turn of the nineteenth century, few doubted that explosive scientific expansion would render us masters of both the objective world we inhabited and our animalness. We would finally be able to proclaim the triumph of *logos* over both of them. Having appeared at that time, psychoanalysis decisively joined this modern crusade. It contributed the crucial knowledge that the study of human beings had to take into account unconscious forces and hitherto neglected contents—humans' infantile and ancestral sexual past. We know now that such aspirations were but an illusion; we will never master real objects or our animalness. We cannot even postulate that the knowing subject and the object to be known are independent. Furthermore, the very technological expansion that gave rise to this utopia also generated immaterial realities where the observed object is pure artifact (Glanville, 1999).

These simulacra, which can blur the differences between subject and object and subvert the space we inhabit, are known by the contradictory name of virtual reality (VR). The latter is part of a larger phenomenon that could be better labeled as virtuality, computer reality, or media reality. All these designations point to the fact that even if we are not hallucinating, our seeing or feeling something does not mean that this something actually exists in the same way as we can say of a material object that it "is." These new realities do not fit into the compartments that had classically served to separate scientific from fictitious, objective from subjective, true from imaginary. VR is neither real nor unreal, neither immanent nor transcendent, neither objective nor subjective, neither true nor false, neither scientific nor fictitious; it transcends categorization. Strictly speaking, we could not even say that it deals with representation because its images *are* what they represent.

This new circumstance also disrupts time and space categories, links, practices, and the conditions of production of subjectivity. To tackle it, therefore, we must first revise our notion of reality. The concept of virtual reality should be considered in the context of the worldview developed during so-called postmodernity or, according to Bauman (2000) and Lewkowicz (2004), liquid modernity.[1] Medieval premodernity believed that the given world already had everything it must have, and hence nothing should be changed. By contrast, modernity's characteristic feature has been the dissolution of the established order. Being modern means being unable to stop searching for a new model to explain reality that is critical of the current model. In this sense, Westerners have been decidedly modern for approximately five centuries. Yet in the past forty years or so the pace of change has dramatically accelerated. Social change is always associated with transformations in contemporary media. Today, information technology in the Web 2.0 format promotes communication among users by way of novel and accessible "social networks" (Cobo and Pardo, 2007).

I start this chapter by examining how the concept of reality emerges in Freud's work. Then I reflect on the significance of the space between representation and the represented, and finally I consider VR and its possible causes and effects.

SUBJECTIVE AND OBJECTIVE

How do subjects distinguish what belongs to them—their subjective world— from the external, objective world? The most surprising aspect of the Freudian perspective on these issues was probably the claim that in human beings the boundary between these two realms is not set by biological heritage, as it is in the other animals. It must develop over time in a never-ending process. At first the infant envisaged by Freud is dominated by the "pleasure principle"; it considers that everything pleasurable belongs to it, while the unpleasurable (whether internal or external) belongs to the outside. Now, since life's demands are pressing and human cubs are not self-sufficient, to relate in a moderately adequate way to their environment they must develop a new principle. Freud called it "reality principle," and it entails the transformation rather than the removal of the pleasure principle. Such transformation, in turn, involves, among other things, infants' adaptation to the discourse that organizes exchanges in their environment. For this reason, individuals' definition of reality depends on the socio-historical conditions of their upbringing.

The necessary trigger for the emergence of the reality principle out of its predecessor the pleasure principle is frustration (and infants' ability to tolerate it). In other words, the environment must contradict infants' primal conceptions. Equipped with this new principle, children are able to associate their perceptions with the representations of their experience and produce new representations that are allegedly more and more "objective." *Objective* here refers to being both more fitting with the real objects' features and independent from the pleasure principle, which is ruled by the attempt to reactivate the primordial archetypes of experiences of satisfaction.

Yet as I mentioned earlier, the transition from the pleasure to the reality principle is never completed. Human beings will hence find it very hard—or rather impossible—to be objective. It is worth highlighting here that this insurmountable distance between psychic and material reality, between representation and what could be its presentation is the basis for all human development. As a result, tolerated frustration is a necessary condition for symbolic production and thought. If the found object coincides with the marks of the yearned-for object, says Freud (1895), thought stops.

It is no less true that if dissatisfaction is excessive and the ego wishes to sleep, *the psychic apparatus* can hallucinate or dream a different reality so as to reduce its charge. This phenomenon is not so foreign to that of virtual reality, as we shall see. I highlighted "the psychic apparatus" in order to point to a significant difference between dream and hallucination, on the one hand, and VR, on the other. The latter is not produced by the subject but imposed from the outside.

PSYCHIC REALITY AND THE REAL

Psychic reality should not be confused here with the real. Psychic reality is individuals' construction of the world they inhabit. It is affected by demands from their fantasy and by the requirement that it be consistent with conventional knowledge, and is regulated by the prevailing social and family discourse. The real[2] is instantaneous, discontinuous, chaotic, and ungraspable, and no cause-effect laws rule its evolution. Psychic reality, that is, reality according to each person, is an illusion that is considered true only by the person who inhabits it; it is a mental construction that conceals its own inconsistency and its inability to account for the real. This construction, this calculation is realized through representations of the external world that are consistently linked. In it the real is manifested only as impasses in the formalization of life experience.

Humans' mastery of increasing fragments of the world where they live (that is, their ability to identify the most frequent laws governing events) may have led them to believe that one day they would fully grasp the specificities of real objects. Yet this belief is as illusory as the idea that we may identify the infinite dots contained in a segment of the real number line because we know a few thousands, millions, or trillions of them. In both cases we are

making progress within infinitesimal infinites.[3] The space between representation and the representable cannot be bridged.

THE IMPOSSIBLE AND THE FORBIDDEN

The heart of psychoanalytic innovation, already announced in the 1893 "Preliminary Communication," might be summarized as follows: apparent inconsistencies present in neurotic discourse are due to the repression of some
elements or their correlations, which have been taken out of circulation from
the conscious-preconscious system of the sick mind. If these elements are
restored or the defense that removes them is overcome, inconsistencies vanish and thought becomes "normal." Although Freud never asserted it categorically, "normal" was generally understood as lacking in contradictions, and
inconsistencies present in neurotic thought were viewed as evidence of the
presence of unconscious or abnormal contents in preconscious or normal
thought. This view, in turn, contributed to the idea that the psyche—now
made up of preconscious and unconscious complementary elements and logics—did not contain indeterminacies but conflicts. If these conflicts were
resolved, everything in "normal" thought would be consistent.

Now, this assertion, which implied significant progress at the turn of the
nineteenth century, implicitly set aside another possible cause of inconsistencies. These may also be due to the fact that human beings' system of representations cannot account for the events that affect it not only because access
to certain key data may be forbidden, but also because its logic may be
unable to produce such an explanation. A paradoxical fact thus emerges. The
great discovery of psychoanalysis, the division of the psychic world between
forbidden and permitted (subsets of the possible) indirectly contributed to
conceal a much more fundamental split: the split between the possible and
the impossible. In this way, for instance, the essential inability to conceive of
the radical difference between the sexes may remain unrevealed if it is formulated in terms of castration theory (Moreno, 1997, 2000c).

THE SPACE BETWEEN THE REPRESENTED
AND PRESENTATIONS

The fictitious "cultural" border separating the forbidden from the permitted,
the admissible from the inadmissible (fictitious in that it conceals the fact
that the space we inhabit actually borders the impossible, not the forbidden)
is not a solid wall but the site of frequent disputes between the established
and the new. Psychoanalysis discovered that the major reason for these struggles has to do with child sexuality, with an argument based on the Oedipal-
narcissistic interface.[4] Humans can produce symptoms, art works, and even

suicides and homicides to tell their imagined father and the conventional construction of reality that neither of them understands their proclamation. The ultimate reason, the smallest unit of the heterogeneity between reality and the real is the radical disjunction between thing and representation. At the same time, even when the mind cannot grasp it, what is not represented may still affect it. It is in this essential caesura of human-ness where every radical innovation has been generated. The mind is affected because its attempt to grasp the elusive real object gives rise to a surplus. Language—any language, whether verbal, pictorial, gestural, or theatrical—is constructed as though custom-made to facilitate the production of unforeseen meaning in the space of incongruence between thing and representation.

The existence of this space is then as critical for the development of humanity as we know it as the air we breathe. If it collapsed by allowing us to fully grasp the real, or if virtuality drew the precise contour of demand, we would melt in a still incandescence. We would be one with the image; there would be no subject-object differentiation. Perhaps this development would be similar to stimulating one's nervous system by inhaling crack. If, by contrast, this space expanded to the point that the real did not affect us and we remained isolated from inconsistencies that might disturb the logic of the psyche, we would become robots with a history as flat as that of a machine or an animal. This history might be similar to that of *Australopithecus*, who apparently imposed no variations on its culture during the million and a half years of its existence. Humans, instead, are traces of the imperfection with which we grasp the world around us. Each of our steps leaves a mark that irreversibly guides our progress. Perfection and reversibility belong in the order of the non-human.

THE SUGGESTION OF THE REPRESENTED

It is very likely that Cro-Magnon paintings in Altamira or Puente Vesgo were attempts to grasp essential animal objects in a primeval, mythical time— attempts to have the beasts or the exploits of the hunt become present again (be re-presented). Yet these images, and perhaps their names, became partly autonomous symbols of what they had initially designated. Differences were thus generated between thing and representation that opened the way for artistic, religious, and mythical meanings that had not been envisaged in the original representation project.

Artistic productions have always played in this space. Their mode of representation defies convention. They strain as far as possible the distance between established reality and its representation within a space that used to be called virtual before the advent of VR. It is said that artists have license to play in this interstice—not too much, but some. In artworks as they have been defined to date the distance between conventional and artistic representation must be big enough to produce a certain vacillation without creating a different reality. It must suggest without disorienting. Spectators must be transported by the painting, the play, or the symphony, while remaining aware of the fact that the artwork is a produced reality that cannot be confused with "the truth." Even though they may enjoy the gap between the represented and the evoked, those who look at a painting by Velázquez or Picasso, attend a Hamlet performance, or listen to a symphony by Berlioz know that it is a representation. Suggestion is not possible when the gap vanishes or is excessive.[5]

ESSENTIAL IMPERFECTION

Our very survival as a species may have depended on the development of this mysterious capacity for partial incorporation, this distance between name and named that culture renders bearable, a distance that, in turn, generates culture. Instantaneous experience is not just inaccessible; it may also be unbalancing. We are not equipped to make contact with the world without the mediation of signs. By mediating and imposing their inertia on our psyche and on the real, signs—arbitrary, necessary, and always articulable—protect us from unbalance. That is why most of the significant activities performed by our species are accompanied by some form of rite or ceremony that integrates them into the social realm—that renders them consistent and eliminates immediacy. Being born, eating, making love, getting married, leaving childhood behind, dying, and even entering and leaving a significant place require a ceremony that takes *time*.

I highlight the word *time* because this dimension constitutes a crucial value in an age so influenced by the media. Present-day culture favors the instantaneous, the ultra fast. Time has become one of our most precious goods, and we dread its loss (J. Gleick, 1999). For this reason, to save time these ceremonies, rites, distractions—everything that may seem redundant— are being eliminated in search of accelerated precision. In 1995 Jean Baudrillard metaphorized the danger of immediacy as follows: if time were instantaneous and we could see the stars without the mediation of the X thousand or million light years that separate us from them, a deadly incandescence would burn us. It would seem as though in these pauses something essential about humans, or at least about the humans we know to date, were at play. Furthermore, these breaks serve to maintain the illusion that it is we who control the entry of the real object into our world.

If I insist on exposing the labile nature of this vital gap that both bridges and separates representation from the represented, it is because this gap is indissolubly linked to the emergence of radical newness (which characterizes human-ness)[6] and, at the same time, is precisely the space occupied by VR. Through this half-open small window dividing reality from the real—the heart and the Achilles heel of our connection with the outside—chaos can interfere to some extent with our orderly and illusory notion of the world. That is why since humans have become humans, unlike every other species, we have constantly spawned variations to our surroundings that expand our domain.[7] This gap has been as pivotal to human development as we know it as the presence of "flaws" in parental genome copies during genetic transmission has been to biological evolution.

Now, the chaos that enters through that small window must do so in minute quantities so as not to provoke unbalances in our psyche, which is essentially rational. As shown by shifts in our relationship with the world that line our 40,000 years of history, humans are capable of coming into contact with perceptions, events, and experiences ungraspable by our logic and thus renew our conception of the world.[8] Yet so far we have done this gradually, without derailing the fragile logic whereby we explain the world around us.

VIRTUAL REALITY

As I was saying, this small window of vital imperfection that connects us with, and separates us from, inconsistencies stemming from our relationship with the world (including our own productions) is the specific target of the technological simulacrum capable of virtually generating realities, that is, so-called virtual reality. This name was coined on June 7 1989, when software company Autodesk and computer company VPL announced the birth of the new technology as follows:

> VR is shared and objectively present like the physical world, composable like a work of art, and as unlimited and harmless as a dream. When VR becomes widely available, around the turn of the century, it will not be seen as a medium used within physical reality, but rather as an additional reality. VR opens up a new continent of ideas and possibilities. At Texpo 89 we set foot on the shore of this continent for the first time.[9]

The term "virtual reality" is powerful because it suggests a broad range of meanings linked to simulation, hyperreality, the effects of information technology, and postmodernism/postmodernity. Yet for this very reason it is also ambiguous. Strictly speaking, it is an oxymoron. In the world where adults over forty grew up, virtuality and reality were antonyms. Other terms that have been used to define this dimension are synthetic environments, cyberspace, artificial reality, simulation technology, media reality, and computer reality. VR is the most common way of designating these phenomena, and that is the meaning it has in this chapter.

While most define VR by focusing on the technology employed to develop it, Jonathan Steuer (1992) does so by way of the notions of presence and
telepresence. Presence refers to the natural perception of an environment, and
telepresence to the perception of this environment mediated by communication technology. Based on this definition, H. R. Rheingold (1991) claims that
VR is an environment perceived through telepresence. To these two categories we could add that of absence, which I define as the ability to evoke an
environment by way of imagination without it being present or telepresent.
From this point on, the notions of presence and absence take a different
meaning, and modes of relating emerge that we do not know how to classify.
The interplay between these concepts enables us—in fact, urges us—to ask
ourselves a question that may very well be crucial in the domain of links:
What is the difference between realms that can be defined as "present,"
"telepresent," "evoked," or "absent" in the case of human relationships? It
also leads us to wonder about the difference, for instance, between an episto-
lary, a "face-to-face" and an "IM" relationship, and relationships over the
phone or Skype.

THE OCCLUSIVE EFFECT OF VR

The truth is that the ingenious technological ability to simulate what subjects
allegedly want and thus affect the emergence of frustration is becoming
available to us in the most varied ways. Where an impossible (a sign of the
real) appears, there emerges the technological-virtual attempt to remove its
condition of insurmountable barrier. Such an attempt may be a frenzy of
superficial sensoriness that hinders perception; excess information that de-
luges and saturates, and in certain cases even cancels the desire to know (in
the fashion of anorexia); body transformations that aspire to abolish the
effects of aging, maturity, death, and linear time in a frantic search for perpetual resurrection; or high-definition pornography, which disrupts eroticism
and sensuousness by lifting the veils that evoke the lack through the presentation of hyperrealistic images of pure animal sexuality.

We should note here that all these examples constitute points of impossibility, sites where it becomes evident that our system of representations
cannot surpass the limits set by real materiality. Virtuality thus directly aims
to occlude the gap between representation and the represented. It does not do
so, however, through a symbolic grasp of the real, as modernity had
dreamed; it does or attempts to do so by way of a simulacrum. The latter
consists in generating a "reality" that is neither real nor unreal, neither scientific nor fictitious, that is, virtual reality. Images do not represent; they are.
This production is not limited to the visual. In the same way, we could state
that "all" information about something *is* that something; that the full ge-

nome is man or woman; or as in Borges's story, that the infinite Library of Babel is the Universe (Borges, 1941a).

Moreover, since present-day technology is digital and thus all information (visual, aural, written) tends to be interchangeable, it is foreseeable that VR's sphere of action will vastly grow in the near future. Our understanding of human biological determinants has ceased to be analogical (the body as a machine) to become digital (determination depends on a code, a sequence) (Sibilia, 2005; Moreno, 2009b). This shift opens the possibility for a direct connection between "data" and the senses.

HYPERREALITY

Everything in VR occurs in high definition. Details of surface (micrometric), time (instantaneous), sound (high fidelity), or memory (total recall) are so highly defined that they exceed our threshold, thus clogging the crevices through which the suggestion of the non-existent would traditionally emerge. As Eco (1986) has claimed, VR aims to be more real than reality itself. The lack, which, as Lacan taught us, is the bait after which our desires metonymically file (thus thwarting the presentation of a fatal *jouissance*), vanishes. Yet it vanishes not because of the raw presentation of *objet petit a* (according to Lacan, the object cause of anxiety), but because it is filled with simulacra that anticipate the allegedly demanded object by copying it up to the smallest detail. In VR, therefore, representation lacks independence or autonomy. It is anchored to the represented, which is representation itself. This situation would approach the scientific ideal of perfect designation save that, being a simulacrum, it eludes any real anchorage and does not provide access to any inconsistency or truth.

The body, the most crudely real entity that we inhabit (or that inhabits us?), does not halt VR in its endeavor. Nonetheless, VR seems to have found unique obstacles there. The more we project images on an apparently complacent human body through surgery, collagen injections, hormones, genes, and prostheses; the more insistently we seek eternity or indefinite puberty; the more radically we attempt to erase all remnant of difference between the sexes, the more will the sinister face that betrays the simulacrum resurface. In this way, VR forces us to face a key question: Can the representation of an object contain the products of its presentation? This question is consistent with the following ones: Is there something of the object—in the sense of "entity"—and of its effects on us that cannot be subsumed into the information contained in it? Or, is "existence" equivalent to "information"? Or, can the atom be reduced to the bit?

Answering negatively ("There is no difference between the atom and the bit or between the object and the information originated in it, and so representation subsumes the effects of presentation") would prophesy a bright future for VR and for epistemological approaches to human problems. It would reveal the mistake of those who have believed that there are discrepancies between matter and information—the ontological difference between being and entity viewed by Heidegger as essential. The topic is very up-to-date because we seem to have overcome old technological obstacles and are now able to handle as numerous and precise data as we want.[10]

The other option is to state that between the sum total of information coming from an object and the real object there is an irreducible difference; that something essential to the object cannot be translated into information; and that the effect of a real object on us cannot be deducted from our representations of it, no matter how numerous they might be. In other words, the ontological difference between being and entity cannot be canceled. It is neither a difference of knowledge nor an epistemological problem. Thinking along these lines would lead us to equate "existence" with "essential indetermination" and would bode an end to the tremendous progress generated by VR and the informational era we have entered. An essential aspect of beings would be irreducible to knowledge.[11]

I am sure that many readers will be, like me, in favor of this second option. Yet we should know that while we discuss these ideas, a thriving billion-dollar technology is determined to make the transmutation phenomenon ("teleporting") real. The goal is to transport an object as far as we want by transmitting information stemming from it. This technology relies on the idea that atom and bit are equivalent and has already experienced some significant success with elementary particles. Those who have placed their hopes in it think that in the future we will "travel" by teleporting.[12]

WHAT'S NEW?

Modern thinkers, Freud included, believed that scientific triumphs would narrow the space separating us from the object, thus finally completing the picture of progress that goes from monkeys to human demigods (absolute owners of the world they inhabit). As we all know, this scientific utopia has failed. Like most innovations, technology came to us through an unforeseen flank—the deactivation of the interaction between reality and the real through simulation. It is hardly surprising that the Freudian theory of a homogenous, synthesizing ego was developed at the height of solid modernity, when events were quite predictable compared to present-day ones. This ego, therefore, was solid, had no heterogeneous fronts,[13] and faced a relatively stable, consistent reality.

What is happening today, instead [as Beatriz Sarlo (2000) points out], is similar to what happens in post-film and contemporary clips, where the time of classic cinematographic shots has ceased to be a key element. The clip is not interested in the duration of the shots but in their accumulation. As if following instructions mediated by the discourse of immediacy, shots must be extremely brief. We are dealing here with a high-impact discourse founded on the speed with which an image replaces the previous one, which it must surpass. Image 1 must be erased by image 2, which will be erased, in turn, by the appearance of image 3, and so on and so forth. The art of clips and advertising shorts demands that previous images be weakened, compacted, and superimposed to leave room for the next ones. In other words, this is an example of the obsolescence required by the liquid medium to give rise to the new. [14]

What I particularly wish to highlight here is that the existence of *one* virtual reality does not cancel the potential for a simultaneous connection with *other* virtual realities. In the same way, a TV channel or an Internet "site" does not interfere with the simultaneous presence of hundreds, thousands, or millions of other channels or sites that swarm everywhere and nowhere. VR has the ability to present and offer itself to "surfing," to the certain subjectivization of each of us, without interfering with other "realities." We can thus become several, in a way. Compared to the era of solid modernity, the reality faced by the ego in our times is manifold.

Moreover, two critical features of the so-called Web 2.0 (the form of Internet that emerged in mid-2007) speak clearly of the drastic difference between modern productions (even those of the most emulated TV heroes) and computer reality productions. One is that the growth, effectiveness, and improvement of Web 2.0 products depend in a homogeneous and increasing way on the number of participants who are summoned to interact in innovative social networks (what is already happening, for instance, in wiki pages, blogs, and so on). The other is that their preannounced obsolescence is a sort of in-built requirement of information technology productions.

In 2004 Prensky established a compelling division between "digital natives" (who were born into this technology) and "digital immigrants" (who were not born into it but learned to use it). I would add to these the "digital illiterate." The three groups coexist today in overlapping worlds. For natives, the power lies in sharing knowledge. They are not concerned with understanding, associating, or synthesizing the various ways of being in informational reality. Immigrants, by contrast, still believe that power lies in knowledge and that associating syntheses are necessary, while illiterates are stunned by these transformations.

Furthermore, in these times individuals are in charge of, and responsible for, being who they are—or at least that is what the media proclaim. The "given" pigeonholes we may simply inhabit or occupy have vanished. Consequently, it seems that it is each person's job to "be" what he or she is. There is an instability, a feeling of pluripotentiality that forces men and women to be in constant motion without the promise of final completion. In a way, individual identity (including gender identity) is conceived of as self-creation—as the result of playing the character we are or, what appears to be the same thing, the character we have decided to be. In the virtual world of the Second Life website, for example, this is the main issue.

Present-day children must prepare themselves from birth to face an always uncertain, liquid, novel, and variable world with means that are rapidly proclaimed as obsolete.[15]

From this perspective, an ego with multiple fronts, which might also be called a "split" ego, could be a way of both disavowing painful realities and surviving in contact with an ever-changing environment (Moreno, 2009a). The definition of normal and abnormal that prevailed when dealing with the issue of sexuality, identity, and subjectivity (in the sense of "way of being") has also changed. The norm was not abolished, and did not become unnecessary either; heterosexuals (formerly "normal") may continue to be heterosexual and to see themselves as normal, if they wish. Instead, other places were created, other pigeonholes, so that there are many norms, many "normal" ways,[16] and each new space has a norm that coexists with the rest.

Nonetheless, speaking about "many norms" is itself contradictory. Moreover, nothing prevents us from simultaneously abiding by different rules. Just as the tendency toward symptoms and neurosis predominated among modern children, so is an incipient yet powerful tendency toward splitting emerging among children today (and probably among adults as well). Splitting may occur between the manifold realities provided by the media and society and/or in the face of difficult situations or horrific presentations, as Freud explained (Moreno, 2009a).

Besides, individuality—the solitary, progressive figure of the hero in modern biographic productions—vanishes today into a blend of anonymous authors and readers who operate together in the time of the instant. This phenomenon is noticeable in blogs, photologs, Wiki pages, You Tube, MySpace, Facebook, or Twitter or, outside the Internet, in the popular, expanded version of graffiti. The pervading idea is that of collective intelligence, which emerged full force in so-called Planet Web 2.0 under the guise of fast-food media and has continued to develop in a noticeable way. Collective intelligence has been depicted by means of eloquent and diverse notions, among them, Berners Lee's (2000) intercreativity, Lévy's (1997) collective intelligence, Rheingold's (2002) smart mob, or Surowiecki's (2004) wisdom of crowds. It would be a mistake, however, to believe that this trend is simply a consequence of the arrival of a certain technology. Pardo and Cobo (2007) claim that Web 2.0 is above all an attitude that favors social networks. Solid, homogeneous structures (such as the pre-splitting Freudian ego, with no cracks or diverse fronts) could pose an obstacle to our ability to face the world we inhabit.

IS THIS GOOD OR BAD?

One of the reasons why VR is frightening is that its success could imply the collapse of the space that fueled mental development as we had defined it to date. In view of the obvious prevalence of phenomena linked to connection[17] and virtual reality in our culture, the pressing question is, does VR entail an impasse in human growth and creativity or a desubjectivation process? Or are we witnessing the appearance of a new form of creativity, subjectivity, and growth? Is this the final defeat of our Promethean quest? Are we returning to our ape past, as Jean Baudrillard (1995) seems to think? Or is our mind expanding, as Andy Clark (2009) bluntly suggests when he states that thinking no longer fits in our brains? Does informational development aim to alter our reality and our contact with the surrounding natural environment and destroy the cultural tenets we inherited from our entire history since the Greeks? Or are we facing a different reality that was not even accessible to us in the past because we lacked the technological means we now possess?

I recently heard a renowned lecturer make the following statement, which I found striking: "This fad [sic] of so-called VR is but a heap of insignificant innovations. Didn't Greek sophists already question the status of reality without so much ado?" he said with unperturbed solemnity. When we deal with these issues we may easily fall into two dangerous temptations, namely, technophilia and technophobia. Since substitutions are so fast-paced, it is not easy to take distance in order to examine them, and so it is very hard to answer the questions posed above. We should not rush. We may not be in a position to identify the costs and benefits of current changes. As they say, these changes are just starting. We would be living in a sort of Old Stone Age (that of *Homo habilis*) of the Informational Age. When a process is in its infancy it is not easy to distinguish between transforming events and imminent catastrophe.

To the world of 2050, the production of subjective meaning may not be as useful as it is in present-day psychoanalytic offices or artists' ateliers. Maybe by then the decisive avoidance of the so-called subject effect (the source of error baptized with the eloquent name of "human factor") that takes place in the production spheres most influenced by technology will take place everywhere. While psychoanalysis and modern art pursue the human factor, technology focuses all its efforts on eliminating it. Fortunately (an expression that betrays, perhaps, the modernity of my quest), the very same efforts to do away with the human factor tend to produce it, and attempts at eradicating it have failed so far (Moreno, 2010).

FOUR VERSIONS OF VR

Due to the feeling of powerlessness that overwhelms us when we cannot control the course of events, in the face of matters as significant as the effects of VR we often think in the line of "somebody is doing it for a reason." In other words, we presume an acting subject, a designer of the changes we are suffering. This attitude has always been one of our chosen ways of dealing with the incomprehensible. Already in the nineteenth century famous British naturalist P. H. Gosse (1857) made up a Simulating God who was responsible for our living in perpetual virtuality. According to Gosse's conceit, all geological and fossil remains from the evolution of the species (including the human species) were but a simulation envisaged and created by that Simulating God five thousand years earlier, on the day he had created the world according to the Bible. This was, claimed Gosse, a magnanimous gesture by a good God who wished us to amuse ourselves and be happy thinking we had a history.

Of course, we might just as well think of this God as evil, but that does not really matter. What does matter is that Gosse was capable of envisaging a Subject-God who could incorporate a true virtual reality into the scene of his creation. This idea in itself dismisses every human creative aspiration and precludes the potential for any form of radical novelty in the planet. Every novelty has already been created by a superior mind. Gosse's scenario is sketchier than those of superior deterministic thinkers such as Plato, Laplace, Newton, Leibnitz, or Descartes. Yet it is not essentially different from theirs, for it contemplates a transcendent superior order that turns our journey, no matter what it may be like, into a simple ride through roads traced by a calculating Other who does not even need to play dice.

Not coincidentally, the same matter is portrayed in three movies from the turn of the twenty-first century. These are *The Matrix*, *The Truman Show*, and *Wag the Dog*. These movies reproduce the noteworthy possibility that someone will make up a reality so that those who are immersed in it will believe they are actually living in this simulacrum. In this way, they will become an easy prey to superior minds. In *The Matrix* (1999), directed by the Wachowsky brothers, this virtual reality was created by evil computers that use humans as voltage generators. After a war that decimated the planet, computers (The Matrix) have taken over, and they need humans as a source not of intelligence but of energy. Immobilized in cells, human beings "experience" a virtual reality by way of direct connections into their sensory system. This virtual reality turns out to be very similar to life as we know it. The Matrix thus keeps humans alive and distracted while machines extract their coveted volts.

In Peter Weir's *The Truman Show* (1998) a media director organizes a colossal staging thanks to his power and (perhaps artistic) ambition. He creates an entire town packed with simulators and hidden cameras, where poor Truman Burbank has been forced since childhood to experience a different reality, which we might call virtual. Notably, this reality is witnessed, in turn, by millions of passionate TV viewers, who follow it as if it were a soap opera. Twofold virtuality? Perhaps it does not matter, for unlike those in the non-virtual world, shots in the virtual world are symmetrical and duplicable. This situation is very similar to reality shows. The third film is *Wag the Dog* (1998) by Barry Levinson. In it the U.S. government stages a war simulacrum in the media with the help of a publicist who is an expert in creating virtual realities. The goal is to distract the world from the potentially scandalous affair between the president and a teenager.

In all four cases (the movies and Gosse's conceit) there is a subject who organizes the simulacrum with a particular goal. Suggestively, the characters embodying this realizing subject are God, rulers, the media, and computers. In the three films the simulacrum fails due to the interference of the human factor, which simulation has failed to eliminate. Part of the films' drama stems from their representation of humans' fight against a technified dominator that, as in Orwell's *1984* or in the manner of bait fishing or hunting, uses a simulated reality to control its victims.

WHO IS DOING THIS TO US?

Deleuze asserts that humans prefer a tragic to a random fate. For the same reason, the chaotic intrusion of confusional psychosis becomes more tolerable when the sufferer can organize a paranoid delusion. While I am aware that these issues have a political or ideological vertex that cannot be easily avoided, I believe that the plots mentioned above are the effect of a kind of relapse. The situation is less persecutory but more decisive. I do not think that anyone is actually directing the course of things. Computer or virtual reality's increasing relevance in our culture is not the act of a creating subject. Nonetheless, there are some who are able to take advantage of the situation—who can speculate or foresee the future and are usually seen as "visionaries."

I believe, instead, that what is happening reflects to some extent the object's impending domination over the subject. Rather than an organized conspiracy, the picture probably resembles the evolution of biological or computer viruses. The latter have no other intention than replicating; whether or not they harm their hosts is a different matter. It is an infection of a complex structure by a more primitive one that can penetrate through those places where the complex structure displays inevitable inconsistencies.[18] Computer and biological viruses infiltrate through the crevices present not in the most sophisticated but in the most basic programs. In this sense, viruses behave like VR, which gets in through that elementary, basic little window that joins and separates representation and the represented.

This reference to biological viruses may have something to tell us. There have been germs that, far from destroying their hosts, were incorporated into them and gave rise to more complex, better-equipped structures. Without going any further, this is the origin of mitochondria. They were first infecting bacteria and are now irreplaceable cell components. At the same time, thinking that technological development is the only factor responsible for the boom of VR would be equivalent to believing that the fall of the Roman Empire was due exclusively to the appearance of the barbarians. It is my contention that the current prevalence of VR-related phenomena is tied to the decline of the hegemony of Aristotelian causal logic and the waning of the idea that words are the only means of communication at humans' disposal. These naturally favored (perhaps excessively) the notion that the human universe is composed only of words and *logos*.

We may be witnessing the end of an era, a situation that certainly leads subjects who grew up in this era to adopt an apocalyptic outlook. Times of crisis like ours may be followed by catastrophes, it is true. Yet radical innovation may also develop that, as is well known, disturbs the established order. Be that as it may, our efforts ought to be directed toward understanding the reality we are experiencing, for as Wittgenstein (1921, 1.1) put it, "the world is the totality of facts," and the worst thing we could do is believe that what is happening is a mistake.

NOTES

1. *Liquid* and *solid* define two types of modernity according to their state. I think liquid modernity is a more suitable term than postmodernity.

2. This term became popular among Argentine analysts because of Lacan's use of it. It corresponds, to a certain extent, to Freud's "material reality" and *das Ding*, Badiou's "inconsistent multiplicity," Deleuze's "chaos," and Castoriadis's "magma."

3. Humans can more easily conceive of an external infinite, an infinitely vast universe, than of an internal infinite, among other things, because an external infinite allows for divine suture while an internal one leads us straight into the impossibility of rendering the infinitesimal consistent.

4. See chapter 5.

5. This is the case of art tied to VR, or cyberart. Cyberart seeks to make the virtual real (Roy Ascott, 1999). The intended artistic effect is for spectators to enter non-conventional realities that are not separated from the established reality by a frame so that they may become another component of "the work."

6. See chapter 1.

7. See chapter 1.

8. See chapters 1 and 9.

9. VPL Research at Texpo 89, quoted in Rheingold (1991), p. 154.

10. The superior mind envisaged by Laplace (1814, p. 4), who masterfully summarized the peak of deterministic thought in his *A Philosophical Essay on Probabilities* (a superior intelligence "which would comprehend all the forces by which nature is animated and the respective situation of beings who compose it—and intelligence sufficiently vast to submit these data to

analysis—it would embrace in the same formula the movement of the greatest bodies and the lightest atoms; for it, nothing would be uncertain and the future, as the past, would present to its eyes"), would face few technological obstacles to carry out this task today.

11. Believing that being may be translated into knowledge means, so to speak, paying the consequences for the forcefulness with which we say that something "is" when the quality of being is still unknown to us. Our entire language is plagued by ideology hinging on the verb "to be" (Berenstein, 2007).

12. Heisenberg's indeterminacy principle (one cannot simultaneously learn the position and the speed of an elementary particle) does not seem to be an insurmountable obstacle (see A. Zeilinger. 2000).

13. At least until 1927.

14. In Sarlo's own words, "spectators can erase images with their lids, as if the latter were windshield wipers, because they know that the icon remains and guarantees the illusion of a continuity that has been infinitely fragmented by the syntax of the clip" (Sarlo, 2000, p. 200).

15. Obsolescence is ingrained in innovative presentations. We are now dealing with "for now" instead of "forever."

16. Regarding sexual identity, one can be a normal heterosexual, or a normal gay person, transvestite, transsexual, cross-dresser, bisexual, drag queen, metrosexual, and so on.

17. See chapter 3.

18. One of the derivations of the Gödel theorem says that there is no computer capable of preventing infection by a virus (Dawson Jr., 1999). Nothing can be utterly consistent.

Chapter Three

Connection and Association

INTRODUCTION

Connection and association are two different ways of relating to the environment we inhabit, and are ruled by heterogeneous logics. Together they form an active screen that unites us with, and separates us from, the inconsistent multiplicity surrounding us. While the mechanism of connection, as we shall see, is quite manifest today because of the preeminence of phenomena linked to virtual and computer reality, our relationship with our environment has always been mediated by both logics. Still, the notion of the world we inherited from Greek rationality, which was well suited for premodernity and solid modernity,[1] favored the interpretation of that relationship in associative terms. This preference for association occluded the evidence of the role of connectivity, placing the latter within the realm of magical thinking or irrationality.

One of the distinctive features of virtual or computer reality is that its images are not associated—the way representations are—and do not produce meanings that allow us to identify the subject of association.[2] They connect with each other, and the connecting subject is diluted through this act (Moreno, 2010). It is worth discussing contemporary children's passion for virtual technology in order to illustrate the prevalence of connection over association in the world of computer reality.

VIDEOGAMES

Present-day children are mad about on-screen reality, where they somehow participate through commands activated by buttons, that is, videogames. Each new character or story fad that invades children's domain like a shock wave traveling through our globalized planet is usually accompanied by the appearance of the corresponding videogame, a huge array of toys, TV series, websites and links, clothing, cards. In addition, a sort of dialect emerges among fans that alludes to a specific knowledge, a knowledge that excludes adults and non-fans. Children's preferences are increasingly directed toward videogames that present their own reality rather than evocatively represent-ing another one.

Furthermore, it would be a mistake to believe that videogames appeal only to children; there are adult fans as well. A new audience of teenage-adults (whom someone has decided to call "adultescents") is equally passion-ate about new videogames and often reactivates the old ones that had been built for Commodore or Nintendo. In addition, flight and war simulators, true sophisticated videogames, have become indispensable for military training. [3] In fact, it is estimated that most future trainings will be carried out with the aid of simulators. This development is favored by the interactive nature of virtual technology, which renders operators' performance into another vari-able in the game.

Modern thinking, prevalent during the formative years of today's older adults, leads us to consider that training and learning must be based on "understanding" through associative practices. Yet in keeping with the way of the future as we foresee it today, VR requires that we connect acts and images without understanding their logic.

CHILDREN IN FRONT OF THE SCREEN

What happens when children play videogames, a customary scene these days and a true training for their interaction with VR? If an image appears on the screen (which becomes the children's universe while they play, as shown by their annoyance when they are asked to stop), trained children make no associations with it; they simply connect it and activate a button that triggers another image. This process lasts as long as the speed of their reflexes. It is not just that associations with the traces evoked by this image in the chil-dren's internal world hinder game performance; such associations are simply out of the question. Moreover, interpreting children's behavior within the associative realm, which we grew accustomed to doing thanks to psychoanal-ysis, might not be appropriate here.

This prevalence of connection over association is favored by the fact that, as is the case with most interactive applications and in VR in general, in videogames there is not one but a multiplicity of potential realities preceding any associative reminiscence that might be stirred in users. The proposition is not "*either* this *or* that" but "this *and* that." The logic of connection enables us to travel simultaneously through bifurcating paths, as in Borges's story

(Borges, 1941b).[4] This possibility is facilitated by computers' ability to keep manifold variants of "reality" activated at the same time.

Videogames' virtual reality images do not aspire to be anything but themselves or to promote anything other than connections, which are utterly reducible to mechanical logics. For this reason, videogames usually include a command that incorporates the instructing device into the game. In this realm machines are unbeatable; when it comes to connecting computers are superior to any human, among other reasons because associative logic interferes with humans' connecting ability. In this sense, videogames offer a kind of test of how mechanical human beings can get. The reverse, however, is not true. Despite being science fiction's favorite topic and the ultimate goal of computer programmers, the production of machine-subjects has not been accomplished even by the most sophisticated devices.

In a psychoanalytic consulting room or an artist's atelier the free association of representations is always encouraged. In these spaces connection seems useless or, at least, not essential. Artistic production, traditional play, dreams, and symptoms are hence apt for interpretation, which involves presuming the existence of non-explicit meanings. That is why free association has been psychoanalysis' main tool and creation's resource par excellence. Its course, which systematically follows the most significant marks in the history of the subject of association, allows us to surmise and identify this subject.

Yet association is not very sensitive to the ties that already exist in the surrounding world (created by resemblance or contiguity); rather, it models this world according to its own logic. Contrariwise, the logic of connection, which is external to subjects, is much more sensitive to a situation's objective relations. For instance, images presented by videogames and VR, dominated by connection, do not admit interpretation because they are what they represent, just as the logic of Internet links is set by the network. The threads woven by connection are there for everyone to travel through, but do not lead to a subject. The characters at play are the ones that appear on the screen. Whether or not the child-operator identifies with them is a different matter. VR's proposition to whoever enters it is to take any of the manifold paths that have already been outlined which, like a hypertext, are there waiting to be trodden upon, even if the travelers believe they are embarking on an unprecedented experience.

TWO TYPES OF GAMES

The nature and pervasiveness of connective games force us to revisit the notion of play. We should distinguish between two different ways of playing based on the prevalence of connection or association. In games where the logic of connection predominates, playing means negotiating logical-mechanical sequences that, by way of images, simulate reality on a screen. Connective play entails traversing prewritten paths with no space for subjective participation—a way of playing that leads to the dilution or vanishing of the subject during the game. Traditional play, discussed by psychoanalysis, is very different. It is the site of association and of the emergence of meaning. Child and adult players can become creators. In Freud's words, a subject may "link *his* imagined objects and situations to the tangible and visible things of the real world" (Freud, 1908, p. 144; emphasis added).

Just as in connective games the external object dominates and prevails over a vanished subject, in associative games subjects imprint their meanings upon an external object that conforms to their fantasies. Psychoanalysts have repeatedly pointed to associative play as the model for free association and even for the cure. The clear prevalence of connective play among children today may have something to say in this regard. There are associative and connective games, and even though they engage in both kinds, young people nowadays show a clear preference for the latter. Should we deplore this situation and teach our wayward children how they ought to play? Should we lead them toward what we believe are true games? I do not think so. Without abandoning our critical position, we should let ourselves be led by our children to some extent, so as to reencounter in their games the characters of their fantasy. We should understand that it is not a distortion but a new kind of practice where frustration is also present, albeit fragmented, in a different scale, or with a different mode of participation.

I would venture to say that perhaps we should accept that the partial prevalence of object over subject characteristic of connective games is not a pathological deviation but a fact of present-day reality. The respite provided by predictability may constitute a haven for subjects overwhelmed by the whirlwind world we inhabit. Our thinking of this form of play as pathological might lead us to find in it two of its symptomatic modes, namely, addiction and phobia to connective media.

When I became interested in these topics I almost unwittingly began to pay attention to the games, videogames, and videos children are currently playing and watching. I started asking my patients what Pokémon, Dragonball, Carmaggedon, Counterstrike, Digimos, Ranma 1/2, and Ben 10 were about. I even bought and learned how to play with Magic, Sakura, Pokémon, and Yu-Gi-Oh cards, names that had been leaving traces in my office without my attaching any importance to them, I must admit. I am slowly becoming quite knowledgeable in these matters. Even so, I cannot follow the fads as they substitute one another, an inability that is constantly being brought to my attention by my patients' scorn. Once their astonishment at my change in attitude had passed, they explained many details unknown to me.

For example, in 1999 six-year-old Martín enlightened me about the 150 different Pokémons, whose names, skills, powers, and potential evolutions he knew through and through. In 2002 (when this book was first published in Spanish) there were already more than 300, and according to Martín they could now be cloned to create new species. It should be highlighted that the courage of Ash, a Pokémon trainer hero, or the wickedness of Team Rocket, their evil counterpart were irrelevant; the key issue was the powers wielded by the little monsters owned and trained by human protagonists.

Pokémon (whose name is the contraction of Pocket Monsters) have no particular intelligence, only powers. Their ability to talk is very limited and unique; except for Meowth, they can only utter their own names. Pikachu, the most popular of the creatures, can only say "pikachu" with different inflections, but can cause great destruction by emitting highly powerful electric discharges, or by "evolving" into Raichu or "involving" into Pichu. Trainers' obsession is to have as many powerful Pokémon as possible. Whether we like it or not, this feature is syntonic with children's behavior, a behavior that turns them into privileged objects of consumer society, as Corea and Lewkowicz (1999) claim.

This dynamic can be extended to most contemporary games. The power granted to characters by objects tends to be much more significant than characters themselves. The attack and defense value, the ability to charm and block, or the weakness of a Magic or Pokémon card depends neither on the creature illustrated on the card nor on its intentions. Rather, it depends on its powers. Such preeminence anticipates perhaps what technological development forebodes—that technological objects will dominate subjects. In most games, furthermore, characters can "transform" into different characters. Is this ability another preview of what technology has in store for the future, when today's children will be adults?

Andrés, an eleven-year-old pubescent boy, taught me some of the thrilling inner workings of Ranma 1/2. When exposed to cold water Ranma Saotome, a teenager of unknown age and student of the Anything Goes Martial Arts School becomes Ranma-chan, an exuberant, attractive red-haired girl. Hot water, in turn, will restore his original male form, Ranma-kun, a brave young man. In the series they call him an aquatranssexual. None of this happened to typical modern heroes[5] such as Tarzan or Prince Valiant. Tarzan's power was his own, and so was Prince Valiant's. They underwent no transformations save the ones brought about by their upbringing and valor, and of course they were proven heterosexuals—machos from head to foot. Superman and Batman only dressed up as Clark Kent or Bruce Wayne to hide attributes that were always part of them.

There is a critical difference between mutation, the pure alteration of contemporary characters, and changes undergone by modern characters, which represented the unfolding of powers inherent in their essence. Tarzan's powers stemmed exclusively from his generous humanity. It is true that his friendship with chimpanzees, lions, or "savages" could be of help. His powers, however, did not depend on objects he possessed but on his own qualities as a subject, namely, his history of orphaned nobility (which could resonate strongly with readers) and his heroic courage. In contemporary games, by contrast, power is permanently granted by objects and by the ability to mutate, not in the sense of changing or dressing up but in the sense of becoming another. It might be advisable at this point to examine separately each of the logics underlying child play.

ASSOCIATIVE LOGIC

The logic of association imposes a condition on the elements with which it operates; they must have an explicit, implicit, or alleged meaning, either conscious or unconscious. This meaning is ruled by a code that responds to translation laws. According to Peirce (1998), the relationship between designation and the thing that is being designated is one of thirdness. Formally, the signs with which association works can be articulated with each other like the terms of a complex mathematical equation. They may be enigmatic but not inconsistent. Heterogeneity can only make its presence evident in associations as an impasse or an inconsistency. In the face of something new, like an unrepresented presentation or a product of the association itself that cannot be assimilated, the psyche's associative system displays its signifiers, repressed or not, and associates this new element with them through condensation or displacement (metaphor or metonymy). In this way, the psyche generates meanings that facilitate understanding. In other words, it reduces the new element to the particularity of a combination of what it already knows. This process also makes it possible to identify the subject of association.

It has been traditionally understood that by means of association psychoanalysis can reveal meanings that were already present in the mind. From the theoretical perspective I am discussing here, association itself produces these meanings. Within this logic, therefore, everything is determined and interpretable in terms of the history of the associating subject. This viewpoint constitutes the core of the method created by Freud and his patients to find the hidden cause of symptoms. It is in this context that we should read the classic recommendation to analysts to be as neutral as possible so that the reality of the session—and if practicable, the vicissitudes of patients' lives— does not interfere with the association process.

The same premise underlies Melanie Klein's suggestion that the toys in the basket of a child patient be as simple, as non-representative as possible. Today we can say that these recommendations are based on the assumption that low sensory stimulation favors association by thwarting connection. The goal is then to let the purest form of child and adult unconscious fantasies unroll based on inconsequential presentations. The materiality of presences should interfere as little as possible so as to keep connection minimal.

CONNECTIVE LOGIC

According to connective logic, elements may be "connected" with each other without articulating them with psychic representations. Connection travels automatically through a network that is external to subjects. Meanings at play here are neither produced nor surmised by subjects, and neither are they enigmatic; they are external. Like the preset steps of a videogame or the paths of a hypertext, the roads of connection exist outside the subject who is connecting them. An example that may illustrate my argument is the TV. Hundreds of TV channels travel through the air or through cable, just as millions of Internet websites constantly broadcast shows and pages regardless of the existence of spectators or readers. Every time spectators activate a channel they start experiencing the reality emitted by the screen. At the same time, thousands of other possible realities circulate uninterruptedly through the ether, ready for connection, and spectators' decisions do not affect their existence.

Viewers become aware of their lack of influence by zapping and substituting other realities for the one that impacts their eyes. They may believe that they are in command, but they can only choose among preexisting realities over which their interventions have no effect whatsoever. It is true that, as polls reveal, we may identify statistical trends concerning subjects' alleged choices. Yet as was the case with Borges's Babel Library, all potential paths have already been written in a preexisting Universe—that of a network—before our alleged discovery.[6] Subjects traversing these paths do not open new roads, nor do they leave their trace on them; their steps effect no alteration. What is more, current technology enables the website or channel—not spectators—to detect users' most frequent "choices." In this way, the current tendency is for the medium, not the spectator to be in command of preferences, thus producing something noticeably similar to Ingsoc's telescreen—to the Big Brother in Orwell's *1984*.

All this may appear natural because we experience it daily, but before information technology flourished, it would not even have been possible to envisage a situation of this sort unless we thought of a spectator running madly from theater to theater. The potential for different realities to circulate simultaneously and be activated by a button is a product of present-day technology and is associated with the existence of manifold realities, so important nowadays. Nonetheless, I think that connection has always been present in human beings. Today's colossal technological progress only renders it more significant and easier to detect.

OBLIVION AND DELETING,
REMEMBRANCE AND TOTAL RECALL

Oblivion, an essential operation to signify and historicize "realities," is exclusive to association and does not exist in connection. The production of signs, basic entities of association, involves forgetting their origin. In this sense, a sign is like a monument commemorating the burial of the event that generated it (Milner, 1988). Of this event only a name and oblivion are left. The name swells the archives of the psyche, where it may produce associations and meaning. We do not remember the facts tied to the quest for that name, which are specifically excluded from the signifying world of associations. It is, therefore, impossible to ponder the origin of the sign; its emergence involves forgetting the event that gave rise to it. The sign is hence a node where necessity and randomness intersect.

Each point of oblivion (of origin of signs) imposes an irreversible direction on time. Time is here a fundamental category, as is Euclidian space, where the subject of association resides. The sense Freud (1924) gave to the burial of the Oedipus complex is paradigmatic of this process. The Oedipus complex must sink, founder, be forgotten so that its marks may be inscribed and rule the associative order forever. Consequently, although the process is rendered more complex because of resignification, in associations there is a time that moves in a certain direction and a space with places where events occur. There are stories, order, and sequences. There is no simultaneity; each "thing" has its own place and time, and these coordinates must be respected. The associative system is ruled by Aristotelian determinism and operates in chronological time.

In the connective system, instead, there is no oblivion or remembrance, strictly speaking. I call this system's operations that are correlative to oblivion and remembrance *deleting* and *total recall*. To delete means to annihilate in the literal sense of turning into nothing, erasing without traces. Total recall, in turn, means being able to record everything, like Funes the Memorious in Borges's short story (Borges, 1944).[7] Deleting and total recall are thus equivalent. Like inactivating a website on the Internet, deleting memory chunks on a PC leaves no traces and involves no forgetting. Furthermore, since there is no oblivion and all records have the same value, as was the case with Funes's mind, in the connection process there is no memory either, only total recall. In practical terms, in the connective system memory is always the same as total recall.

The operation typical of association is inscription, which is essentially imperfect and involves surplus marks, specific exclusions, and oblivion. The operation typical of connection, by contrast, is transcription, which leaves no mark but what has been transcribed, is exact, and generates no surplus. Many of us have lost one (or all!) of our computer files. There is nothing more distressing about this calamity than the fact that the deleting act leaves no traces and is oblivious to the quality and quantity of the information erased. There is no difference between annihilating the phrase "my mother loves me," the letter "u," or the manuscript of *Martín Fierro*.[8]

In the same way, total recall is completely oblivious to the quality and quantity of the information recorded. In addition, since traveling through connective roads leaves no evocable mark, these roads are reversible. Time, therefore, has no direction, and space, no places. As paradoxical as it may seem, Internet websites do not take any space. Whatever their topology may be, it does not seem to be Euclidean. Undoubtedly, it is much harder to approach connective logic intuitively than to do so with associative logic. Such difficulty may stem from the discrepancy between the logic of connection and everyday experience as well as from the strong mark left in our thinking by the Aristotelian, deterministic view of the world.

Nonetheless, we should not be discouraged. After all, something notably similar happens with quantum physics' discrepancy with Newtonian physics. The latter cannot conceive of the behavior of an electron, a negatively charged tiny particle that swarms in varying numbers around all atoms. Electrons behave as though they were in many places and in no place at the same time. Only their observation creates a specific place for them. In this sense, they are similar to websites, TV channels, or videogame characters. These only remain in a specific location while they are being watched.

If we throw a tennis ball against a wall, it bounces. Yet if an electron collides with a wall, it may either bounce or go through it. This aspect of electron behavior is the basis for the workings of transistors and present-day electronics. As Tom Siegfried (2000) states, "quantum mechanics shows no respect for common notions of time and space (. . .) observers, by acquiring information, are somehow involved in bringing reality into existence" (Siegfried, 2000, p. 10). The coincidence with the connective world is noticeable, although similarities may be due just to the fact that the logics ruling these systems are not Aristotelian.

SIGN AND ICON

Perhaps in order to understand the most radical aspects of the difference between the associative and connective systems we should analyze the nature of what, following Peirce, we would call their representamen.[9] While this analysis is necessary, it exceeds the purpose of this book, so I will only outline some ideas. In association, designations are subject to the laws of translation. Between the sign and the designated object there is hence a distance mediated by a code. Consequently, while it becomes necessary once it is established, the relationship between the designator and the designated is utterly arbitrary and loses all naturalness. It is precisely the lack of a natural relationship, or relationship of firstness, in the associative route that makes it possible for sign combinations to generate unforeseen meanings. These meanings, in turn, facilitate the identification of the subject of association, especially in analytic practice.

In the realm of connection, by contrast, the representamen is not a sign but an icon. The latter operates without a code (a law) that ties it to the denoted object. The designated and the designator operate in the same plane of firstness (Peirce, 1998; Corea, 2001). The icon does not produce meaning by following the law of translation. Rather, it "exhibits the same quality, or the same configuration of qualities, that the denoted object exhibits" (Ducrot and Todorov, 1972, p. 86). The icon is anchored, in a way, in the object it designates, and its association produces nothing.

Let us take the well-known videogame Pacman as an example. Between the name *pacman* and what it denotes there is a distance mediated by the laws of translation. For this reason, depending on context, punctuation, and the previous and subsequent associations the word provokes, within the associative regime the person saying "pacman" could be designating the game itself, the yellow Pacman icon or "character" (a yellow, circular head with a wedge removed for the mouth) a backpacker, a bulimic (because in the game the icon eats everything that crosses its path), or thousands of other things, depending on the direction taken by the associative course.

What happens in the realm of connection is very different. The Pacman icon is both the figure and what it designates, and it means nothing other than that. In the *Pacman* videogame world, gamers operate with this icon, and in the practice of the game the icon generates no meaning that exceeds it. Gamers do not associate anything with it. They maintain the relationship between the icon and the Pacman in the dimension of firstness. It is a natural correlation that is not mediated by a law translating or ruling its existence and does not produce meaning outside.

If I ask people what "mother" means to them, it is unlikely that they will draw a sign, write a name, or show a picture. Above all, the sign "mother" supports an absence. Conversely, in the practice of the game the Pacman icon is the unrepresentable presence of the Pacman trace. Consequently, the icon, contrary to the sign, is not arbitrary but natural. Neither is it necessary, for the representamen and the object are the same and hence do not lead to each other. A "forgotten" icon will not necessarily leave a trace; the designator and the designated coincide in the icon, and if one disappears, so will the other. In connection there is no forgetting, only deletion.

Another critical difference between the associative and connective systems is the speed with which they operate. The inertia of association is far greater than the inertia of connection. Association always lags behind processes. Every time the world surrounding the psyche is altered, farewells, usually accompanied by rites, become necessary. When something new occurs we may be able to understand it after a working-through process that may be lengthy and costly at times. Within the associative system, understanding something means redirecting it toward what we already know and attaching meaning to it.

Associative logic naturally tends toward homeostasis and toward viewing everything as a variant of what already exists. Connection is immediate. Its time is the instant, and it does not tend toward homeostatic regulation. That is why although they have some effect on the psyche, connections themselves may be impossible to grasp, as we shall see in the next chapter.[10]

HOW SHOULD WE APPROACH THIS DEBATE?

In my view, there are two radically different ways of addressing this matter. One is thinking that everything related to connection and presentation is a spurious remainder that is irrelevant to the undisputed reign of *logos*. The other is considering that connection (and its current prevalence) makes present what had been violently expelled from our conception of the world and the psyche by the tyranny of words and reason—traces that do not represent but are.

According to this second consideration, the obvious emergence of connection in our times is not just the product of current technological developments. It is also tied to the fall of the rational utopia that manifested itself in the psychoanalytic milieu as a tendency to attribute every existing meaning, every possible creation to an effect of words or to an associative articulation among representatives of absences. It is evident that the deification of *logos* was an exaggeration. Yet we should point out that it was in this logocentric climate that psychoanalysis was born, with all its power to explain. Having developed in this context may have led psychoanalytic theory and practice to set aside what I call connective phenomena and the effects of unrepresentable presentations which, as we shall see, are an essential aspect of the emergence of the radically new.

NOTES

1. See chapter 2.

2. The meanings of the associative process converge in a locus where all signification allegedly concentrates, a locus that corresponds to the notion of subject.

3. The use of helmet-mounted displays simulating a reality that may be intuited based on data perceived by radars (which is already being used by civilian pilots) is now common in many armies.

4. "The Garden of Forking Paths," in *Labyrinths*, New York: New Directions, 2007. (T.N.)

5. See chapter 8.

6. The author is referring here to the short story "The Library of Babel." The library in Borges's story holds everything that has been written and that could ever be written. (T.N.)

7. The character in Borges's short story has an incredibly accurate perception of every single detail of the world around him and can remember absolutely everything he perceives. (T.N.)

8. "*Mi mamá me ama*" (my mother loves me) was a typical phrase of Argentine elementary school textbooks. *Martín Fierro* is a classic of Argentine literature. (T.N.)

9. Firstness, or the category of *feeling*, corresponds to "an instance of that kind of consciousness which involves no analysis, comparison or any process whatsoever, nor consists in whole or in part of any act by which one stretch of consciousness is distinguished from another (. . .) A feeling, then, is not an event, a happening, a coming to pass, . . . a feeling is a *state,* which is in its entirety in every moment of time as long as it endures (Peirce, 1998, p. 1.306). According to Jay Zeman (1977), "firstness is immediacy, firstness is the prereflexive. When refection does occur, however, we enter the realm of secondness. Secondness is the category of the *actual existent* (. . .) Something is a second insofar as it is." Thirdness, by contrast is "the category of law" (Zeman, 1977, p. 23). The categories of firstness, secondness, and thirdness correspond to the semiotic categories of icon, index, and symbol, respectively. Every act of semiosis has an object, a representamen (icon, index, or symbol), and an interpretant (the mental representation, or thought, that the semiotic act tends to determine).

10. Either of these logics has prevailed in different ways at different times, depending on the availability of information resources. While in earlier times (which compared to our own were characterized by a scarcity of information) association predominated, today's plethora of data has led to the preeminence of connection.

Chapter Four

The Link I

Theory

FATES OF THE NEW

When something (a theory, an announcement, a piece of news) with an ambition to innovate bursts into a discipline, it provokes two reactions that, albeit seemingly contradictory, produce a similar effect. The first one is to consider that as this emergent has shed light on major issues in the field, any other option, whether past or future, should be dismissed. The second reaction rids the alleged new thing of its novelty by claiming that it is a mere reformulation of what had already been written in. . . . It is not, therefore, rare for those who appear to speak in the name of a revolution to be eventually accused of being renegades, ignorant, or opportunistic.

Doubtlessly, this alleged novelty might not actually be new. Nonetheless, if it were a genuine event, both reactions would be partially right. It is as true that its precursors created the necessary platform for the new to emerge as the impossibility to reduce an event to its antecedents. Radical novelty is more than the result of any of the potential combinations of these antecedents. The two reactions that usually follow the emergence of new discoveries (blind acceptance or early rejection) share in fact the same goal. They both aim to avoid the disruptive effects that these discoveries might have on instituted knowledge. When something threatens such knowledge, a kind of struggle breaks out between the structure's conservative inertia and the force with which the new truth tries to carve out a place for itself.

The term "link," which despite its popularity in the Argentine psychoanalytic realm was not easily incorporated into the field, has given rise to similar reactions. This concept poses problems, among other reasons, because of the

53

questions it prompts, among them the following: Is there more to the link than the unfolding of representations contributed by each individual participating in it? Those who believe that the answer is negative see no reason to consider this term unique in any way. At the same time, those who think that the consequences of an encounter transcend any reckoning based on participants' prior history and that "link" is, in a way, the name of this surplus have trouble explaining the concept and the cause of its effects. I will address this quandary step by step, going from the periphery into the core.

SOURCES OF DISTURBANCE

Why is it that sometimes, without any apparent reason, we are disturbed by a presence or circumstance that seems foreign to us? There are two answers to this question that we must differentiate in view of our subsequent discussion. One, which was masterly developed by classic psychoanalysis, is that subjects are disturbed by a struggle between the repressed, which strives to clear a path toward consciousness, and our defenses, which attempt to prevent the repressed from achieving its end. Subjects are thus unsettled by the recurrence of a repressed past that aims to reemerge—the return of what had already been dislodged from consciousness and stored in the unconscious. For example, excessive concern regarding a love encounter might be due to the return of incestuous fantasies typical of the Oedipus complex that had not been properly buried.

The other type of answer claims that the new that is attempting to burst in is disturbing because its presentation faces the psyche with an impasse; the logic of the psyche is inconsistent when it comes to understanding something that lies outside its system of representations. For instance, the announcement to the father-to-be of the arrival of his first child may be unsettling not because of the return of some aspect of repressed childhood sexuality, but because the prospective father's psychic apparatus had specifically excluded everything related to "being a father" from its formulations. Or to give another example, the disturbance brought about by the love encounter we discussed above might be due simply to the fact that this encounter opened a door into territories hitherto untrodden by the person in love.

The disparity between these answers—something disturbs either because it had been repressed or because it is inconceivable—is highly significant for psychoanalytic practice. While in the first case it is natural to maintain that in order to promote psychic change we must unlock what was locked by the defenses raised against the repressed (Freud's "making conscious the unconscious"), in the second we must be aware that the radically new will face the most tenacious obstacles to its entering the psyche merely by virtue of its newness. In this sense, we should distinguish obstacle from resistance. Obstacles are generated by the emergence of the inadmissible, the previously nonexistent. Resistance, by contrast, is the opposition to the return of the repressed, that is, of something that already exists but was buried. Since obstacle and resistance are deeply intertwined, they are usually hard to differentiate. How much of the symptom is produced by resistance and by what is being resisted, and how much is a manifestation of the inadmissible and its obstacles? Elucidating this question might be pivotal to clinical work.

Generally speaking, classic psychoanalysis decidedly favored the approach to disturbing aspects of "normal" thinking in terms of resistance. This approach led to the dismissal of the notion of obstacle. As a consequence, the role of the undetermined and the radically new was neglected in both theory and practice (Moreno, 2000a). Such neglect is not trivial in the least. As we discussed in Chapter 1, humans are distinguished by their use of consistent signs to represent the situation they inhabit, but more so by their ability to come into contact with experiences or situations that exceed this system of signs, that is, with inconsistencies.[1] Yet as we shall see, these paths do not diverge that much in practice. Every psychic change involves both bringing into play resistances opposing conscious remembrance and overcoming obstacles to our opening to the unknown. Furthermore, obstacles to the new and resistance against the repressed are often intricately entwined.

JUST SIGNS?

In the previous chapter I suggested that a sort of screen composed of two heterogeneous systems (associative and connective) both separates human beings from the world surrounding them and binds them to it. I will now attempt to delve into the ways in which this screen participates in the specific mechanisms that mediate relationships among humans. It is true that a "newborn,"[2] whatever this actually means, emerges into a world populated by speaking fellow-beings but lacks the resources to engage with them. To become one of its kind, it will have to develop such resources. Babies are welcome into a world packed with signifiers. The smallest unit of this world, which postulates itself as whole and free of inconsistencies, is the sign.

Some students of subjectivity believe that the world of signifiers and signifieds is the ultimate determinant of any type of subjective development—even of any potential meaning of the links that babies will build over time. Nonetheless, scholars increasingly suspect that the effects of links defy explanations based solely on the codes and signs of the representational world, or at least on the codes and signs used by each of the psyches involved in those links. When we talk about aspects of the other that produce effects on us despite our inability to subsume them into our system of representations, we usually refer to "the alien in others" (Puget and Berenstein, 1989;

Berenstein, 2001, 2007). This approach, however, poses two problems. First, we need to assess whether the alien in others actually exists, or if we are dealing with our own inability or lack of knowledge to evaluate the effects of representations. Second, if the ungraspable in others does exist, we must find out how it affects us (for instance, if it has its own inscription).

Since extralinguistic qualities have generally been viewed as a remnant of our instinctive, animal past, it is common practice to dismiss them as a potential cause of human effects or to cast them into the discredited realm of magical thinking. This is certainly understandable; it was very hard for psychoanalysis to develop the notion that humans are different from animals and that this difference, this "breach in the functional efficiency" discussed by Freud (1900, p. 594) is a source of neurosis. Yet such an approach may suffer the same fate as those definitions that set boundaries to the problem they want to address. If we claim that humans inhabit a world of words, everything affecting them will be by definition an effect of words, and anything that is not a word will be non-human. My viewpoint is different, as we shall see.

WHAT MECHANISMS REGULATE RELATIONSHIPS AMONG HUMANS?

There are two basic ways of addressing this general question, and we should distinguish them from the start. We may claim either that subjects determine the link, or that the link determines the subjectivity of those involved in it. According to the first perspective, the traditional one, it is in the "we," in one and the other subject that we must search for the cause of occurrences in the link. What takes place there is hence the result of the combination of elements that are already present as potential in participating subjects and unfold in the act. That is why, regardless of changes in environmental conditions, we cannot expect to find radical differences between the subjects *in* the link and those same subjects *outside* the link. From this point of view, subjects have a definable, delimited set of individual potentialities that may develop in their link experiences. There is no reason for these experiences to alter the essence of subjects, who are viewed as fairly stable structures.[3]

To illustrate this position, we may think of two subjects, Juan and Maria, each possessing a psychic world that is a complex, stable organization. These subjects determine ("<" and ">") what will happen in the in-between, in the link:

Juan > between < Maria

We may read this diagram as "the link between Juan and Maria is determined by the properties of Juan plus the properties of Maria."[4] Still, this approach usually acknowledges that due to the huge number and delicate subtlety of the variables at play, chance (epistemological chance, which is grounded on the observer's lack of knowledge) hinders efforts to calculate these determinations. Consequently, without abandoning this position we may claim that predicting what will happen in a link based on the total knowledge of participating subjects' psyches may be impossible in practice.

Nevertheless, and this is a crucial point, such prediction is not impossible in and of itself. Rather, its immense complexity makes it unfeasible. It is worth recalling here Voltaire's words: "What we call chance can be no other than the unknown cause of a known effect" (Voltaire, 1764, p. 142). Chance plays no role in links. The unexpected is but the effect of our ignorance of previously existing forces that remain dormant in the linked subjects. According to this conception, then, the effects of the encounter are determined. In addition, there is a tendency toward homeostasis and a limit to the range of developments set by the potentiality of the subjects involved, who are not changed by the link.[5]

The second approach ("the link determines subjects") is less traditional and more at odds with our usual way of thinking. It does not consider that the "we" can determine the in-between, or that even the most complete knowledge of the psychic apparatuses at play in the link would allow us to foresee the latter's nature or its effects on linked subjects. Such inability, moreover, is not due to the number of variables at play or to the complexity of the interaction. This perspective is radically different from the first one. In each instant the in-between, the relationship itself defines each of the terms making up the "we." An inevitable surplus emerges that alters every element of the link. There are no stable, fully assembled, or constituted subjects who forge relationships. The linkage they traverse constantly redefines them.

Maria and Juan are outlined by their link. Perhaps it would be easier to think that there are a Juan and a Maria who precede the encounter, and a different Juan and Maria who follow it. Such view, however, is a weakened version of this viewpoint. It would be similar to what Borges (1964) remarked about the way in which the first meaning of Heraclitus's thesis—"The river is another"—is related to (and, I would add, obscures) the second one—"I am another at every instant." The diagram in this case would be the following:

Juan "<" between ">" Maria

This diagram should be read as "The link determines Juan and Maria." The potential effects of the encounter, therefore, are not determined in advance and will differ for each subject of the link. Furthermore, such difference is not complementary in any way.

THESE PERSPECTIVES CANNOT BE ARTICULATED

These two perspectives—the one that stresses that the future relationship is defined by what already is, and the one that claims that it is the relationship itself that determines its components—cannot engage in a dialogue. Their connection seems to be empty. Neither position can rebut the other, but both seem reasonable. Moreover, each speaks of aspects that may be verified by experience. Nonetheless, they coincide in one way. Neither one by itself allows us to ponder the historicization of the link. In the first case, because every mark 2 generated in the link refers to the combination of marks 1 contributed by the subjects. Identities and contiguities are preserved in renewed combinations, but there is no place for the products of the new. The present of the link can always be reduced to its individual antecedents. Historicization, therefore, is only possible if it is understood as the unfolding of what already existed. In fact, the word "link" does not designate a novelty.

According to the second approach, in turn, historicization is not possible because we cannot even claim that linked subjects are identical to themselves—they vary at every instant. Pure present, with no marks to determine it, cancels historical thinking. Marks 1 of instant 1 are not related to marks 2 of instant 2. The latter might very well be called 1, as there is no temporal continuity or sequence. From this point of view, the word *link* designates something with no boundaries. While they share the inability to explain a relationship, these approaches do not engage in a dialogue and cannot rebut one another, as I already pointed out. There is hence a gap between them. We might think that their inability to contrast or debate is due to their use of different premises and modes of reasoning. I believe, however, that the cause should be sought elsewhere.

THE LINK: CONNECTION-ASSOCIATION

I address inter-human relations from the perspective that both views on links are valid, or rather, that each view is partly right but neither can fully account for the linking phenomenon. This phenomenon entails a complex interaction between both viewpoints. In other words, we are not dealing with different approaches to, or alternative explanations of, a single phenomenon, but with two utterly different mechanisms that operate by creating a fractal interface or border (Gleick, 1987) between them. Through this border travels what we call the link as if it were a unity. In actuality, one of this book's major theses is that the uniqueness of our species—its ability to change—is due to the interplay between the two mechanisms (each setting boundaries to the other) in every relationship between humans and their environment.

We may thus consider two poles with different logics that form a sort of screen on the border of mental activity and thus mediate all inter-human relations. The poles are the connective and associative systems, and the phenomenon known as *link* develops between them.

association]. . . . . [connection
link ↑

While these systems are heterogeneous, their actions are always coupled because each system's productions modify the operating conditions of the other (hence everything constantly varies). I call this coupling a link. We should start by looking at each pole separately.

THE ASSOCIATIVE POLE: THE PSYCHIC COUNTING

The associative pole, whose meanings are the product of the association of homogeneous elements, may also be called representation pole because it is composed of representations. Or we could simply call it psychic counting. I am drawing here from Badiou's (1988) notion of count-as-one.[6] The psyche counts particularities of what is already known but overlooks anything that is singular and, as such, uncountable.

Lewkowicz's (1990) differentiation between singular and particular may be of use here. Singular refers to those aspects of a given object that cannot be reduced to the object's properties. Particular, by contrast, alludes to perceptible differences that facilitate the distinction among components of the same group. We can count individuals as one, two, three, and so on because they display traits that identify them as different. In this way, the psyche neutralizes singularity by attempting to reduce it to a particularity of a class that is part of its system of representations. The psychic counting, then, specifically excludes singularities in order to be able to count-as-one. In the next chapter I will go deeper into the reasons for choosing the term "one."

Operations typical of the associative pole are consistent with the deterministic spirit stressed in Freud's work. This pole's way of functioning might be formulated as follows: the psychic counting renders what happens around it and what affects it comprehensible by means of frameworks forged in the past. It verifies the repetition of this past in the present, and makes time and space continuous so that experiences taking place in them are homogeneous and articulable. The psychic counting acts in the model of the Aristotelian machine I described earlier.[7] It has verifying frameworks, that is, frameworks that set the course of perception so that anything that happens may be seen as a particularity or as the unfolding of what is considered possible. Consequently, subjects can view every result as already determined.

According to the logic of the associative pole, compulsion to repeat is verifying repetition[8]—the return of the same that shapes the present as a recapitulation of the past. It homogenizes the heterogeneous, articulates what cannot be articulated, and particularizes the singular. In this way, the contemporary, unique elements that might stem from a presentation (either external or the product of the psychic counting itself, a creative emergent whose understanding exceeds its own logic) are transformed into a particularity within the system's code—a new term of the old sequence. Like the Egyptian geometer who transformed all the irregularities left by the receding water of the Nile after a flood into polygons so as to calculate its area, the psychic counting transforms singularities into countable units. It specifically excludes (we should remember this term) what is inconsistent within the geometric framework (irregularities that cannot be reduced to polygonal forms) because such inconsistencies might affect this transformation.

Consequently, those features of the presentation that cannot become marks or signs to be articulated by the psychic counting[9] are specifically excluded, and no sign is left of the exclusion process beyond the implications of this suturing operation. The psychic counting cannot capture the Two as an essential difference; it can only transform presences into Ones and articulate these Ones based on a law. It thus counts by Threes[10] to formulate in its own fashion—that is, by way of signs—the irreducible differences (the Two) of the inconsistent multiplicity it inhabits, thence the "counting" in psychic counting. In the associative pole the singularities of a presentation tend to be, so to speak, destroyed by the internal object, whose production, like that of any symbolic representation, involves forgetting the event that generated it.

Representations (the elements with which the associative pole operates) are divided into two complementary subsets. One is the subset of the forbidden or repressed, and the other, the subset of the permitted or non-repressed. Everything that happens in the associative world may be explained by the complex interplay of the elements of the two subsets, as Freud attempted to do. For the psychic counting, nothing exists outside these subsets in the world of signs, which is the only thing it takes into account. The repressed and the non-repressed operate with common, articulable elements.[11] So much so that we could say that in the psychic counting there are only mixed formations. Classic psychoanalytic theory considers that inconsistencies occasionally present in the subset of permitted representations dissolve—in Freud's (1900) terms, thinking becomes "normal"—if we can incorporate the elements cancelled by repression into its explanatory framework. The principle of the excluded third (in this case, this principle establishes that a representation can only be repressed or not repressed, and so nothing exists outside these two categories) is fully valid here and supports the unity of the whole.

THE DREAM AS A MODEL FOR THE ASSOCIATIVE SYSTEM

If one had to illustrate the associative mode of functioning of the psychic counting with a model, I think it would be that of dreaming, as Freud masterly interpreted it in 1900. Those who dream have shut their windows to the world. From then on, everything that happens in their psyche is the product of the association of lingering representations that hamper sleep like a fly buzzing around. They are a residue of daytime concerns, and have received a transfer from an unconscious movement to form an oneiric desire whose realization constitutes the dream. The latter is utterly comprehensible and interpretable based on the laws of condensation and displacement. Furthermore, since it is the product of the combination of representations already present in the psyche, nothing in it is radically new.

The power of associations to interpret everything in terms of repetitive frameworks may be illustrated by the effects on sleep of an external stimulus, as is the case with Maury's famous dream (Freud, 1900). Reclining on his bed during an illness with his mother sitting next to him, Maury dreamed he was living during the French Terror. After witnessing a series of terrifying assassination scenes, he is taken to the revolutionary tribunal, where he sees Robespierre, Marat, Fouquier-Tinville, and the other heroes of the time. He is interrogated, and after some incidents he can't remember he is sentenced and led to the execution site, surrounded by a huge crowd. He climbs to the scaffold. His head is placed on the guillotine, and he feels the blade falling on his neck—he can even see how his head detaches from his body.

Maury woke up feeling terribly anxious, and realized that the headrest had fallen and hit his neck just as the guillotine blade had done in the dream. The external stimulus "headrest brushing the neck" had been absorbed by Maury's psychic counting and transformed into an almost pure verifying repetition, with the troubling presence of castration. The quality or features of the external element that had affected the psyche scarcely mattered.

This account is but a sample of the power of association when unchecked by connection. Associative logic, both unconscious and preconscious, works by generating a product that is first and foremost an interpretation of current occurrences based on existing frameworks. Dreaming is here a regressive, narcissistic time when dreamers relate only to the reflections of their remembrance. To be able to keep sleeping, they veil whatever is troubling them with these reflections. Such turn of events is the extreme form of what customarily takes place during waking life in the associative pole, although with less autonomy—we protect ourselves from unexpected events.

THE CONNECTIVE POLE

The other basic system is tied to the notion of connection discussed earlier.[12] Yet when we are dealing with relationships between people, the quality of the *traits* with which connection is established is more complex and special. The psychic counting of the person creating the link must view these traits as inadmissible, excluded, and hard to associate. In other words, connections are created with the alien aspects of others. The classic cause-effect, space-time categories are not valid in this pole; the time of connection is the instant. If we attempted to translate the development of connective events into a graph, we would draw scattered dots rather than the lines or itineraries that are suitable for the metaphoric and metonymic steps of the associative process.

As we saw in the previous chapter, the basic units of connection are not ruled by the laws of thirdness (Peirce) or by a code that makes it possible to articulate them. Contrary to association, which only operates with elements admitted by the psychic counting, connection can bring elements into play that have been specifically excluded from the psyche. Those aspects of others that are inadmissible from the point of view of associative logic can thus make contact with areas of inconsistency, blind spots in one's own psyche. In reality, it is likely that both inadmissible and admissible aspects may be connected. Yet the latter are quickly incorporated by the psychic counting and integrated into the already existing set of associations. Consequently, the meanings produced are typical of the associative pole (as happened to the dreaming Maury, whose psychic counting fully absorbed the stimulus of the headboard).

It should be noted here that *inadmissible to the psychic counting* applies to two different instances. From the point of view of associative logic, it is the repressed. From that of connective logic, it is the inconsistent, which was excluded to preserve the consistency of the system of representations, and therefore poses an obstacle. I am referring here to the second meaning. Connection involves the potential coming into play of the two sets of traits that belong in the category of the excluded. One set comprises those traits of the real external object[13] that, not being marks, have no place in the system of representations. In the case of links, these traits include the other's alien aspects. The other includes traits present in an area of the psychic counting that does not have the consistency to grasp these aspects—a blind spot that cannot perceive the other's traits. In a link, then, specific exclusions of a subject participating in the link are connected to those qualities of others that are alien to the subject. Such qualities, in turn, could also be specific exclusions from the subject's own psychic counting. By way of connection, inconsistencies can meet in a link, and these meetings cannot be explained from the associative viewpoint.

Naturally, not everything is ready to be connected; only the meetings between what has been excluded by the psychic counting and the latter's blind spots can produce a connection. When the psychic counting captures a trait, that is, when it incorporates this trait into the associative weft by way of representation, this trait ceases to have a connective effect (or at least the effect is weakened). If a trait does not encounter areas of specific exclusion in the psychic counting, a connection cannot be established, or at least not a connection that may become part of a link (for this to happen, the trait must disturb the prevailing associative system, which somehow stabilizes the disturbances brought about by the new). This is important because of its implications. The areas of the psychic counting that are highly consistent or whose logic is impeccable are not the most suitable for connection. It is easier for the latter to take place precisely in those areas where associative logic is somewhat lax. [14]

In the connective pole, repeated elements remain outside the system of signs like flaws in the weft that insist on appearing as pure difference with no representation. I call this kind of repetition (which is part of Freud's compulsion to repeat) "repetition of differences" to distinguish it from the repetition of the associative system, which I called "verifying repetition." [15]

AUTISM: CONNECTIVE PREEMINENCE

If I had to offer an example close to pure connective functioning, I would mention autism. In autism connection is increased to the maximum, probably due to a deficit in the associative system that may be organic and/or produced by development. Autistic people usually evince a lack of awareness of the interiority where their emotions are displayed, as well as an overall deficit in their understanding of the associative meaning of words. They seem to experience time as circular and repetitive and cannot make sense or understand new linking experiences from an associative viewpoint. For instance, they "don't understand" that others may have different thoughts, plans, and perspectives. This feature may likely be the cause of their tendency toward uniformity, their difficulty to face new situations and forge relationships, and their need to avoid contact with others, particularly visual contact.

This analysis, of course, is valid as long as we consider that humans live in a chronological "time" and that "understanding" is an associative process (Moreno, 2010). It is also suitable to address what might be considered the deficits of autism. In addition to an eccentric behavior that shares some of the features mentioned above, a group of autistic people called savants (a clinical picture also designated as Asperger's syndrome) exhibits certain "high-level" skills. Among them we might mention exceptional memory, the ability to perceive, record, and connect incredibly fine details that would go unnoticed by most, and striking math, music or painting abilities. They also tend to be highly proficient with computers in their attempt, as Meltzer (1975) points out, to make the units they perceive countable. [16]

It would seem that some deficiencies and exceptional skills are related. Autistic people may not distinguish a fork from a spoon because they are entirely focused on a single aspect of the piece of silverware. At the same time, their focus allows them to perceive subtleties (of color, for instance) that are inaccessible to others. A sort of compensation may be taking place here. Since their associative ability is deteriorated, autistic people develop exceptional connective capacities.

Kim Peek, who inspired the character in the film *Rain Man*, is a good example of this peculiar and astonishing combination of skills and deficits. He knows the content of 7,600 books by heart and read the first of these books when he was 16 months old. He can read and memorize eight pages in less than a minute and read two texts simultaneously. Memorizing seems actually to be redundant; Peek does not seem to be able to forget. His math skills (for example, he can mentally multiply three- and four-figure numbers in seconds) are as stunning in reality as they were in the movie, and so is his sharp perception of minute details. Yet right before the film was made, when he was about thirty-five years old, Peek had met fewer than twenty people [17] (Treffert and Wallace, 2002). Fox and Smolka (2002) tell us that a savant named Joseph could immediately answer the question, "What number times what number equals 1,234,567,890?" The answer was 137,134,210 times 9. When she was fourteen, without ever having taken piano lessons, Leslie Lemke (a blind, brain-disabled savant who has become a well-known musician) flawlessly played Tchaikovsky's Piano Concerto No. 1 after having heard it on TV several hours earlier (Treffert and Wallace, 2002).

I am offering these anecdotic examples to illustrate the connection process and facilitate our understanding of it. I believe that autistic people possess unique skills tied to the operation of the connective pole because their associative system is deficient. That is why these savants exhibit something approaching the total recall described in the previous chapter, along with an ability to focus on insignificant details by detaching them from the perceived object. Perhaps autistic people's use of connection is so pervasive in inter-human links as it is in their interaction with external objects. Such exacerbation would endow these links with traumatic intensity, resulting in autistic people's isolation and fear or rejection of emotional contact despite their hypersensitivity to others' emotional states.

Maybe we are naturally much more capable of connecting than we realize. We may be born with exceptional connective ability—with almost perfect pitch and the ability to perceive everything. Yet in order to be "socialized"—to incorporate the agreed-upon meanings and associative understanding that allow us to live in society—we must sacrifice these skills, something neither Borges's Funes nor savants can do. As Miller (1998) states, autistic people retain these gifts at the expense of losing linguistic meaning.

The loss of these skills, which becomes obvious when we compare savants' memory or perceptive ability with that of "normal" people, would be the price we pay for the intervention of the associative pole. The latter, in turn, makes it possible for us to understand, historicize, and perceive experiences as our own. In some cases we may verify this kind of connective compensation of associative flaws. Nadia, an autistic savant who could produce incredible drawings at three, lost this ability as she acquired symbolic verbal skills thanks to intensive treatment (Treffert, 1989).[18] Perhaps the oft-highlighted, frequently striking intuition of children, psychotic patients, and seers, which allows them to grasp meanings and circumstances that remain obscure to others, is due to the increased operation of the connective pole, facilitated by a relatively weak or lax psychic counting.

THE LINKING EVENT

Meetings typical of connection, in turn, may generate unique events that, albeit repressed, cannot be excluded. Like truths, these events may demand to be named, an indispensable requirement to be granted "citizenship" as signs and to be included as part of the associative system. Nevertheless, due to these events' uniqueness, inclusion only occurs if something changes in the psychic counting's deciphering key; association tends to include events as particularities, that is, as variants of the same thing. These connective encounters, therefore, may set in motion a supplementation process that can violate the principle of sufficient reason.[19] In this way, encounters between elements that do not exist for the psychic counting (blind spots, excluded traits) can generate transformative events.

In other words, considered from the viewpoint of the associative world these events are effects without a cause, unmotivated. They lie beyond the realm of determination. Consequently, the second approach described above is valid for the connective pole; the unique, novel aspects of an event disturb the psyche, and encounters determine the subjects of the link. In the associative pole, by contrast, what is disturbing is always tied to a repressed past, and the already constituted subjects participating in the link determine the particular aspects of their relationship. The first approach described above is appropriate in this case.

Excluded elements generate events that may, in turn, become truths demanding faithfulness and inclusion in the psychic counting. If the counting itself lacks the resources to transform them into particularities, inclusion occurs through supplementation. This sequence constitutes an event called *link*. The link is hence an emergent that involves the work of both poles and is capable of transforming the subjects participating in it. Now, like any event, the link erases itself as a cause when it is inscribed in an associative history. Once it has taken place, therefore, it may be interpreted in terms of preexisting or "hidden" causes.

Nonetheless, any of the stages of the sequence I just described may fail to occur. We may have traits and blind spots with no encounters, encounters that do not produce events, events that lead to no change or are absorbed by an unchanged psychic counting code, or truths that do not generate the loyalty needed for their inclusion. Moreover, because of the psychic counting's homeostatic tendency, the emergency of the linking event always faces obstacles.

THE CONNECTION/ASSOCIATION INTERFACE

The link takes place in the connection/association interface. The word "interface" comes from the study of thermodynamics of irreversible processes, where it designates a surface separating two states.[20] Interfaces are not clear boundaries but extremely active fractal fronts. Events occur there that are irreducible to the laws regulating occurrences in each of the faces. The screen I suggest as the link would thus be composed of two systems with different logics that juxtapose and intertwine. I am intentionally refraining from saying "different logics that articulate" or "complementary logics"; we are dealing here with an irreducible tension between two principles.

I will try to clarify this further by contrasting connection and association, on the one hand, with multiplication and addition of natural numbers and Freud's (1895) notion of primary and secondary processes, on the other. Multiplication and addition act on the same elements (numbers) and may be articulated, as illustrated by the fact that we can write equivalences between them. For instance, "y + y + y" is an exact equivalence of "3 x y." Unlike these operations, connection and association are not variants of the same operational logic. Neither can we compare the intertwining of association and connection to that of the primary and secondary processes in the Freudian psychic apparatus. These processes can also be seen as operating with the same elements (representations) and forming mixed products through their articulation. Conversely, association and connection do not articulate, form mixed products, or operate with the same elements.[21]

Yet neither could we say that they are wholly independent, for the product of the operation of one alters the starting conditions and affects the functioning of the other. In this sense, they resemble independent enzymes that are coupled during enzymatic activity either because the substrate of one is the product of the other, or because the products of one alter the structure and functioning of the other. To put it differently, association and connection are entirely different operations that do not articulate but operate jointly, to the extent that the result of their operations appears as a whole called link. Still, the word link, it is true, suggests some sort of unity. [22]

The link is then the result of two essentially diverse but coupled operations—the association of representations and the connection of alien features. Each sets boundaries to the other's functioning. Connection demands that association incorporate unnoticed elements, which become quite evident in the formation of dreams and in the attempt to sleep, as Freud (1900) has shown. Association, in turn, limits connective scattering, so manifest in autism. If we wished to conceive of the link as pure association and include it in the world of representations, we would be in trouble. We would find ourselves facing an impervious, closed, and irreversible apparatus. Objects within it would be easily replaceable, and we would not be able to grasp, among other things, the magnitude of mourning processes, the certainty and specificity of passions such as love and hatred, or the customary need for the presence of others in the performance of human acts.

In this sort of mental bubble, the Platonic ideal of obsessive thinking or of Laplace's Superior Intelligence would be partially realized. The cost—or perhaps, from a solipsistic perspective, we should say "the benefit"—would be the exclusion of every external disturbance, resulting in a process deprived of wonder or transforming newness. As I mentioned before, the model that I find closest to this mode of functioning is a dream that occurs while the gates that open into the external world are completely shut. According to Freud himself, nothing new can take place there.

If we attempted to think of the linking phenomenon exclusively from the connective vantage point we would fare no better. Instead of finding the peace of reversibility and deterministic equilibrium of a homogenous, linear time and a Euclidian space with clearly defined borders, we would clash with a coreless chaos, a dedifferentiation around an amorphous alienness that bars us from viewing it as either our own or others'. It would be impossible to produce even the minimal alterity dividing the "I" from the "you" that makes thinking possible. There would only be unconnected instants with no special containers.

Viewing the link as something that happens in the middle of a homogenous line representing connection or association would not work either. My outlining the link as a segment with associative and connective poles may have generated this false impression. Connection and association do not operate disjointedly or in parallel. They neither form independent compartments nor constitute complementary figures making up a whole, like yin and yang. They are not branches of the same tree, but their foliages always overlap in intense activity, constituting a kind of phenomenal unity (like an interface) where the link occurs. Connection detotalizes association's hegemonic aspirations, and association sets boundaries to the scattering typical of connection. Yet between association and connection there is no linearity or complementariness. Even so, their simultaneous existence is the source of the infinite richness and variability that renders us both different and comparable and facilitates our interaction in relationships. It makes it possible for us to consider ourselves similar to each other when we are actually unique.

The conflict and core of psychic change may now be understood as the struggle or interplay not only between childhood repetition and defense (in the traditional manner perfectly compatible with the associative realm), but also between the associative and connective poles—between what is representable and what is inassimilable or alien in others. Perhaps this discrepancy between two logics should have a different name, such as "obstacleness."

SPALTUNG?

Would it be possible to consider the space separating the connective and associative poles as a (the?) fundamental human *Spaltung*? Barely a century ago psychoanalysis introduced the enlightening revelation that human relations, elections, and desires are determined somewhere other than in the conscious surface accessible to memory and will. Such discovery allowed the identification of a pivotal split between conscious and unconscious that displaced the determining core of human-ness from the ego to the unconscious.[23] From our perspective, however, there would be no determining center. The essential feature of human-ness would not be the displacement of its core but rather the fact that *there is no core*.

That is why in more than one case the psychoanalytic operation of tracing back effects to their unconscious causes may actually conceal the emergence of unmotivated effects. The notion of truth as the process whereby an inadmissible content demands a place, thus disturbing the order established by the psychic counting, alludes to a subject of that truth. And rather than split, this subject is above all decentered.

Each link entails the resonance of heterogeneous traits, and therefore its results are incalculable. Reason—the Oedipal-narcissistic counting that provides meanings[24] —would never be able to subsume the connective pole, not even by means of a hypothetical access to all unconscious signifiers. Moreover, what belongs in this pole can only survive by demanding inclusion in the psychic counting's terms. Essential difference (the Two) can only affect us by way of the connective system. Yet we cannot assimilate the effects of this difference unless we shift the angle of comprehension to facilitate its incorporation, a move that will necessarily involve changing the psychic counting's deciphering key.

NOTES

1. Strictly speaking, both aspects are correlative. It is by using representations that inevitably leave an opening between them and what they represent that human beings can come into contact with points of inconsistence in their representational world. A closed system would not allow for such contact.

2. For perspectives that presume a definite origin, "being born" is the starting point of the "life" sequence. Interestingly enough, it has not been possible to reach consensus regarding this origin. In my view, such inability illustrates the weakness of any conventional answer to this question.

3. These ideas about subjects' stability are also expressed by the claim that it is the subjects' *position*, not their structure that changes.

4. Juan may be defined by a (huge) set of "j" elements: $(J = \{j1, j2 ... jn.\})$, and Maria, by a (huge) set of "m" elements: $(M = \{m1, m2 ... mn\})$. The link stems from a cross-section of the resultant of the total possible "j-m" combinations. According to this proposition, the link does not radically affect J or M; j and m elements that may be brought into play by a specific situation are particularities that are not heterogeneous with the J and M sets.

5. In "Analysis Terminable and Interminable" Freud (1937) appears concerned by the fact that the transference does not succeed in stirring all the dormant (or potential) elements that are present in a certain subject. Freud's concern may be based solely on the belief that such a goal is actually attainable. Rooted in Aristotelian philosophy, this conception maintains that only what exists as potency may become act and that the unconscious is both the ultimate source of potency and the origin of every act.

6. The latter is based on the supposition that the One, the essential unity of something, is not, and therefore every effect of one—essential for the associative system—is the product of counting, of counting as one.

7. See chapter 1.

8. See chapter 5.

9. See chapter 1.

10. See chapter 5.

11. Whether these are twice-inscribed or dynamically differentiated representations, as Freud (1915) put it in "The Unconscious."

12. See chapter 3.

13. See chapter 1.

14. At the same time, encounters happen without the intervention of the psychic counting of the subjects involved in the link. We might say that they happen despite the associative system's demand for repetitive consistency, which is why linking escapes associative determination.

15. See chapter 5.

16. In an article published in *Wired* magazine, Silberman (2001) suggests that it is for this reason that the autistic and savant population is significantly larger in California's Silicon Valley than in the rest of the United States.

17. According to Oliver Sacks (1995), forty-year-old Franco Magnani (perhaps another example of Asperger's syndrome) would paint his hometown, which he had left when he was twelve, with meticulous detail and in a highly realistic manner.

18. Neurological approaches to this issue seem to indicate that connective skills are located in the brain's right hemisphere, and associative skills in the left. In most savants with brain damage it is the left hemisphere, linked to symbolic mechanisms, that is compromised (see Miller et al., 1998; Ansermet and Magistretti, 2004, and www.wiscosinmedicalsociety.org/savant).

19. This principle, whose formulation has been attributed to Leibnitz, states that for every entity, event, or proposition there has to be a sufficient explanation. (T. N.)

20. Or "faces," like water and air or dermis and epidermis. The other possible origin of the term is equally suitable. It refers to mitotic division, where the interface signals a state of apparent stillness between the phases of mitosis, when decisive preparations take place.

21. Association operates on marks or signs, and connection, on elements that have been specifically excluded from the domain of the psychic counting and may lack associative meaning.

22. A clear, remarkable example of the ways in which absolutely diverse systems may intertwine is the following, taken from Stewart and Cohen (1997, p. 63): "There is a parasitic flatworm that spends part of its life inside an ant, while its reproductive stage is inside a cow. The technique that it has evolved to affect the transfer from one animal to the other shows just how subtle the effects of "blind" evolution can be. The parasite infects the ant and presses on a particular part of its brain. This interferes with the normal behavior of the brain, which causes the ant to climb a grass stem, grasp it with its jaws, and hang there, permanently attached. So when a cow comes along and eats the grass, the parasite enters the cow."

23. Laplanche (1992).

24. See chapter 5.

Chapter Five

The Link II

Manifestations

This chapter tackles the notion of the link in its interaction with clinical practice. I discuss the topics introduced in chapter 4 in more detail and examine the clinical manifestations of the link in three areas, namely, the mother-infant relationship, mourning, and the transference.

THE OEDIPAL-NARCISSISTIC INTERFACE

Just as inflamed tissue surrounds a splinter, so does the psychic counting envelop what it deems unknowable by means of a structure at whose heart lies an interface between narcissism and the Oedipus complex. Everything that is "real" to us is the result of the passage of our perceptions through this interface. The very act of recording events—determining what will be included as a mark or representative and what will be specifically excluded—is also performed by this interface. While they refer to concatenated libidinal stages within the developmental history described by Freud, narcissism and the Oedipus complex also structure the psychic apparatus and determine the psychic counting's way of functioning. We might say that both result from events whose occurrence in the life of "normal" human beings has been programmed. In the manner of all events, as they launch a new system they erase the traces of their quest. Those individuals who do not traverse these stages properly have a hard time curbing the dispersion typical of connection and sharing their experiences with their fellow beings.

Understood as the psychic act that founds the ego as a libidinizable object (Freud, 1914a), narcissism is the mark of a One, the delimitation of the image of what we are supposed to be. This One that designates the ego constitutes the essential unit that is counted by the psychic counting. It is the ego subject of my utterances, the subject of my experiences, the point of reference and comparison with other fellow beings. Without it there would be no libidinal or cognitive stability. Moreover, through this One the ego views others as variants of itself—as fellow beings. Even so, this One stems from an experience that, as Lacan initially explained in 1938, can only oscillate between anticipation and insufficiency (Lacan, 1949). Pure narcissism, therefore, is always alienated, and amalgamates symmetrical territories that cannot be semanticized or articulated. The pure narcissistic One can account for no human relationship other than the simple specular apprehension of one in the other.

The psychic counting, furthermore, cannot conceive of an original Two as an essential difference between heterogeneous elements, such as "I" and "other"; it counts them as particularities of the One. The original One is above all the suture of the Two. For the psychic counting to be able to count or relate these Ones perceived from the perspective of narcissism, it must incorporate them into a structure that can articulate them by way of marks that represent them, that is, by way of representations. This is the role of the Oedipus complex. The key to the relationship between narcissism and the Oedipus complex and their interface may be found in the phase designated by Freud (1923) as the phallic phase of psychosexual development.

During this phase the narcissistic value of the ego is transferred to the penis. Through the castration complex, this shift makes it possible for the privileged value bestowed on the ego during narcissism, and transferred to the phallus during the phallic phase, to become a sign capable of processing crucial matters such as identity and difference, particularly the difference between the sexes.[1] In this way, the Two of essential difference has been doubly eluded. The One results from a forced apprehension of what is not—the ego created by the narcissistic psychic act based on an image or a surface. The ego's attributes and particularities are hence seen as essential differences in relation to the egos of other Ones when, strictly speaking, they are sutures of these differences.

I suggested elsewhere[2] that by accounting for the difference between the sexes through castration theory ("women lack it, men have it"), children seek both to explain the presentation of illogical differences and to protect themselves from it. This attempt is certainly a step forward in relation to the theory of the phallic phase, according to which there is only one sex. At the same time, however, it is a real defense against the inability to represent the pure, irreversible difference between the sexes. Indeed, castration theory does not state that sex change is impossible. It only points out that this change would bear consequences and even indicates the course it would take.

To belong to the other sex, it says, one must wait for the restoration of the penis or pay the price of castration.

Within castration theory, the difference between the sexes is thus so reasonable and predictable that in Freud's view we spend our lives fearing and/or yearning for this change, which is constrained to the possession or lack of just one element.[3] Phallic theory, which veils the very existence of the most obvious difference between human beings, collapses in view of the presentation of the irreversible, illogical nature of the difference between the sexes. This theory's inability to account for an essential difference gives rise to the emergence of castration theory. The latter proposes a fictitious world where complementarity and reversibility may be found in a beyond that lies either in the past ("hers was cut") or in the future ("it will grow").

Castration anxiety, according to Freud, is based precisely on the belief that men and women are potentially equal or may be seen as equal. For this reason, as I mentioned earlier, the outcome of the Oedipus-Narcissus interface is a twofold distortion of the question of identity and difference. Moreover, negative times negative turns only virtualities positive. The psychic counting would count One, Three, two, but the last two is no longer the Two of essential difference. In no way can such difference be inscribed in the psychic counting. The only way the psyche can tackle singularities is by way of the two, that is, by replacing them with particularities of what was already established.

In any case, this Two cannot be apprehended. It does not cease to produce disturbing effects on the associative regime by way of its connection with specific exclusions in the psychic counting. The latter cannot grasp the inconsistent multiplicity it inhabits, and yet this multiplicity permanently changes it.

THE FEELING OF SATISFACTION AS A LINKING EVENT

According to Freud, humans do not have innate or instinctive structures that are suitable for survival. Unlike other animals, the basis of their mental functioning and behavior is forged during development. There is an original time before the advent of repression, sexual positioning, and the establishment of individual reality. Out of this multiform biological readiness, dams will emerge that will eventually produce a normal psychic apparatus.[4] These are primal in the sense of primitive, first and founding, and their description logically shares something of the mystery of creations ex nihilo. So when Freud discovered that the psychic apparatus tends above all to repeat satisfactory experiences, he did not consider that this repetition was instinctive, as it is in every other animal. He thought it must emerge somewhat randomly through a primal structuring experience.

This experience, which he defined as an experience of satisfaction, involves the transformation of a mode of functioning that tends only toward reflex discharge into a different mode of functioning in which the traces of the experience of satisfaction will forever determine the direction of repetition (the "fulfillment of the wish"). According to Freud, this founding step takes place within a link. What the experience of satisfaction produces is in fact what we have called the psychic counting and the associative mechanism. Yet the sense of satisfaction is based on an earlier mechanism, namely, on connection. This step is necessary for linking practices to inscribe their mark in the psychic counting.

Let us see how this process unfolds in the experience of satisfaction described by Freud:

> . . . that apparatus [of the adult] has only reached its present perfection after a long period of development (. . .) its first structure followed the plan of a reflex apparatus, so that any sensory excitation (. . .) could be promptly discharged (. . .) But the exigencies of life interfere with this simple function (. . .) [They] confront it first in the form of the major somatic needs. The excitations produced by internal needs seek discharge in movement (. . .) A hungry baby screams or kicks helplessly (. . .) A change can only come about if in some way or other (in the case of the baby, through outside help) an *'experience of satisfaction'* can be achieved which puts an end to the internal stimulus. An essential component of this experience of satisfaction is a particular perception (that of nourishment, in our example) the mnemic image of which remains associated thenceforward with the memory trace of the excitation produced by the need. As a result of the link that has thus been established, next time this need arises a psychical impulse will at once emerge which will seek to re-cathect the mnemic image of the perception and to re-evoke the perception itself, that is to say, to re-establish the situation of the original satisfaction. An impulse of this kind is what we call a wish; the reappearance of the perception is the fulfilment of the wish . . . (Freud, 1900, pp. 564-65; author's emphasis)

Here Freud describes how a link experience leads the apparatus to appropriate and connect two elements that had not previously existed in the mind as representations. These are the thrust provided by the exigencies of life ("the major somatic needs") and the cross-sections of the external world (the traces of the "particular perception of nutrition"). In the experience of satisfaction the meeting of these two disorganized magmas produces an event that leaves marks. From then on the dominant, determining tendency will be for every future experience to travel through these marks. In other words, the psychic counting will exist based on that experience. Yet the meeting itself, which precedes the existence of the psychic counting, can only be understood as a connective event.

In any case, the experience of satisfaction may be explained in two different ways. Along with Freud, we can view it as the (theoretically necessary) original moment that sets in motion a repetitive trend affecting every psychic act. In this context, the experience of satisfaction is understood in associative, deterministic terms. It is the necessary, original milestone that separates a before (free of marks, mythical) and an after (comprehensible, determined, and ruled by the pleasure principle and desire). From then on, "the system cannot do anything but wish" (Freud, 1900, p. 476).[5]

I believe, however, that it would be more appropriate to understand this experience in a different way. We should look at it not as the mythical origin of a system but as a kind of model of what takes place in every link. There would thus be not one but manifold origins, and the experience of satisfaction would be a manifestation of the sequence of occurrences that constantly unfold in the connection-association interface. The unstructured, both "internal" and "external,"[6] can be connected and produce events that demand new inscriptions in the psychic counting.

On the inside, like the tension produced by needs, the unstructured (that is, the unrepresented) corresponds to those aspects of subjects that transcend their marks. We could say that this tension is the pressure (*Drang*) of the drive that is not represented by, or exceeds, psychic representatives. We should also include here those meanings emerging from association itself that are inconsistent in the context of associative logic (a production that is incomprehensible to the system that originated it), as well as the unknown, alien aspects of ourselves. On the outside, in turn, there is the presence of the ancillary agent, which encompasses the non-comparable (Freud, 1895), alien (Berenstein, 2001) aspects of others. If a connective encounter takes place, an event may be generated whose marks will supplementarily swell the psychic counting, as they do in the experience of satisfaction.

It is important to stress the difference between these two explanations. The first one ("the experience of satisfaction is the origin") implies or suggests that as of this experience, every mental occurrence must be processed by way of representations, marks, or inscriptions. Certainly, Freud himself asserts that this state of affairs may be enriched later through new experiences capable of enhancing the psyche's complexity. In his own words, "the bitter experience of life must have changed this primitive thought-activity into a more expedient secondary one (. . .) [that allows it] to seek out other paths which lead eventually to the desired perceptual identity" (Freud, 1900, p. 566), that is, to properly examine the external world so as to avoid confusion. Nonetheless, we must not think that the power of repetition, grounded on that origin, is cancelled as a determining cause. On the contrary, Freud goes on to state that "all this activity of thought merely constitutes a roundabout path to wish-fulfilment (. . .). Thought is after all nothing but a substitute for a hallucinatory wish"(Freud, 1900, p. 566).

The second explanation ("the experience of satisfaction attests to the nature of the link, that is, that there are multiple origins") assumes that unrepresented surpluses will always exist. Such surpluses will be ready for connection and capable of promoting experiences in the fashion of the experience of satisfaction. From this perspective, representations can only partially account for the internal and external "worlds." The system of representations is either insufficient or inconsistent to grasp what happens in those worlds. Inevitably, specific exclusions will occur that, without being part of the psychic counting, can produce effects by connecting the unrepresented. Freud's following statement suggests something of the kind:

> "Properly speaking, the unconscious is the real psychic; *its inner nature is just as unknown to us as the reality of the external world, and it is just as imperfectly reported to us through the data of consciousness as is the external world through the indications of our sensory organs*" (Freud, 1900, p. 486; author's emphasis).

According to my thesis, however, the unknown can be connected. Much of the significance of Freud's assertion, it is true, will depend on how we define *unknown* and *imperfectly*. The approach I am suggesting here assumes that something essential of the real psyche and of the external world is inevitably unrepresentable, and therefore cannot participate in the associative commerce. Nevertheless, and this is crucial, it can still produce effects through meetings and events based on connection.[7] We may find that this is the case in the Freudian description of the experience of satisfaction.

The other option—that the unrepresentable does not produce effects on the psyche—would result in a mechanical mode of functioning[8] that would utterly exclude the potential existence of connectivity. The combination of sign operations such as metaphor and metonymy would hence account for every occurrence, without the incorporation of heterogeneous elements. This system would be either closed or in a state defined by thermodynamists as "stationary equilibrium."

FELLOW BEINGS

The issue becomes more complex because at least two people participate in a link (such as the one that produces the experience of satisfaction). When Freud (1895) analyzes the question of recognition and representation of fellow beings, he claims that this process has two different facets. One is variable and may be viewed as memory work involving comparisons with (visual and aural) sensory impressions of one's own body that may serve to understand the other human being. Through this mechanism we are able to understand those aspects of the other that are similar to ours. Yet there is another facet of our fellow beings, something new (allegedly, he means new in each case). He calls this part the "thing" because it is incomprehensible, unassimilable (p. 423), and non-comparable (p. 394). In this way, a relationship is established through primary facilitations (that is, without ego involvement).

According to Freud, therefore, there is something in the other that is mysterious, incomprehensible, unassimilable and non-comparable, and hence cannot be represented. It is my contention that this alien aspect of others can actually establish connections with those aspects of oneself that are also beyond comprehension and representation. We may state from several different angles that the world of representations is incapable of accounting for everything that takes place in a link. The experience of satisfaction itself, which starts from a mythical zero level of representation, can aptly illustrate such inability. Attempting to analyze the ways in which human beings create links with their environment only through the articulation of representation and the represented is a limited approach.

THE MOTHER-INFANT LINK

We will now look at the link between a mother and her baby from this perspective. In actuality, Freud did not tackle this relationship specifically. Rather, he used it as a sort of myth of origin of human desire. Yet his work left numerous clues to reconstruct the focal points of this approach.

There have been many different ways of studying this link. Some think that children are a kind of clean slate where maternal contents are inscribed. Others have suggested that children are born with determinant instinctive guidelines that can only be modulated by the link. The viewpoint I am advancing here does not reject these formulations. Rather, it deems each of them incomplete. I first examine what elements of the mother are at play in the link. Then I look at the infant's contributions. Finally, I discuss the ways in which the two interact. I follow this order for clarity purposes and not because I believe that this is the temporal or logical sequence of events.

What aspects of the mother are at play in this link? Mysteriously or not, Freud's depiction of the experience of satisfaction disregards the mother. Furthermore, in his portrayal of the first contacts between mother and child, when pondering how the infant sees its mother, he hesitates—is she a simple part-object, or a person or whole object?

In the mother's contact with her baby her desire for a child will certainly be present. Freud did talk about the longing to be a mother as the culmination of the feminine desire par excellence, that is, the desire for the phallus. Children represent the finish line of a long history—the history of women's femininity, which starts with a passionate attachment to the mother (*Muterbindung*). When the girl realizes that she has been deprived of the penis, a dramatic disillusionment ensues. Disillusionment, in turn, leads to the shift of the demand from the mother to the father. The girl asks him for restitution for the humiliation she has suffered. She expects from him, finally, the yearned-for penis-child. When the child arrives a kind of happy ending follows that is depicted in the image of the proud breast-feeding mother. Theoretically, in this image the child is undergoing the experience of satisfaction discussed above.

Whether or not we agree with a conceptualization that took Freud so much effort to develop is immaterial in the context of my argument, even though it is hard to concur with the idea that this is all a child means to its mother. What matters is that the child is inscribed in the mother's psyche in the Oedipal-narcissistic history. Her psychic counting provides a privileged place where to embrace this child, where to adopt a "maternal attitude." When children undergo the experience of satisfaction they are not alone with the nipple, the breast, and the milk; they are with that mother.

Is that all? We should not think so. As sweet and natural as the picture of mother and child might appear to us, as many Renaissance images so dear to our modern roots as it might evoke,[9] we cannot help thinking that those elements that could not be organized by the mother's Oedipal-narcissistic interface will also come into play. The actual presence of the child transcends the mother's representational world. There will be many traits that did not acquire signification and were excluded from the mother's psychic counting because they did not produce encounters or significant events. These traits can still participate in the link via connection. We need only recall the beautiful Mrs. Graf, little Hans's mother, or the famous unhappy Young Homosexual Woman—or witness the tremendous emotional upheaval of a mother who loses a child—to verify to what extent the psychic counting cannot fully encompass the question of motherhood.

Let us turn now to the infant. While it is sucking, it appears to relate only to *its* breast. However, unlike most animals,[10] to develop into "normal" adults infants need more than being well equipped instinctively to suck their mother's breast. In the link with their caregiver human pups must create a history that leaves essential, unique marks—the marks that will set the course of their sexuality (in the broadest sense of the term). Now, clinical data show that infants are very sensitive to the mental state of this external helper, probably more than to milk or to anything else coming from their mothers. Infants are certainly capable of grasping much more than what might be suggested by Freud's picture of the experience of satisfaction. In reality, it is essential for these events to happen in the mother-infant link; it is essential for mother and infant to connect.

What would we add to this landscape if we addressed it from the perspective of links? First, we would show that the vision that assumes a mother → child determination as the relationship between a constituted and a to-be-constituted subject denies that events take place in this link that transform both mother and child into subjects of the link, in other words, into new subjects. Of course, not everything that occurs in the link becomes a transforming event. The mother and infant's mutual captivation is so ordinary to us that we tend to think that it is simply part of our nature. Yet the existence of both biological and cultural conditions that make this space particularly apt (even predetermined) for the development of encounters should not conceal the fact that events (irreducible singularities) happen here.[11]

The mother's desire, unconscious and somehow alien to her, exceeds any "what does she want from me" questions that the infant might ask in its own way. This excess will necessarily produce effects on the infant, both through an attempt by its rudimentary psychic counting to incorporate the comprehensible aspects of the other and through events favored by connection (the alien aspects of the other). There will be encounters between the enigmatic facets of maternal desire and the huge cracks left by the lax logic of the infant's psychic counting.[12] The mother herself will engage in a relationship with her baby that will not involve pure repetitions of her clichés. Beyond the yearned-for penis, something incomprehensible about the child will open up for her whose presentations, alien to her, may eventually make contact and create a link. The existence of the connective pole of the link, where these alien aspects of child and mother intertwine, is pivotal to accounting for the unforeseeable elements that emerge in the link.

MOURNING

The mourning process that is triggered after the death of a loved one has always been a favored ground for psychoanalysis. The Freudian approach to mourning gives the impression that there is a dimension of the problem that cannot be addressed, which is suggested by the following question: Why does the death of a loved one create so much work for the human psychic apparatus? Or, to put the question in Freudian terms, why is it so hard to get rid of lost objects?

This question makes a lot of sense for those who delve into the world of associations and object relations. If internal objects are representations and representations are easily transferrable, displaceable, and replaceable, it is logical to wonder why—or to what—links remain anchored or fixed, as mourning shows. What is it that ties subjects to the real other beyond the incorporation of the latter's marks or representations into their psychic counting? Is there something more than that?

We may verify the ease with which this type of replacement occurs in dreams, which take place mainly in the domain of associations. Yet in the real world the work of mourning is so vast and arduous that those who lose a loved one sometimes prefer to abandon reality testing and dismiss the fact that the person they have lost is no longer there, having delusions or even hallucinations of his or her presence, and other times may go as far as dying to be with that loved one. Perhaps, as Freud says, the significance of the question is concealed by the fact that we understand mourning subjects very well. In other words, our human condition makes us understand that there are irreplaceable objects and that the notion of object representation does not cover all the effects that real objects may have on us. According to Freudian theory, however, since object relations are mediated by representation, object libido ought to be capable of replacing lost "objects" more easily than it actually does. That is why Freud was so intrigued by mourning.

We may examine the problem posed by the difficulty of replacing the other in a mourning process by inquiring into the development of this topic in Freud's paper "Mourning and Melancholia," written in 1917. In this essay Freud states the following:

> In what, now, does the work which mourning performs consist? I do not think there is anything far-fetched in presenting it in the following way. Reality-testing has shown that the loved object no longer exists, and it proceeds to demand that all libido shall be withdrawn from is attachments to that object. This demand arouses understandable opposition—it is a matter of general observation that people never willingly abandon a libidinal position, not even, indeed, when a substitute is already beckoning to them. This opposition can be so intense that a turning away from reality takes place and a clinging to the object through the medium of an hallucinatory wishful psychosis. Normally, respect for reality gains the day. Nevertheless its orders cannot be obeyed at once. They are carried out *bit by bit* (. . .) Each single one of the memories and expectations in which the libido is bound to the object is brought up and hypercathected, and detachment of the libido is accomplished in respect of it. (Freud, 1917, p. 244-245; emphasis added)

And he adds later:

> Each single one [of them] (. . .) is met by the verdict of reality that the object no longer exists; and the ego, confronted as it were with the question whether it shall share this fate, is persuaded by the sum of the narcissistic satisfactions it derives from being alive to sever its attachment to the object (. . .) this work of severance is so slow and gradual that by the time it has been finished the expenditure of energy necessary for it is also dissipated. (ibid., p. 255)

Why so much work, Freud keeps wondering. And then, as if he had found the answer, he states: "The quick and easy answer is that 'the unconscious (thing-) presentation has been abandoned by the libido.' In reality, however, this presentation is made up of *innumerable single impressions (or unconscious traces of them)*, and this withdrawal of libido is not a process that can be accomplished in a moment but must certainly (. . .) be one in which progress is long-drawn-out and gradual" (Freud, ibid., p. 256; emphasis added).

It is true that Freud's reasoning is based on the explanation of something empathetically understandable that happens to us all. Still, it is intriguing that the farewell must be performed bit by bit, that it takes so long for it to be completed, and that it is mediated by this kind of decision on the part of the ego. Is there something of the unrepresented presentation of the dead or disappeared other at play here? My opinion is that mourning exposes the inability of the system of representations (which can wrap around the real object like a spider web until it is convinced that the object has become another component of its sequence) to explain all the effects of the real presence of the object or of the connection established with it. The object produces effects that transcend representations' explanation capacity, and after the death of the other, its impresence (Badiou, 1988) cannot be replaced by the elements of the psychic counting.

Impresence and absence differ in meaning. Absence is the reverse of presence. Impresence, by contrast, is generated by the lack of material existence of the unrepresented aspect of presences. Impresence has no reverse and does not belong in the symbolic register. Representations can substitute for the representable aspects of the other and shift to new investitures, but these aspects are anchored in something of the presentation and are incapable of shifting. Would it be possible to consider that Freud (1917, p. 256) is alluding to such an impossibility when he writes that the "[thing-] presentation (. . .) is made up of innumerable single impressions"?

This conjecture rests on two paths of thought. One is considering that "single impressions" refers to what is left as an alien trait outside representation, ready for connection and the repetition of differences. In this sense, we should view the thing-representation as an attempt to embrace the innumerable single impressions of the world's unknowable thing discussed in the *Project for a Scientific Psychology*. The other one is thinking that for a system that is above all a counting system, "innumerable" is equivalent to "impossible" and designates what the psychic counting cannot encompass— specific exclusions, which undeniably belong in the domain of connection. In this sense, "innumerable" would be somewhat synonymous with "impossible to represent."

In other words, the death of a loved one makes apparent the fact that the beloved's effects on our psyche cannot be subsumed into our representations of him or her. The real impresence of the alien aspects of others produces its effects through the connective pole of the link. The work of mourning, then, involves intense efforts on the fractal border of the link (where connection and association interact) to ensure that unrepresented presentations (impresences) may somehow be incorporated into the psychic counting which, by way of a mourning process, will eventually suture their effect. In this sense, rather than a farewell, the model for mourning ought to be scar formation—the healing of the irreplaceable aspects of the other.

THE TRANSFERENCE AS A LINK

The transference, that series of key events that develop between analysand and analyst, is actually a link. It should, therefore, be possible to distinguish its associative and connective facets. The associative nature of the transference is nothing new to us; Freud thought of it in these terms from the start. The role of connection in the transference and in the analytic process, by contrast, is not so evident, but it is manifested through this simple and forceful fact: for a person to be analyzed, the real, effective presence of another human being is indispensable. In a genuine analytic process the psychoanalyst cannot be, for example, a computer or a figment of the analysand's imagination. [13]

When Freud encountered the transference back in 1895 he did not hesitate in considering it "the worst obstacle that we can come across" (Freud and Breuer, 1893–1895, p. 301). He thought it was due to a *mésalliance* (false connection) whereby the presence of the interpreting subject might hinder the sweet associative flow of psychoanalysis as he defined it back then. In fact, until 1914 the role of the transference in Freud's theory was relatively minor. He related its appearance to a tactical need—resistance made use of it. What follows expresses the culmination of this perspective: " . . . the transference-idea has penetrated into consciousness in front of any other possible associations *because* it satisfies the resistance" (Freud, 1912a, pp. 103–4; author's emphasis). The author adds in a footnote: "This, however, should not lead us to conclude in general that the element selected for transference-resistance is of peculiar pathogenic importance" (Freud, ibid., p. 104). Moreover, he claims that "transference in the analytic treatment *invariably* appears to us in the first instance as the strongest weapon of the resistance, and we may conclude that the intensity and persistence of the transference are an effect and an expression of the resistance" (Freud, ibid., p. 104; emphasis added).

Yet two years later Freud makes an astonishing statement that somehow goes against his earlier claims. In "Remembering, Repeating and Working-Through" he argues that transference repetition is the result of a new, enigmatic process designated by a term explained in the succinct glossary: repetition compulsion. [14]

> In these hypnotic treatments (. . .) the patient put himself back into an earlier situation, which he seemed never to confuse with the present one, and gave an account of the mental processes belonging to it (. . .) transforming the processes that had at the time been unconscious into conscious ones (. . .) Under the new technique very little, and often nothing, is left of this delightfully smooth

course of events (. . .) the patient does not remember anything of what he has forgotten and repressed, but acts it out [*agieren*]. He reproduces it not as a memory but as an action; he repeats it, without, of course, knowing that he is "repeating" it (148–150) (. . .) "Remembering," as it was induced in hypnosis, could not but give the impression of an experiment carried out in the laboratory. "Repeating," as it is induced in analytic treatment (. . .), implies conjuring up a piece of real life. (Freud, 1914a, p. 152)

"From then onwards," he adds, "the resistances determine the sequence of the material which is to be repeated" (ibid., p. 152). Before, in the lab experiment, everything was about associations between representations. The technique consisted in a kind of information operation—translating or transferring information from the unconscious to the conscious "file." Now it has inevitably become something else. Repeating is not just the opposite of remembering; it is different. Neither is it a simple resistance tactic. Rather, it obeys a new command, a kind of compulsion not to remember but, one might say, to connect. If that were the case, we could understand why the appearance of the transference obstacle became a sine qua non of the analytic process. It is the way in which connection summons the psychic counting's specifically excluded elements and exposes them to analysis.

Nonetheless, the associative pole of the transference—the displacement of parental imagoes onto the analyst—exists and plays a very significant role in the process, as Freud pointed out in 1912: " . . . each individual, through the combined operation of his innate disposition and the influences brought to bear on him during his early years, has acquired a specific method of his own in his conduct of his erotic life (. . .) This produces what might be described as a stereotype plate (or several such), which is constantly repeated—constantly reprinted afresh—in the course of the person's life" (Freud, 1912a, p. 99). These "stereotype plates" make it possible to elucidate "object relations." In this operation analysts perform the role of observers, to some extent. They are placed in a position that transcends events. There may be moments in an analysis when this is really what takes place, or when one may at least identify a trend in that direction. Invariably, however, the connective pole interferes and puts a stop to this "delightfully smooth course of events." The associative course inexorably runs into the presentation of something that cannot be associated or, at least, cannot be subsumed into association. This obstacle to the flow of remembrance points to the imminence of connection.

In its connective pole, the transference alludes to potential encounters between alien elements stirred up by the analytic situation and inconsistencies (specific exclusions) of the analysand's and (it goes without saying) the analyst's psychic counting. Consequently, analysts here are anything but a screen. Like everything that takes place within the connection mechanism, analytic work is immanent. For this reason, transference is not resistance but the mode of presentation of the connective system. What is involved here is not actually the repetition of something that already exists.[15] In the connection process the non-existent, what has been excluded from the psychic counting emerges, seeking to be produced or to be by means of encounters.

Consequently, any interpretation of what emerges in the session as a repetition of the past fails to recognize the connective side of the transference. The transference phenomenon is hence the result of a complex interweaving of the connective and associative dimensions of the analytic situation. It is a fact that the analytic device tends to favor a certain repetition of the past, even of the repressed past. Yet these sites of repetition and disruption are rapidly compressed around knots that are real symptoms of transference neurosis. Like any symptom, they express both fulfilled and forbidden desires and constitute an effort to suture disturbing emergents. The latter are disturbing in that they represent inconsistencies for the psychic counting.[16]

Around these sites, which are blind to presentations, the psychic counting weaves a thick net of symptom formations. Once the analytic process is underway, these formations are "loosened" by the analytic situation and tend to open themselves to connection. Encounters, events, and truths may then be generated that will demand incorporation into the psychic counting. This process detotalizes and thwarts the attempt to conduct what Freud referred to ironically as a lab experiment, which typically inaugurates an analysis. Yet it is the only thing that can promote supplementation and change in the psychic counting. Supplementation and change unblock the associative process and launch it into new paths, in an effort to incorporate the new into the psychic counting so that it may be transformed into countable elements. In this way, the presentation of the Two by means of connection detotalizes the psychic counting, which must now count again.

Of course, the sequence of events need not follow this order. Transference is actually a complex process where both vertices are constantly intertwining, each checking and triggering the work of the other. As Freud (1914b) suggests, the sites that show the highest production levels are those where the two poles knot and past and present meet. What happens in analysis, therefore, cannot be referred only to the past; there is something in its reality that is irreducible to verifying repetition. Neither can it be referred only to the present, since in order to exert their transforming power, connective emergents must be incorporated into the psychic counting.

It is precisely in the presence of these emergents, not in their explanatory power that analysis's ability to transform is at play. Interpreting what emerges in analysis with the past as the only key, or only in terms of resistance, means surrendering to the obstacle represented by the presentation of the new and avoiding the wager entailed by interpreting the presentation of connectivity. Without connection no psychic change is possible.

THE ROLE OF THE INDETERMINATE

Irrational emergents are the greatest threat to logical systems. The customary way of rendering these occasional "enemies" harmless has been to consider them the effects of a superior cause. Traditionally, this superior agency, the origin of seemingly absurd events, was considered divine, and the irrationality of events, proof of the existence of God. In this way, a miracle could be viewed both as caused by God and as evidence that he existed. Since its inceptions psychoanalysis tried to make those aspects of the psyche that appeared as illogical fit into rational logic. It did so mainly by creating a site—a different site—with determining power: the unconscious. We may find this course of action very clearly described in the first pages of the essay "The Unconscious," which Freud published in 1915. There he states in his singular style, which involved imagining critical readers: " . . . the existence of something mental that is unconscious (. . .) is disputed in many quarters. To this we can reply that our assumption of the unconscious is *necessary* (. . .) and that we possess numerous proofs of its existence" (Freud, 1915b, p. 166; author's emphasis).

What are these proofs, and why is the concept of unconscious necessary? "It is *necessary*," says Freud,

> because the data of consciousness have a very large number of gaps in them; both in healthy and in sick people psychical acts often occur which can be explained only by presupposing other acts, of which, nevertheless, consciousness affords no evidence. These not only include parapraxes and dreams in healthy people, and everything described as a psychical symptom or an obsession in the sick; our most personal daily experience acquaints us with ideas that come into our head we do not know from where, and with intellectual conclusions arrived at we do not know how. All these conscious acts remain disconnected and unintelligible if we insist upon claiming that every mental act that occurs in us must also necessarily be experienced by us through consciousness; on the other hand, they fall into a demonstrable connection if we interpolate between them the unconscious acts which we have inferred. (Freud, 1915b, pp. 166–7)

This explanation is very similar to the one that might be offered by an advocate of the magical or divine origin of human acts. It relocates the inexplicable, disconnected, full of gaps, unheard of (even those "ideas that come into our head we do not know from where, and intellectual conclusions arrived at we do not know how") within rational, causal thought and assumes that it has been determined by a different source. The spirit of this quote, moreover, indirectly dismisses any alleged presence of unmotivated psychic acts. Their apparent existence is but the effect of our ignorance of their unconscious determinants. *Unconscious* is actually a way of transforming what is apparently illogical into something logical, what is apparently new into a repetition, and what is apparently different into the same.

The problem with this type of reasoning is that it leads to a trap—the unconscious is the cause of what we thought was undetermined, and what is undetermined becomes evidence that the unconscious exists. Do not misunderstand me. I am not overlooking the difference between considering that psychic acts have a divine origin and contending that their origin is unconscious. Neither am I ignoring the transcendental nature of Freud's discovery. What I want to point out here is that both explanations of the unprecedented or undetermined have in common the creation of a site that makes it possible to render logical what was hitherto illogical. Absurdity itself becomes proof of the existence of an entity whose determining power renders it a superior agency. The origin of the missing element that will make coherent the incoherent matters very little; it could be Mount Olympus, the Holy Father, or the unconscious. What matters is noting that the consequence of establishing this origin is that the unreasonable becomes reasonable, which leads to rejecting the existence of undetermined events or experiences.

At the same time, it is no less true that analytic practice is consistent with Freud's thesis. Such consistency may be observed clearly in this author's clinical histories. Every time an incomprehensible, hostile thought appears in the Rat Man's mind, it is located in the unconscious. If a dream presents an odd or grotesque image—such as Irma's strange throat or Uncle Joseph's distorted face—this image is seen as the product of displacements and condensations of unconscious content. If, what is more, the Young Homosexual Woman throws herself (*niederkommen*) from up high onto the railroad tracks in a clear and serious suicide attempt, this act becomes logical once its unconscious motivations have been revealed. Freud constantly refers these apparently incoherent emergents to their unconscious preexistence. Besides providing the basis for an effective clinical practice, his approach renders these emergents consistent from a causal perspective.

We could then claim that Freud's postulations are not wrong but incomplete. They account for much of what is apparently unmotivated in the psyche, but this is not necessarily everything. There is unconscious determination, but this does not mean that indetermination does not exist. The repressed and the undetermined do not entirely overlap. It is time to admit a true fact: the dramatic impact caused by the unveiling of the repressed concealed the presence of the unmotivated, a concealment that had, and still has, significant clinical consequences.

Psychoanalysis was born under the modern deterministic paradigm and abided by its tenets. The theory's novelty—that even the strangest psychic acts are unconsciously determined—affected culture and psychotherapeutic practices to such an extent that it prevented the study of indeterminacy in the psyche. Perhaps for this reason connectivity was neglected. I will not dwell here on an issue I have discussed elsewhere.[17] Still, I would like to stress that this development was favored by the fact that events erase themselves as a cause, thus eliminating the connective traces of their genesis. Consequently, after an event, which constitutes a true disruption of the causal flow, everything may be explained once again by way of association.

CONNECTION AND EXCEPTIONS IN DIFFERENT PSYCHOANALYTIC THEORIES

To be fair, we must say that psychoanalytic theories did not overlook unmotivated effects. Rather, they produced adjustments, exceptions, and additions to make some room for them. In my opinion, however, incorporating them in this way has prevented these exceptions from challenging the basic postulation of the deterministic functioning of the psyche.

Integrating exceptions into a theory has a twofold effect. On the one hand, it makes the theory more flexible, facilitating the explanation of the phenomena it describes in a more precise way. On the other hand, it conceals the theory's potential inconsistencies, making its logic harder to rebuke and reducing its transforming power.[18] As we saw in chapter 1, thanks to their inconsistencies, theories evolve in their effort to find explanations. However, they stagnate when no real world data contradict them.

As I mentioned earlier, the idea that there are effects that are not produced by repetition has probably given rise to new developments in all psychoanalytic theories. Let us start with Freud. Allusions to connective phenomena in his theory might be, for instance, the depiction of the effects of incomprehensible phenomena in his never fully abandoned seduction theory; the enigmatic references to the dream's navel;[19] the manifold suggestive notes on the role of coincidence in the genesis of symptoms, notes that are scattered across his clinical histories; his work on telepathy; and the (also enigmatic) reference to the possibility that "the unconscious of one human being can react upon that of another, without the conscious being implicated at all" (Freud, 1915b, p. 194).

We may find clearer signs of his support for the potential existence of connective phenomena in Freud's not always clear (as Laplanche and Pontalis point out) distinction between memory trace and representation (*Vorstellung*). According to the creator of psychoanalysis, everything we experience is inscribed in the unconscious as a memory trace. If there is something we do not remember, it is not due to a loss of charge or the lack of inscription but to repression. Now, the Freudian psychic apparatus works with affects and representations. The latter are "the cathexis, if not of the memory-images of the thing, at least of remoter memory-traces derived from these" (ibid., p. 201). In other words, representations entail an investiture on a certain chosen number of "innumerable single impressions" (1917, p. 256) or memory traces. The latter become permanent and will only participate as thing-presentations when they are invested.

We could thus state quite effortlessly that thing-presentations and word-presentations with which the Freudian psychic apparatus operates neglect memory traces (inscriptions of events) that are not part of representations.[20] These memory traces have been specifically excluded from representation. To put it differently, there is always a surplus of inscriptions, traits, or specific exclusions that do not become representations and are, therefore, available for connection.[21]

I cannot thoroughly describe here the ways in which connection has been present in other theories, nor is it my goal to do so. I can, however, point out where to start looking for this phenomenon in different theoretical developments. In contributions associated with the Kleinian school we might look at the notions of *projective identification* and *depressive position*. As I understand it, these concepts deal with potential effects of experiences, affects, or thoughts that may transcend the system of representations.[22] Bion's notions of *catastrophic change* and *transformation in O*, as far as I can see, also point to the possibility of transcending this system. Finally, in Lacanian theory I would inquire into the idea of the Real as a cause, expressed in *objet petit a*, in Seminar 10;[23] to the opposition between *Tyché* and the Automaton in Seminar 11; and to the mystery involved in "traversing" something that, like the fundamental *fantasme*, lacks signifiers.

By way of these concepts, the above-mentioned theories may aim to show the relevance for psychic determination of elements that are not part of representational logic. In any case, as I was saying, incorporating exceptions weakens theories while rendering them impregnable. That is why, in my view, it may be advisable to eschew these exceptions. It is true that in doing so we may be left with the impression that nobody actually supports these theoretical positions, but this may be the best way to be faithful to theories. If, as I believe, the productivity of a theoretical perspective hinges on the emergents it produces but is unable to address, the goal should be not to conceal these emergents but to bring them to light.

DESIGNATIONS

As readers will have probably noticed, some of the concepts I am developing here have progressed in my thinking through a field laden with obstacles. Ambiguities typical of rudimentary thoughts always project shadows on the naming process. Categorial hesitation is thus the inevitable manifestation of an unfolding thought. For instance, what I called *object relation* earlier[24] I now call *association*, what I called *link*, *connection* and what I called *rela-*

tion, link. The advantage of the previous over the current names is that they were familiar to practitioners of psychoanalysis. Yet it was this very quality (among other things) that made me abandon them. Object relation is a very common term in Kleinian and post-Kleinian theories, which were (and still are) greatly influential in the Argentine psychoanalytic milieu. This designation, however, overlooked significant differences between representation and internal object or between unconscious and internal world.[25] In addition, *object relation* might also create confusion between *object* as in *object of the drive*, whose random nature was stressed by Freud, and *object* as in *object relation*, which highlights the unconscious determination of the choice of, and relation to, that object.

My prior use of the word *link* to name what I now call *connection* was also problematic. First, because link is a somewhat fashionable word that refers to what happens between two or more people, as opposed to what happens to a single person. Bion also used this notion to describe potential interactions among internal objects. Berenstein and Puget (1989), in turn, suggested that *link* should designate what takes place in a specific *intersubjective* space, independent of the transubjective and intrasubjective spaces.

The concept of link, or substantial link, [26] is also present in the work of Leibniz and the scholastics (Ferrater Mora, 1979). I would like to point out the interesting analogy between Leibniz's notion of substantial link and the idea of connection I am advancing here. Both allude to a kind of escape from determinism. According to Leibniz, to the various relations among things we must add the substantial link, which constitutes a real, perfect relation between substances that may lead to the emergence of new elements.

CLARIFYING THINGS FURTHER

Challenges to accuracy are also posed by other names that refer to crucial yet complex concepts such as presentation, presence, absence, alienness, and alterity. I will attempt to specify them further, though I generally use them in a very similar way as Berenstein and Puget (1997), who introduced them into the Latin American psychoanalytic field. Presence and absence are mutually implied and refer to a symbolic structure that only applies to the associative pole. Since this pole operates with psychic representations, it does not matter whether or not the referent is there.

This is true for nouns but not necessarily for proper names. I have met obsessive neurotics who show that they understand this difference very well. True promoters of generalizations and mathematical formulations of the kind "for every x, such that . . . " take to the extreme the structuralist thesis that it suffices to name the place occupied by an object in a structure to predict its effects. They thus avoid mentioning the name of the person they are talking about, saying, "there was someone there," "a friend," or "one of my children" instead of Martha, Chuck, or Johnny. The reason for this behavior is that unlike common nouns, proper names usually evoke something of the dimension of the presentation that exceeds representation. We know that names kill singularities by turning them into nameable particularities—a simple term in a series of possibilities. Symbolic operations, then, aim to sanction existences simply by mentioning the attributes of the named thing: "If it has four legs and can be used to set things on it, it is a table." Yet such is not the case with proper names. Along with them, something of the presentation, of the unique aspects of what is named that exceed its categorization as part of a class seeps through, so to speak, and responds to evocation. [27]

The question is, can the effects of someone's actual existence be reduced to the enumeration of his or her attributes? This question leads to another: Can the wrappings of associative representatives account for the real object? These questions, which we already asked when discussing humans' relations with objects, [28] become decisively meaningful when referred to inter-human relations. It is obvious that names do not exhaust the effects of the represented on subjects. In reality, every human experience speaks of the effects of presentation that are not encompassed by representation, and even more so if what is being named or represented is a person. What remains outside names or representations but still produces effects—those aspects of the other that exceed any potential representation by the psychic counting—is what I call presentation. [29]

Presentation names elements of a situation but cannot be included as such in a structure; it is not part of a dichotomy such as presence/absence. Even though it may have served us to differentiate it from absence when we talk about mourning, because it lacks an opposite, in presence or non-presentation transcends associative logic. As we may have surmised, just as presence and absence refer to the associative pole of the link, *presentation* alludes exclusively to the connective pole. Associative operations with presence/absence pairs never succeed in suturing the connective effects of presentation. The question is, how can the effects of presentation be inscribed in the psychic counting? While I am not answering this question, I would like to note that events promoted by connective encounters must have a name. Naming, in turn, will demand some form of change in the psychic counting. The name, as we pointed out earlier, kills something in the thing it names. Now we can add that it kills only the effects it names, and it does so by incorporating them into the prevailing logical and imaginary system. Nonetheless, these effects are but an infinitesimal fraction of the potential consequences of presentations.

Now, the fact that the named other has been incorporated as an alterity in no way means that the connective effects of his or her presentation are cancelled. There will always be something alien in that other that can have connective effects. Just as association does not encompass connection, so is alterity unable to subsume the effects of alienness. For instance, within castration theory, castration would be the name whereby the Freudian psychic counting alludes to the effects of the ungraspable essential difference between the sexes. Yet this difference keeps generating effects that go beyond the meaning produced by the phallic/castrated dichotomy. Castration anxiety would thus be the product of the presentation of this essential difference. The latter exceeds the psychic counting's potential explanations based on representations of this pair.

The term presentation is associated with alienness. Alienness, however, does not allude only to those aspects of the other that cannot be subsumed into the psychic counting. It also speaks of elements that are part of us but are alien, for connection does not distinguish between "I" and "other." Even so, the alien aspects of others may promote the incorporation of marks that name, and are understood as, other in the sense of fellow being. Still, alterity, otherness, and fellow being are but representations that account for a tiny portion of the effects of presentation. This limitation is especially clear when the other becomes impresent, as is the case with mourning. Alterity, then, involves the existence of a supplementation that has led to the recognition of the other as a particularity within a series rather than as an ungraspable singularity.

TWO SOURCES OF REPETITION

There is a psychoanalytic concept upon which these ideas exert a decisive effect, that is, the notion of repetition. From beginning to end Freud viewed repetition as a foundation for the psyche. The neurological basis of this operation, established in the *Project* (1895) and recalled in *Beyond the Pleasure Principle* (1920), is facilitation. "Neurons," he writes in 1895, "are permanently altered by the passage of an excitation (. . .) their contact barriers become more capable of conduction and less impermeable (. . .) We shall describe the state of the contact barriers as their degree of facilitation (*Bahnung*)" (pp. 298–99).

Since the passage of energy through a certain path leads to reduced resistance, the apparatus conceived of by Freud tends to repetition. Repetition itself contributes to a decrease in resistance in the path that is being repeatedly traveled, which leads, in turn, to the further intensification of the repetitive tendency. The experience of satisfaction, which founds desire, makes use of facilitation, on which it is partially based. Nevertheless, the apparatus's repetitive tendency precedes and is more basic than desire. The latter becomes a kind of attractor that tends to shape every foreign emergent (internal and external) according to its framework. Like a web, the basic repetitive tendency will aim to model everything on the encounter with the lost object.

What is repeated, however, transcends desire. The existence of repetition outside desire is the main pronouncement in *Beyond the Pleasure Principle*; the apparatus's basic repetitive tendency, repetition compulsion, goes beyond this principle. In our allegory, it inevitably escapes the foundational attractor. We are then faced with two repetitions. One seeks pleasure and tension reduction. As far as possible, this repetition transforms emergents into particularities (countable Ones) that fit into the already existing series in the psychic counting. It interprets everything within the framework of desire. This type of repetition, which I have called verifying repetition, molds the present based on frameworks created in the past.

The other kind of repetition is the primitive tendency to repeat what lies outside the law of the psychic counting, and includes everything that has not been bound or transformed into countable Ones. I am referring to the memory traces or traits that have not been incorporated as representations or marks and that, like *fantasmes*, insist on presenting themselves and may eventually be connected. I call this type of repetition a repetition of differences. Its content is not revealed until encounters and occurrences take place that may require being named by the psychic counting. In other words, there is a basic repetitive tendency; the Oedipal-narcissistic attractor partially appropriates presentations and shapes them in the model of past experiences. Nonetheless, specifically excluded aspects will persist, promoting occasional encounters by way of connection. In this way, desire and the representable conceal the unrepresentable alien, just as the castration complex conceals the nameless horror of the unrepresentable presentation of the difference between the sexes.

Of course, the most obvious and highlighted aspect of traditional clinical practice is the product of the work of the great Oedipal attractor, tied to repression and verifying repetition. Yet the repetition of differences, which involves the unsignified that is searching for connective ties, has effects *and* is essential. In sum, castration and the end of the Oedipus complex (through the institution of the Law that regulates the thirdness typical of association) cannot exhaust the meanings of the difference between the sexes. The burial of the Oedipus complex lays the foundations for the psychic counting while perpetuating the presence of heterogeneity, which will always be specifically excluded. That is why vortices (specific exclusions) remain outside the psychic counting. Not having been understood as a product of the Oedipal articulation of child-father-mother, these exclusions cannot be buried.

Rather than repressed, these elements have been specifically excluded from the system of representations. Nonetheless, every time their effects appear the Oedipal-narcissistic attractor will attempt to fill these signification gaps by reinforcing the Oedipal weft. Such reinforcements are often betrayed by a surplus in the use of the elements of the Oedipal set gathered around so-called unconscious formations—overly or insufficiently desiring parents, too many unpaid or hidden debts, overly or insufficiently loving mothers . . .

Reinforcements are symptoms that try to cancel those elements that have not been buried and return under manifold guises. It is as though the symptom could "understand" that, for instance, by reinforcing the meaning of "making the other, my parent, desire me" we could eventually repair the Oedipal defect, which has failed to provide signification for something essential and alien in us. Or in the case of obsessive neurosis, by believing that helping a parent pay what was left unpaid or thoroughly settling accounts we will be able to restore the deficit generated by his or her ineffective action. These are the *hidden causes* suggested by every neurosis. In an analysis, however, we inevitably reveal that these causes are not hidden but . . . non-existent. They are non-existent in terms of the psychic counting or the great Oedipal attractor, but ex-sistent in that they lie outside the consistency of the psychic counting. To put it differently, what is not named by the structure exists nevertheless. We cannot reduce the impossible surrounding and constituting us to the forbidden, which is regulated by the psychic counting.

NOTES

1. Since Lacan's reading of Freud's work, we should consider narcissism–phallic-stage–castration not as a temporal but as a logical sequence.

2. Moreno, Julio, 1997.

3. According to this theory, "woman" is simply "not-man." In this it resembles structuralist theories, which consider that the presence/absence pair (associated with the notion of place) can explain all forms of diversity. Nonetheless, certain feminist conceptualizations that demand equality also see men and women as symmetrical beings.

4. Freud's opinion that this "construction" is typical of the species and is even biologically programmed does not take away from his idea.

5. In 1920 he was forced to change this statement as follows: "The compulsion to repeat also recalls the past experiences that include no possibility of pleasure" (Freud, 1920, p. 20).

6. Quotation marks serve to highlight the arbitrariness of dividing the link's components into internal and external, for the topology of links is far more complex.

7. While it is true that childhood experiences have greater power than adult experiences to set the course for repetition (e.g., see Freud, 1918), this does not mean that they are unique.

8. See chapter 1.

9. See chapter 8.

10. See chapter 10.

11. As it happens during adolescence, the structure may point to the site of an event but not to its unique content (Moreno, 1999).

12. The period of the first mother-child contacts may be particularly suitable for connection, both from the point of view of the mother (due to her emotional condition) and from that of the baby (due to its lax logical weft).

13. Furthermore, there is no self-analysis. The first psychoanalysis, Freud's, did not lack a real other. The latter was no less (or should I say "no more"?) than W. Fliess, who was seen as a fool by some and as a psychotic by others.

14. A term he will not even mention for the next six years.

15. The repetition involved—if we can call it that—is not verifying repetition but the repetition of differences, as we shall see later.

16. Dora's cough, Hans's horse, Isabel de R.'s thighs, Catalina's dizziness, the Rat Man's compulsive efforts to pay his debts are obvious efforts to understand the incomprehensible, to make consistent the inconsistencies that life presented to these famous characters (Freud's triggering factors of illness).

17. See Moreno, 2000b.

18. For instance, if we believed that the sun turns around the Earth, as Ptolemy suggested, when we observed the orbits of some planets we would see that not all these orbits could be considered circles or ellipses, as they ought to be if planets actually turned around us. Their trajectory shows deviations. Nevertheless, we could introduce exceptions (understood as circumstantial or irrelevant irregularities) that would enable us to calculate and predict these deviations. We could thus still accurately predict planets' trajectories. In this way, the central postulates of geocentrism could remain unchallenged for a long time, which was in fact the case.

19. "There is often a passage in even the most thoroughly interpreted dream which has to be left obscure; this is because we become aware during the work of interpretation that at that point there is a tangle of dream-thoughts which cannot be unraveled and which moreover adds nothing to our knowledge of the content of the dream. This is the dream's navel, the spot where it reaches down into the unknown" (Freud, 1900, p. 525).

20. As is the case with the signs of perception mentioned in Letter 52 to Fliess (1896), *S.E*: 1:234.

21. This is tied to recent neurobiological findings on memory (see first footnote in Chapter 8).

22. The Kleinian concept of object relation, however, does not precisely correspond to that of representation.

23. Nonetheless, it is not the same thing to talk about two different logics as to talk about different objects within the discourses that organize a single logic.

24. Moreno,1999.

25. In this sense, see Moguillansky, R., 1999.

26. Leibnitz's notion of *vinculum substantiale* is usually translated into English as "substantial bond," but I kept the word "link" to make the author's argument clearer. (T.N.)

27. "Its singularity exceeds the particularity of the known" (Lewkowicz, "Cultura, inconsistencia, consistencias, dialéctica," unpublished).

28. See chapter 3.

29. A. Badiou (2005, p. 519) defines it as follows: "multiple-being such as it is effectively deployed (. . .) The One is not presented, it results, thus making the multiple consist."

Chapter Six

Belief

VACILLATION BEFORE THE VIRTUES OF BELIEVING

Problems associated with belief connect us with the absolute, that is, with those postulates in which we believe beyond doubt and, at the same time, with those we need to leave behind if we want to develop our own thinking. Beliefs, therefore, are usually tied to this hesitation: we cannot do without them, but neither can we depend exclusively on them. The value attached to their role in our relationship with the world also oscillates between these two alternatives—a faith that erects a signpost impervious to judgment, and a lack of belief that opens the way to truth by doubting and challenging.

Which of these poles will prevail will certainly depend to a large extent on each person's historical context, culture, and particular situation. For example, while blind belief may be appreciated and even deemed indispensable in a military regime or a cult, it might mean the downfall of scientists or detectives. A similar duality exists in a realm where beliefs play a major role, that is, the realm of childhood. As we shall see in the next chapter, credulity constitutes a key factor in the child's link with its parents. Yet for children to have a "normal" development, it is as important to believe what adults say as it is to mistrust it.

In clinical practice with children we may appreciate the significance of the simultaneous presence of these two apparently contradictory attitudes. For instance, children's complete trust in a therapist on their first visit (their bursting into the office when they do not know what they might find there) should set off alarm bells. So should the sight of children behaving as if they knew that everything, save perhaps their mother's lap, represented a danger to them, but the first case is the one that concerns us the most.

IDEAS AND BELIEFS

José Ortega y Gasset took an important step toward the organization of queries about belief. In his 1940 lectures "Ideas y creencias" (Ideas and Beliefs) he distinguishes ideas—which we hold—from beliefs—where we exist. This author claims that we produce, discuss, and disseminate ideas, and may even die for them. About beliefs, by contrast, we cannot say that we have them but that we live in them. They are our world and our being, to the extent that we confuse them with reality itself. According to the Spanish philosopher, while we can detach ourselves from, combat, pierce through, or exchange ideas, we cannot change (or get out of) the beliefs we are, which constitute the backbone of the reality we believe we inhabit. In an even more radical sense, Wittgenstein (1953) states that we can mistrust our senses but not our beliefs.

BELIEFS SEAL POINTS OF INCONSISTENCY

Perhaps now my concern with this topic will become clearer. Beliefs suture the points of inconsistency of the structure where we dwell. These points are of particular interest because, as I mentioned earlier, they are zones that are particularly favorable to connection and to the emergence of truths that may challenge established beliefs. When we inhabit a situation, unquestionable notions are supported by beliefs that constitute, in turn, the backbone of our psychic counting. These are blind spots that render inconsistencies unquestionable.

The matter of origins constitutes a special chapter in the book of enigmas sealed by beliefs. Strictly speaking, rational thought, which is our customary way of thinking and according to which every effect is the result of a cause, cannot provide unquestionable answers about origins. If we faithfully apply this method, as soon as we say that A's origin is B, a question is raised about the origin of B, and so on and so forth. In this way, a genuine origin would actually be an effect without a cause, an undetermined fact.

This conclusion, however, is as abhorrent to the traditional, deterministic thought in which we have been trained as emptiness was for Aristotle. The only way out of the endless maze into which causal reasoning casts us is admitting the existence of an ultimate, unreasonable cause in which we simply believe. Consequently, we can only close off effects and causes by starting from beliefs that, like axioms, cannot be reasoned. While they are being advanced as explanations, therefore, myths of origin in fact mask a void. In clinical practice this process is manifested in the great disturbance generated by the inability to establish credible myths that may function as true points of departure to historicize one's own origin (Berenstein, 1986).

CERTAINTY

Certainty, a notion closely related to that of belief, stops knowledge in its continuous motion. What is typical of certainty is the rejection of questionability. At the same time, since scientific discourse is actually based on questionability, it is driven by a yearning to eliminate the dimension of belief. This wish, however, cannot be fulfilled by human thought; the undisputable dams built upon belief are indispensable for any mental act. Endless inquiry would lead to a maddening vertigo that only beliefs, as axioms or points of departure, might relieve. As a result, the reality principle is not an autonomous construction, for it is grounded on the beliefs that prevail in each situation. While it is true that thinking involves questioning established knowledge, as scientific discourse suggests, it is also true that thinking is not possible without an unquestionable point of departure—without belief.

THE STRUGGLE BETWEEN KNOWLEDGE AND BELIEF

The controversial relationship between knowledge and belief has been expressed in different ways across history. In the Middle Ages the confrontation was between religious faith and knowledge stemming from experience. Anselm, following Augustine, claimed that faith requires understanding (Ferrater Mora, 1979). He thus counterbalanced and opposed Isaiah's assertion that one must believe in order to understand (VV, x9). This contradiction, which traverses the entire Christian thought, becomes extreme in Tertulianus's apothegm "I believe it because it is absurd" (Ferrater Mora, 1979). In the mode of an opposition, this apothegm succeeds nevertheless in establishing a relationship between knowledge and belief, and is consistent with the fact that despite an empty correspondence, at some point the two might require each other.

H. Price (1934) referred to the relationship between believing and understanding by stating that one cannot *simultaneously* believe and understand. I stress the word "simultaneously" because I think it provides an important clue. Doing both at the same time that is indeed impossible, but these two acts could happen at different logical times that are mutually necessary and linked. If that were the case, Anselm's statement would point to one of the possible directions of the relationship between the logic of belief and the logic of knowledge, and Isaiah's assertion would point to the other. Tertulianus's "I believe it because it is absurd," in turn, would mark the boundary between both.

The question, then, is not simply the difficulty in thinking or believing, or the degree of "objectivity" of a postulate. Rather, the very core of human thought is the intertwining of two operations, namely, believing in predications on which the knowledge of reality is based so that, at a different logical time—that of understanding—these beliefs can be questioned. This is but another way of saying that only by means of a thought that assumes itself to be consistent can we point to an inconsistency. It is true that, as we saw in Chapter 1, humans are distinguished by their ability to pierce through beliefs. Yet criticism of old beliefs will only found new ones.

WHAT DETERMINES WHAT WE BELIEVE?

How beliefs are established depends on each situation, and mainly on the discourse that organizes links. We could roughly differentiate three of these organizers of the mode of belief, namely, religious or sacred, scientific, and media discourse. While we could distinguish historical periods based on the preeminence of each of these discourses, they can all determine (and usually do) the conditions that support the unquestionable in different contexts in the same period.

Religious discourse establishes that truths have already been revealed by way of original mythical statements that are beyond any form of judgment. In the face of these statements of the given that may or may not appear as enigmatic, the only option is to believe. Contrariwise, according to scientific discourse (based on the substitution of knowledge for belief), we can only believe what can be verified—what can be established as true by reason and systematic questioning. Even though it is not explicitly stated, the basis of this discourse is that one can refuse to believe and that such refusal constitutes the real path to truth.

In addition to these two discourses, another way of determining what is unquestionable has acquired weight in the last decades. We might call it the media discourse. Within this discourse we believe that what the media announce and present as existing, especially in the form of images, actually exists. Perhaps an incident that took place in my office a short while ago may illustrate the pervasiveness of this discourse. With Martín, a seven-year-old patient, we had decided to write a comic strip based on a system we had devised—each would draw and write the script for one of the characters of a story. Martín asked me to be the first one to draw. I drew a character, and Martín asked me what its name was. I said it was Chinchán, a made-up name I thought might somehow be tied to Martín's life. Then Martín asked, "But does it exist?" "What do you mean, does it exist," I said, pointing at the drawing. "It exists because I drew it, don't you see? It's this one." Then my young patient had to explain to me what he had meant because it was obvious that I had not understood his question. "No," he said, "I'm asking if it exists on TV," he clarified.

TWO VIEWPOINTS ON THE ORIGIN OF "EVERYTHING"

If each predication starts from beliefs it criticizes in order to establish new beliefs, scientists should not escape this process. This is one of the problems encountered by science every time it aims to define a general theory of the universe. When discourse classifies a statement as knowledge, it presupposes a belief. The belief implicit in scientific discourse is that we can dispense with belief.

Let us compare now two versions of the origin of the world, a topic that has always inspired passion. How did everything that exists appear? The first version is in the Old Testament. It is anonymous and was written several thousand years ago. The other is more contemporary. Stewart and Cohen wrote it in 1997, inspired by Stephen Hawking's work. Both try to explain how the universe started.

First, the ancient version. According to Genesis, the universe began like this:

> In the beginning God created the heaven and the earth. And the earth was without form, and void; and darkness was upon the face of the deep. And the Spirit of God moved upon the face of the waters. And God said, Let there be light: and there was light. And God saw the light, that it was good: and God divided the light from the darkness. And God called the light Day, and the darkness he called Night. And the evening and the morning were the first day. And God said, Let there be a firmament (. . .) And God called the firmament Heaven. And the evening and the morning were the second day (. . .) And God said, Let there be lights in the firmament of the heaven to divide the day from the night (. . .) to give light upon the earth: and it was so. And God made two great lights; the greater light to rule the day, and the lesser light to rule the night: he made the stars also. And God set them in the firmament of the heaven to give light upon the earth (. . .) and God saw that it was good. [1]

Now let us look at the contemporary scientific version developed by Stewart and Cohen in *Figments of Reality: The Evolution of the Curious Mind*:

> Fifteen thousand million years ago the universe was no bigger than the dot at the end of this sentence. A tiny, tiny, tiny fraction of a second before that—but there was no fraction of a second before that. There was no time before the universe began, and without time, there can be no 'before' (As well to ask what lies north of the North Pole). There was no space, no time, and no matter. But when the space that was coextensive with the universe had grown to the size of a dot, time had already begun to tick. The temperature within the dot was far too high for matter to exist, but there was plenty of what was required to create matter: radiation. The primal dot seethed with radiant energy.
> During time's first duodecillionth (10^{-39}) of a second of existence, the universe was a 'false vacuum,' a state of negative pressure in which every

fragment of space repelled every other fragment. Space exploded exponential-
ly, and in that near-infinitesimal instant the universe inflated from a tiny dot to
a ball many light-years across as its negative pressure literally blew it apart. As
the temperature dropped the false vacuum gave way to a true vacuum, a state
of zero pressure, and the era of inflation ceased. The universe, now large
enough to be interesting, continued to expand under its own momentum—but
more sedately, at a rate of a few thousand kilometres per second.[2]

When time was one ten thousandth of a second old, the temperature of the
universe dropped to a trillion degrees. Pairs of particles, one of matter, one of
antimatter, were winking into existence and out again, born in and dying as
fluctuations of radiant energy. Matter and radiation were in perfect balance.
However, the balance between matter and antimatter was imperfect. For every
999,999,999 antiprotons there were 1,000,000,000 protons. From that imbal-
ance came everything that we know. (Stewart and Cohen, 1997, p. 1)

With your hand on your heart, tell me which of the two versions seems more
credible to you. As far as I am concerned, being an inhabitant of this century
I find the second one more appealing. Yet I am convinced that my choice has
been influenced by the prevalence in my thinking of the belief that unquestionable explanations are causal explanations that resort to verifiable physical
forces. That is, Ortega y Gasset would say, the belief I inhabit.

OUR PASSION FOR EXPLANATIONS

In any case, even without taking sides, we should call attention on several
issues. One is that during the many years that went by between both explanations, silence did not prevail. Thousands of other theories and myths spoke,
speak, and will speak about our origin, as though there were no room for "I
don't know" or "I'm not qualified to answer these questions" type of statements.[3] Another noteworthy fact is that these two positions cannot engage in
a dialogue because they are grounded on and establish profoundly different
beliefs. Both a worthy scientist and a respectable priest would be opposed to
arguing about the "ridiculous" assertions of the other theory.

The truth is that humans cannot explain what we do not understand. Just
as our bodies need water, so do our minds need to believe that origins can be
understood. The Genesis and the Big Bang versions resemble each other in
that they relieve the uncertainty felt by people living in the time when these
versions are being upheld. For this essential function to be effective, people
must *believe* in these explanations in each situation. Belief turns explanations
into dams that make thinking possible.

I would not like readers to accuse me of relativist and obscurantist. It is
true that the Big-Bang version is more open to modification. In other words,
it is more easily refuted. Several changes have been made to it in the years
that elapsed between the publication of *Figments* and the writing of this

book. For instance, current ideas about the Big Bang claim that it would be one among infinite explosions of "creation out of nothing" that are still taking place (Guth, 1997; Lemley, 2002; Hawking and Mlodinow, 2005). Furthermore, it is unlikely that those who do not support the Big Bang theory would be burned at the stake, as happened in the Middle Ages with heretics who did not believe in the biblical account (although nowadays we have other means of persuasion). My point is that while humans can change the content of beliefs—we can even predict that the "evolution" of a theory depends on the challenge of its unquestionable statements—we cannot do without them.

BELIEFS ARE BOTH FACILITATORS AND OBSTACLES

The inconsistency behind the great enigmas (the origin of the universe, death, the conception of a new being, or the mystery of difference) is not the only thing that is sealed by belief. For instance, the phallic and castration phases, which psychoanalytic theory describes as psychic explanations of the difference between the sexes that prevail during human development,[4] are true beliefs. Actually, we always count on beliefs that seal issues and are part of what we call reality. The advantage of this behavior is that we do not need to ask questions about things we believe, or develop an explanation for them. If we wanted to verify the result of a calculation sensorially by counting marks of units (e.g. downstrokes), it would be very hard for us to know how much is $23,000^3$ (according to my calculator, believe me, it is 1.2167×10^{13}). At the rate of one mark per second and working ten hours a day with no holidays, verifying this calculation with downstrokes would take a suspicious person about four thousand years.

Luckily, since we all know how to multiply (that is, we believe in the method we use to do so), we do not need to spend so much time checking. Nowadays we do not even use paper and pen; we have calculators. In other words, we believe in a gadget. The validity of multiplication or the incorruptibility of a calculator is so established that questioning it would be considered sheer stupidity. Yet our trust is only based on belief; we count on the fact that this is the way it is, and we inhabit this place.[5]

Beliefs may also become true obstacles to the emergence of an innovation that would seem obvious but for the hindering power of faith. For instance, until recently Western culture had no zero and no notion of the void. The reason for this absence, if there was one, is that the Greek masters (Pythagoras, Aristotle, and Ptolemy, among others), whose influence survived almost 2,000 years after the collapse of the Greek empire, did not believe in the void or anything like it; there was no room for "nothingness" (Seife, 2000). The zero did not exist simply because there was no room for it in official knowledge. It was, therefore, impossible to believe in or count with/on it. It is interesting to note that the efficacy of belief in the completeness of the universe and in the absolute validity of *ratio* transformed the zero into a specifically excluded element.[6] As this is no longer the case, if today some-one said that the zero does not exist, rather than being considered a Pythago-rean, he or she would likely be labeled ignorant or mad.

We know now that every symbolic system is incomplete or inconsistent in some ways, to begin with, because it excludes itself from the reality it defines. We also know that observation and the laws of causality we apply reach a boundary where material reality becomes inaccessible. It is true that, for our peace of mind, the range of predications we use in our daily life (for instance, multiplication laws and the calculation underlying the use of calcu-lators), as well as our ability to observe physical events, tends to be suffi-ciently removed from our zone of inconsistencies as to allow us to remain unaffected by those errors. The reassuring belief in official predications has its advantages.

THE VALUE OF BELIEF IN OUR SPECIES

The adaptive value of genetics, which regulates the evolution of all living forms, has been partly displaced in our species by the system of transgenera-tional transmission and accumulation of knowledge. This system travels through an extrasomatic channel, that is, through culture.[7] Now, to make transmission possible, individuals must first believe what is being transmit-ted. For every issue, culture contributes (or actually imposes) starting points that are shared as unquestionable cores and support the given reality in each situation. This is an essential step in the production of the most powerful tool possessed by living beings in our planet—human culture.

Nonetheless, perhaps as a counterpart, we lack the instinctive knowledge that would easily allow us to interact effectively with the world around us. This lack distinguishes us from all other known living beings. There are animals that are born so well equipped with instincts that they do not need to have any contact with their parents (in some cases, not even with other members of their species) in order to survive. Others, in turn, only need their progenitors to shape or "fine tune" the instinctive machinery with which they are already furnished at birth (the jukebox mechanism that affects human beings as well).[8] Yet no other being compares to us in our utter inability to exist without cultural transmission.

With no other justification, in my view, than maintaining our alleged superiority, a certain mythology assumes that human beings have been sup-plied with exceptional intelligence as a substitute for instinctive heritage. This quality would allow individuals who are entirely isolated from society to reconstruct the steps made by humans over tens of thousands of years of cultural accumulation. In reality, we have neither the natural instinctive knowledge of wasps, nor the intelligence to fill the gap separating us from autonomous beings without the help of culture. As far as I know, there is no evidence that human beings isolated from their culture (if we could call those creatures, should they survive, human) are more intelligent than a chimpanzee or a dolphin. Our intelligence is such thanks to the dams we believe in, which are imposed by culture.

INSCRIPTION AND TRANSCRIPTION

Even so, the unique quality of humans' relationship with their environment is that they endlessly transform it.[9] While it may seem incredible, this mode of interacting with reality starts with a kind of blind belief, an undisputed certainty. It is culture that defines the backbone of what each of us calls reality—a series of beliefs corresponding to each situation, age, and region that establishes and discusses what things are like. Believing, in Ortega y Gasset's radical sense, in the statements provided by progenitors (who are, in turn, traversed by culture) constitutes an unavoidable step in human development. Later we may take some distance from these initial beliefs, but this distance is short. Humans can pierce through and change their beliefs, but can only do so by inhabiting them first.

Thus, *human knowledge is critical*; it must be critical. All knowledge is based on and starts from belief. Every contact with the world is founded on statements emanating from an Other or other, but these statements that are believed at first will be challenged later. This would be a "zero"—mythical, and unreal—time of transmission. I am calling it mythical and unreal because human statements are not transcribed but inscribed. We should differentiate, therefore, transcription from inscription.

Ideal transcription is the exact reproduction of the same. Verbatim quotes are transcriptions, as is the information we transfer from one file to another in our computer. In the transcription process, the time separating cause from effect bears no surplus. Furthermore, no elements emerge that are heterogeneous to what has been transcribed. In the inscription process, by contrast, the effect is irreducible to its causes; surplus always occurs. There is always a difference between the message and its effect, and this difference is not proportional to anything. Connection involves transcription, while associations can only inscribe.

If we used the parent-child link as an example,[10] we ought to say that parental statements (even those that work as unquestionable dams) are inscribed in the child. Consequently, their record always differs from the original statement for two reasons: because of perceptual distortions, and because being an active surface, children's mind generates surpluses that set difference on an irreversible path.

KNOWING AND THINKING

We said that human thought is critical. It does not start from a solitary finding but from a difference with established thought. Every truth is a truth about a structure whose blind spot it exposes, and radical newness is such only in relation to an established belief. In other words, there are no ex nihilo revelations. They all refer to something that will seem (afterward) to have been concealed behind beliefs and discovered by critical thinking. In fact, this last statement is fictitious. While we think that these are preexisting truths that are "discovered" or "revealed," the critical process we are discussing here actually generates them. Working on the belief it challenges, criticism produces something that did not exist before.

Following Puget (2000), we could call this process *thinking* to differentiate it from *knowing*. Rather than producing non-existent emergents, knowledge entails guiding the new toward the already known, or explaining the unknown in previously established terms. Thinking, by contrast, works in the space between belief and its criticism, and can produce hitherto non-existent emergents. Consequently, the thinking process will be halted in two cases. One is when inscribed original statements are so powerful that their criticism fails to gain ground. In this case, the option of seeing everything in terms of known and prescribed statements prevails. The other is when original statements are not powerful enough to be convincing, and therefore nothing may be shaken by truth. The first characterized the age of solid modernity; the second is typical of present-day liquid modernity.[11]

MOORE'S PARADOX

In this way, while it may seem bizarre, if we wanted to describe something like the basic cell of human thought we would have to envision the existence of predicates in which we both believed and did not believe. But, how can we simultaneously state our belief and our disbelief without producing a nonsensical formulation? Formal logic would categorically dismiss this option as inconsistent or absurd. Still, there is a type of logic that will allow us to consider this possibility. I am referring here to modal logic, which deals with propositional attitudes. Propositions in modal logic are constructed with verbs such as believe, wish, and doubt. They therefore contain subordinate clauses, which create a context that Frege (1892) called of indirect or oblique reference.

For example, the phrase "I believe that Maria is a thief" is formed, strictly speaking, by two propositions with different truth-value. The two propositions, "I believe" and "Maria is a thief," do not contradict each other, whether or not I actually believe that Maria is a thief. The truth or falseness of the phrase "I believe that Maria is a thief" is hard or impossible to pinpoint within formal logic because the event of the utterance bursts into the statement. The utterance proposes one truth-value (related to the utterer), and the statement another one (related to its content), and these values are not necessarily related.

It was G. E. Moore (1925) who observed that phrases like "It's raining, but I don't believe that is the case," while not being contradictory, cannot be used to make consistent assertions. Wittgenstein (1956) was also interested in this formulation, which he called "Moore's paradox." Moore's paradox has become one of the most debated issues in the realm of modal logic and among those who are interested in the phenomenon of belief from a logical perspective. It is usually formulated as follows: "p, but I do not believe that p," where "p" can be any proposition.

Some logicians think it is natural for a person to assert something without believing it. Others, among them Moore himself, consider that such an assertion is contradictory or, in any case, absurd. The problem, as you can see, points directly to the controversial relationship between knowing and believing. If we demand a close relationship between them, the paradox states something absurd or inacceptable. If we agree that there cannot be a close correspondence between them, the paradox might turn into something more acceptable. In this case it would refer to the ways in which we think about these issues.

In 1967 Griffiths claimed that it was incredible that epistemic logic could concern itself with matters that seemed so absurd. In his opinion, such concern was due to the fact that logicians are more prone to talking about a problem than to trying to solve it. I, instead, believe that in a way, logicians' interest is tied to the fact that in its apparent absurdity, Moore's paradox expresses a crucial knot in the question of human development and difference. Below are three issues stemming from this paradox that are pivotal to our discussion:

a. Every "p" formulation that is believed veils an inconsistency, but the suture it achieves is never complete; what is not veiled by belief is exposed through the "I do not believe that p." Moreover, thoughts and transformations may emerge from the gap separating the propositions that make up the paradox ("p" and "I do not believe that p").
b. Children's approach to parental statements is very well described by this paradox; they both believe and disbelieve what parents tell them. As we shall see in more detail,[12] when children begin to participate in

the link with their parents they believe the latter's affirmations. "To believe" here bears all the power indicated by Ortega y Gasset. We might, therefore, affirm that at this stage children *are* their belief. Their development will thus depend on their ability to differentiate themselves from it. Their differentiation starts at the critical gap, defined by the paradox, between belief (which is what children are) and disbelief. In this way, Moore's paradox allows us to describe how vacillation between two propositions in child discourse[13] relates to transitional space (Winnicott, 1971), which is essential for children's growth. The prevalence of either of the propositions generates severe developmental disorders.

c. As Hintikka (1962) has highlighted, Moore's paradox can be expressed in terms of "knowing" instead of "believing." In this case, it would read, "p, but I don't know if p." Formulated in this way, the paradox expresses the adult problem of "knowing that one knows but not knowing that one knows" proposed by Freud (1916). The content of "p" would be unconscious and stem from parental propositions that had been believed by these adults (original parental statements). The disjunction between "p" and "I don't know if p" would express the division between conscious and unconscious. It should be stressed here that no matter what mathematical logicians may say, the fundamental propositions of a neurosis could be adequately expressed in terms of Moore's paradox.

To illustrate this assertion with Freud's famous clinical histories, Dora might say, "My father is impotent, but I don't believe it" or "I know that my father is impotent but I don't know it." The Rat Man, in turn, would say, "My father is in debt, but I don't believe it" or "I know that my father is in debt but I don't know it," while little Hans might claim that "women have 'peepee-makers' but I don't believe it" or "I know that women have 'peepee-makers' but I don't know it." These apparently absurd formulations are nonetheless extremely consistent with the content of each history. Furthermore, the symptoms of Dora, the Rat Man, and little Hans seem to be designed to support the validity of these absurdities.

ADDENDUM ON MOORE'S PARADOX

I would like to add three points that stress the suitability of Moore's paradox to describe certain mental occurrences.

a. As Wittgenstein indicated, there is no absurdity whatsoever in assuming that the propositions contained in Moore's paradox are both true.

What would be absurd would be to assert that they are. This distinction may be crucial for us. In the evolution of human knowledge and children's minds, the most important thing is to preserve unanswered questions and, as we shall see in the next chapter, such goal may be better achieved through suppositions or conjectures than through assertions. Moreover, the fact that we are dealing with assumptions instead of affirmations is key to understanding mental tolerance to absurdity and the power of paradox to sustain enigmas. Strictly speaking, paradoxes are a privileged way of connecting inconsistencies.

b. The second proposition of the "I don't believe that p" paradox offers no assertion about what it is that one actually believes. It only affirms that it is not true that one believes what one admits that one believes. As Green (1999) maintains, it is not the same thing to say "p, but I don't believe that p" (for instance, "Juan is noble, but I don't believe it) as to say "p, but I believe that not-p" (Juan is noble, but I believe that he is not noble"), and even less to say "p, but I believe that q" (Juan is noble, but I believe he is obsequious"). These formulations affirm something concrete regarding "p" statements. Yet "I don't believe that p" leaves the door open for another—any—affirmation to emerge in the crack between "p" (Juan is noble") and "I don't believe that p" (I don't believe that Juan is noble"). This is precisely the space of the unknown, where unique emergents may appear. In the same way, children's assertion "but I don't believe what my parents say" does not drive them to state what they actually think of this issue. That is why this assertion makes it possible for an optimum site for connection to develop, and hence opens the way for the emergence of singular propositions.

c. If we change the tense of one of the statements of the paradox, or make each of them refer to a different person, the contradiction is dissolved. Consequently, the formulations "It rains, but I didn't believe it" or "Maria is a thief, but Juan does not believe so" are not paradoxical. The dissolution of the paradox is based on the fact that these statements refer either to two different uttering subjects or to two statements uttered by the same subject at different times. Moore's propositions, then, are paradoxical because they intertwine in the same time and person. Since formal logic does not accept this dual position, it sees the paradox as absurd. This absurdity, however, is consistent if we assume that the subject is immanently split into two—one who believes and one who simultaneously disbelieves the uttered proposition.

NOTES

1. Old Testament, The King James Version, available here: http://www.kingjamesbibleonline.org/Genesis-Chapter-1/

2. This quote is from 1997. In 1999 scholars started to suspect, based on quite solid grounds, that the expansion of the universe has a positive acceleration—its speed is constantly increasing. Lately, another new notion about the Big Bang seems to have become prevalent. I briefly describe it in the next section.

3. See chapter 1, section 15.

4. See chapter 5.

5. Up until very recently it was not possible to state "it can be shown that for every n" in reference to Fermat's last theorem. The latter postulates that if n is an integer number, an + bn = cn has no solution in positive integers for n greater than 2 (indeed, if n=2, a=3 and b=4, c=5). To verify that there are no $n \neq 2$ that contradict the theorem, mathematicians and their computers simply needed to try with different values for n: 3, 4, 5, and so on. In 1850 it was proved that the theorem was valid for $n = 100$ or less, in 1983 for n smaller than 1 million, and in 1990 for n smaller than 4 million. Finally, after more than 100 years, in 1995 Andrew Willes mathematically verified the validity of the theorem for any value of n (Aczel, 1997). It seems that we can now confidently believe what Fermat formulated in the mid-seventeenth century with apparently "insufficient proof." However, there are not many cases like this one, where knowledge and belief eventually meet.

6. See chapters 4 and 5.

7. See chapters 1, 9, and 10.

8. See chapters 1, 9, and 10.

9. See chapter 1.

10. We will examine this link in more detail in the next chapter.

11. See chapter 1.

12. See chapter 7.

13. See chapter 7.

Chapter Seven

Childishness

INTRODUCTION

Children and adults are different. There is no question about that. Yet, where does this difference lie? As we shall see in the next chapter, the answer to this question depends on the notion of childhood with which we operate. Our definition of *child* stems to a great extent from our conception of childhood, and this conception varies across history and cultures. Still, even within our own times the difference between children and adults has been diversely explained. Psychoanalytic schools do not have a common view on this topic, which bears important theoretical and clinical consequences. On one end are those who consider that children and adults do not show essential differences from a psychoanalytic perspective; both deal with the same types of anxieties. On the other are those who think that children lack the basic attributes that define adult subjects, and therefore child and adult analysis must be profoundly different. The most radicalized thinkers in this group go as far as to state that child analysis is not psychoanalysis. In this chapter I develop the thesis that children and parents are fundamentally determined by the link that unites them.

FREUD'S POSITION

In the only child analysis he performed (little Hans's case), Freud substantially modified his technique. In 1909 he gave the following reasons for his decision:

> It is true that I laid down the general lines of the treatment and that on one single occasion (. . .) I took a direct share in it, but the treatment itself was

carried out by the child's father (. . .) No one else, in my opinion, could possibly have prevailed on the child to make such avowals (. . .) It was only because the authority of a father and of a physician were united in a single person (. . .) that it was possible in this one instance to apply the method to us to which it would not otherwise have itself. (Freud, 1909a, p. 5)

This statement is usually interpreted as the product of Freud's out-of-date-ness. In 1909 he could not resort to the theoretical and clinical developments that would later enrich child psychoanalysis, nor had he written his critical essays on psychoanalytic technique.[1] This interpretation may be partly true, yet twenty-three years later he stated the following:

It turned out that a child is a very favourable subject for analytic therapy; the results are thorough and lasting. The technique of treatment worked out for adults must, of course, be largely altered for children. A child is psychological-ly a different object from an adult. As yet he possesses no super-ego, the method of free association does not carry far with him, transference (since the real parents are still on the spot) plays a different part. The internal resistances against which we struggle in adults are replaced for the most part in children by external difficulties. (1933, p.148)

For Freud, then, child analysis is not impossible, but it is undeniably different from adult analysis, in the first place, because children and adults are differ-ent objects. This difference is not trivial. It affects transference, free associa-tion, and resistance, the three pillars of psychoanalysis, and has therefore vital clinical consequences. What I would like to stress here is that according to Freud, the disparity between adults and children does not lie in the content they bring to the session, their intelligence, or their mode of expression. Rather, it is directly related to the link between children and their present, "on-the-spot" parents. In children this link takes the place, so to speak, occu-pied in adults by no other than the superego, readiness for transference, and resistance.

Jurisprudence seems to view children in the same way. It clearly distin-guishes them from adults. Children are not allowed to act freely (take respon-sibility for their acts) or enter into contracts, and their parents are seen as their natural guarantors. For this reason, both the justice system and Freud believe that (legal or psychoanalytic) "treatment" of children cannot dispense with parents. I will not dwell on this complex situation here, but there is something I would like to point out. It is as though professionals in both fields believed that what children need to acquire to be considered adults— the superego, transference and resistance in an analysis, and responsibility and commitment in a trial—ought to be provided by their parents. As we shall see, I do not think that the vector connecting *providing parents* → with *children in lack* is appropriate to understand the parent-child link. Yet I would like to stress that both Freud and jurisprudence view the difference between children and adults as inextricably intertwined with the link that connects them.

CHILD DISCOURSE

I consider that the child-parent link is regulated by a discourse (that is, a set of practices and rules that have a subjectivizing effect on those subject to them) that I have called *child discourse*. Seeing discourse as determining subjectivities is the opposite of viewing subjectivities as stemming from subjects' essential or natural features. The first perspective has the following corollary: since childishness is not a content that emanates from Heaven or from children themselves, what a "child" is or is not and what a "father" or "mother" is or is not will depend to a great extent on the definition sanctioned by each society in each historical period. This relationship may be verified empirically. Today's childhood differs from that of Freud's times and is utterly dissimilar to that of the Middle Ages. The same is true for parenthood. I will not delve into this topic because I will discuss it in the next chapter. I just want to clarify that from now on, when I talk about child discourse I am referring to current children, who would be, in my view, the children of modernity in transition.

ADULTS FACED WITH UNANSWERABLE QUESTIONS

As we have seen earlier, while beliefs aim to seal unanswerable queries, humans ask more questions than they can answer. Furthermore, particularly in our times, when beliefs appear to be scarcely effective, questions do not cease to be asked, taxing the psychic counting and its environment's ability to answer them. As do those spots where drives cannot find proper representation, unanswerable questions inevitably cast humans into the land of inconsistency, that is, into those areas where their psychic counting, organized on the basis of the Oedipal-narcissistic interface, is unable to produce consistent formulations.

I could not claim that these queries *are* adult neurosis, but I could certainly affirm that they are, in a way, at its heart. Neurotics behave as though answers were inaccessible to them, and resort to symptoms in an attempt to occlude the distressing effect of unanswerable questions and inconsolable states of mind. Symptoms entail both a reinforcement of the psychic counting's explanations that strengthens it in the face of inconsistency, and a kind of request to the world. Neurotics demand some sort of re-formulation or answer that addresses an impersonal agency (the Other, a superior determining agency, or God),[2] which may be embodied in a person, an institution, or an ideal. This claim, in which Freud ably read traces of the unconscious, is closely tied to their readiness for transference and demand for analysis.

CHILDREN FACED WITH UNANSWERABLE QUESTIONS

Children do not escape the human doom and glory of asking questions that exceed one's ability to answer them. Faced with queries about their identity, their role as the source and sexual object of the parental couple, birth, death, the emergence of their physical body and, above all, with a walk on the edge of an indeterminable, unforeseeable abyss, children also encounter stumbling blocks. Sometimes they can reassure themselves by producing their own answers (the product of a prodigious imagination often tinged with murderous imaginarization) and appear somewhat resistant to the influence of current beliefs.

Yet children's typical response to these dead ends is to stop searching and find consolation in the assumption that another living being knows the answer. They assume that the meaning of their participation in the world, the answer to their uncertainties (including their fate), and everything that seems to be missing for them to see their world as complete may be found in their parents' minds. They expect and strive to receive knowledge and love from their parents, whose live presence is a major reference point for their identity. Their behavior creates and positions them and their parents within the child discourse. By believing that their parents possess this knowledge about them, children can set aside overwhelming questions. They can curb these questions by saying to themselves, "They know it," and continue their path toward development.

In a way, children live their lives as though they were the protagonists of an already written novel whose text (or basic plot, at least) existed in their parents' minds. Children's behavior is a kind of performance whereby they display their attributes in front of their parents (who are supposed to know the plot), so that the latter can keep these attributes in mind or, if necessary, change part of the screenplay. The match between the screenplay and children's performance constitutes an essential coordinate of the territory where the parent-child link and children's development unfold.

THE SIGNIFICANCE OF BELIEVING

As several authors have pointed out, among them, Freud, Winnicott, Aulagnier, Lacan, and Meltzer, it is crucial for children to believe what they assume their parents are saying about them. According to Piera Aulagnier (1975, 1986), reality investiture requires the recognition of parental statements as a guaranteed definition by a first utterer-teacher. The belief in the undisputed validity of these utterances, which, as a monologic voice, leave a founding inscription that is not subject to articulation, is typical of childhood and extends beyond it. Nevertheless, while their value never disappears, these statements gradually lose their absolute determining power as children grow.

How does this transition, pivotal to childhood development, take place? The answer to this question is one of my main concerns. Let us say for now that other statements start emerging that include features typical of each child—unique conjectures evincing the development of a new space in children's minds. This new space entails some degree of mistrust, a refusal to fully believe that those first utterances are true. Moore's paradox "p, but I don't believe that p," which I introduced in the previous chapter, may be of use here. It offers an accurate expression of this odd state of affairs in the child's mind. While still valid, parental "p" statements are now followed by "I don't believe that p." Without contradicting "p," these new statements make up the paradox that will open unique developmental paths.

THE PARENTS' POSITION

Strictly speaking, parents do not necessarily have to know what it is that their children assume that parents know about them. Children are the ones who, by way of their assumptions, set their parents as bearers of the text of their truth. In this more than in anything else lies the key to parents' power over children and to the latter's dependence on their progenitors. That is why when this dependence becomes excessive it betrays children's intention to exert a paranoid control over those who, in their opinion, hold the keys to their being.

Child discourse does not involve only parents and children. It may also regulate other links where a particular type of dependence is created, for the person in the locus of the father in child discourse is in a position of power.[3] This discourse may be present at any chronological age and is common in institutions. Adult psychoanalysis, for instance, necessarily goes through this kind of configuration at first. Furthermore, a large part of its success (or failure) depends on the analytic link's ability to leave child discourse behind and use this first thrust to its benefit.

"Childish" adults, then, are those who position themselves in the link in such a way that they are said by others. Adult symptoms entail an attempt to recompose things in the psychic counting by appealing to imaginary and symbolic resources of the psychic structure. Childhood symptoms, in turn, are mainly directed to the parents (who, according to children's assumption, hold the keys to their being) and respond, among other things, to the symptomatic aspects of the family structure. That is why when parents bring a child for consultation we may be sure that child discourse has made it hard to make room for new situations.

Failure to do so may have manifold causes. The young may perceive that they do not arouse genuine interest in their parents. The productions at play may be too intense for them to assume that their parents have all the answers. In addition, children may feel a) that their parents have unequivocally shown that they do not know what children assume they know (real parents are a mistake), or b) that they are incapable of living up to their parents' expectations (children are a mistake in their parents' view). Indication of treatment in children is hence a more delicate and critical step than it is in adults. Treatment may be necessary for the child but also for the family, the parental couple, or the child's link with either of its progenitors, or there may be a need for just a specific intervention.

PARENTS AND ASSUMPTIONS: A PARTIAL LACK OF KNOWLEDGE

Must parents, who, as I already mentioned, are partly constituted as such by discourse, know exactly what happens in their children's souls? The answer is no, but it is a complex matter, among other things, because children can detect minute nuances in the weft of the link. If children's position in the discourse is foreign—for it implies that they assume but do not know what their parents know—so is parents' position. Not knowing what is taking place in their children's minds, they must act as though they accepted their children's assumptions. They cannot ignore, believe they know, not tolerate not knowing, or reject these assumptions.

None of this is possible if parents are not interested in their children, an interest that serves, in a way, as the platform for child discourse. Still, this interest should not be excessive. This odd parental attitude in discourse is a partial lack of knowledge that is sustained by parents' genuine partial interest in their children. What we do not know is something that we should be able to know. The expression "I don't know that" implies that we assume, or even expect, some type of revelation about what we do not know, even if we cannot predict what that revelation will be. Not knowing attributes an enigmatic quality to the unknown. From this perspective, *not knowing* is opposed to *ignoring*. Ignoring entails having taken something for granted—either not seeing anything mysterious in it or not taking it into account at all. A partial parental lack of knowledge will make it possible for singular productions typical of development to emerge from the tension between the two terms of Moore's paradox ("p" and "I don't believe that p").

I fear that the notions of *partial lack of knowledge* and *partial interest* may be understood as another indication of what "good fathers" and "good mothers" ought to be like. That was not my intention. In any case, if someone did ascribe such meaning to these notions, they should keep in mind that parental lack of knowledge cannot be manufactured, and parental interest even less. Neither can children make up their assumption of their parents' adequate knowledge. It is discourse that produces these attitudes.

In any case, we should recall that the child discourse I am discussing here is grounded on the belief that children are fragile, naive, and can be educated, and that parents can and must protect them and place their own conscious and unconscious expectations on them. The reason why I say this is that these beliefs have not always existed nor, it seems, will exist in the near future.[4] This is what I was talking about when I said that I would discuss modern children in transition.

SOME LITERARY EXAMPLES

Like in many other instances, it is easier to examine cases that show deficiencies in the parental position in discourse than to look at normal cases. While they do not necessarily portray child-parent relationships, the following literary examples illustrate the potential effects of flaws in child discourse.

Hamlet's ghost is a typical instance of a father who knows too much, even after death. Prince Hamlet has no space of his own that is veiled from the knowledge he assumes his dead father possesses. This lack overwhelms him to the extent that he cannot perform any acts. Even though he is an adult, Hamlet assumes that his father's knowledge is overwhelming. In this sense he resembles Freud's Rat Man (Freud, 1909b). As a child, the Rat Man was convinced that his parents could hear his thoughts. Once he reached adulthood, he hesitated before every action, and was unable to define himself in relation to a dead father whose alleged knowledge left no room for independent thoughts. In terms of Moore's paradox, in both cases the invasive presence of "p" impedes the emergence of "I don't believe that p."

Laius, Oedipus's father, is a good example of a father who ignores his son. Other than feeling apprehensive about the future, neither he nor his wife Jocasta has shown any interest in Oedipus as a son. This attitude becomes evident in two different instances. First, when the king and queen order Oedipus to be killed on Mount Cithaeron before even naming him. Second, when Laius faces the teenage Oedipus at the crossroads and dies pierced by his son's sword without recognizing him. As we read in the tragedy, the consequences are tremendous. Oedipus's arrogance and excess—the omnipotence that can be inferred from his ceaseless questioning, as Tiresias points out—show that the paternal dams have failed. In terms of Moore's paradox, "p" does not set appropriate boundaries to "I don't believe that p," which expands and generates the manic tone of curiosity, arrogance, and triumph of Oedipus, King of Thebes.

Max Graf, in turn, constitutes an apt illustration of a father who can neither satisfy his wife's disproportionate desire nor tolerate his own lack of knowledge about his child. Consequently, little Hans will try to replace his father with an original invention—the horse. As a phobia-generating object, this animal does mark territories, set boundaries, and build dams. The father's partial lack of knowledge is blatantly absent, and his (and his wife's) partial interest has become excessive and suffocating. Hans cannot attribute to his father a knowledge that might offer suitable containment to those mental productions he cannot curb on his own.

The cure occurs when the boy succeeds in assuming such knowledge in Professor Freud. "If you don't know that naked women wear chemises or that giraffes wrinkle, ask the Professor, he will tell you," says Hans to his father near the end of the treatment. In terms of Moore's paradox, we could say that little Hans struggles to find suitable "p" statements to halt the tyrannizing emergence of the "I don't believe that p" assertions of his boundless curiosity.

For different reasons but due to a similar motivation, Hamlet, Oedipus, and Hans are thus left to face the emergence of the drive, represented in the stories by the lusty mother (lewd Gertrude, incestuous Jocasta, and beautiful Mrs. Graf), without proper mediation. Since they are supposed to know too much, to ignore, or not to tolerate not knowing, all three fathers fail to maintain that foreign but irreplaceable position of partial lack of knowledge.

LACK OR READINESS?

Based on these ideas, the so-called helplessness of children should not be understood simply as a lack but also, and perhaps primarily, as a point of departure and a readiness for supplementation. Supplementation is what happens when a radically new emergent detotalizes a previously established conception. In terms of Moore's paradox, supplementation refers to the possibility of the promotion of singular transformations based on the tension between "p" and "I don't believe that p." In this sense, supplementing must be distinguished from complementing. Complementing means using something that is allegedly missing to achieve a preconceived unity without altering it this unity.

We should, therefore, distinguish between two types of readiness in children, both tied to child discourse. One is a readiness to complement (in the sense of completing an alleged totality) what children assume that grownups want from them. Parental ideals (stemming from parental narcissism) transferred to His Majesty, the Baby play the main role here. It is to such readiness that traditional modern education appeals. Children must fulfill educational expectations.

The other readiness, perhaps the most specific of child discourse, is a readiness for supplementation. With their imagination and ability to connect in the link, children can travel unexpected roads and produce undetermined encounters that exceed what might have been wanted from them. In this process they will be greatly assisted by a partial parental lack of knowledge, which will place at their disposal a malleable space where to assume what parents know about and expect from them. In this way, children will not feel that their creativity disturbs the container that, according to their assumption, is provided by their parents. Retrieving or restoring children's readiness to supplement is the main goal of child psychoanalysis.

In any case, this is a complex matter, because parents' interest in their children, which, as I mentioned earlier, constitutes the platform for child discourse, necessarily entails something of a transferred narcissism. In this way, both forms of readiness intertwine. Now we can understand that *lack* and *helplessness* are associated with the notion of child as a void that must be filled. From the viewpoint of readiness for supplementation, by contrast, children do not lack anything. Rather, they are the starting point for connective encounters that can produce events.

THE "SACRED YES" OF CHILDREN [5]

Children tend to be more tolerant than adults of unprecedented and new situations. Suffice it to look at an exhibit of children's paintings to see their ease and the creative freedom they enjoy. Young artists may lack technique, pictorial language, or compositional harmony, but they usually have plenty of courage and spontaneity, and can cover entire surfaces with vivid colors and shapes that express deep feelings. This is no different from what happens when children let us enter the unconventional world of their prodigious imagination. It is remarkable how these young artists find amusement in creation, unlike adults, whose creative moments are marked by a tragic, suffering atmosphere. Why is this the case? Whatever the answer to this question, it must be related to their age; as young artists grow their creativity tends to vanish.

I don't think that this tolerance of creativity is solely due to the lesser strength or effectiveness of repression, or that their lack of experience causes children to be less influenced by convention. While these factors doubtlessly play a role, there is another one that decidedly contributes to children's joyful walk through the unknown. This factor is connected with child discourse. There is nothing adults dread more than venturing outside convention into realms that have been sanctioned as impossible in the situation they inhabit.

Crossing the barriers of convention leads them to the following alternative: either they enter zones that are not part of established reality, or they penetrate forbidden territory, a deed that may be conceived of as a parricidal triumph. Still, the second case is the most tolerable.

Children, instead, are protected from these alternatives to a certain extent by child discourse. They view their foray into the creative world in the same way as travelers view their entry into a territory that has already been explored, or a person who gives the right answer looks at a riddle whose solution has already been found. There is no room for trepidation. They believe they are just successfully representing a role in a screenplay (or at least the outline of one) that, according to their assumption, already exists in their parents' minds. Consequently, parents will not be overwhelmed by children's creativity.

Strictly speaking, the young's work may be an utterly unique, even potentially disruptive creation. Yet thanks to the protection of child discourse, they believe that it is made up of things they have found in a trunk full of known objects that were somehow waiting to be found. Perhaps this is the context for children's joy of thinking or for the happiness (neither euphoria nor excess) they often show when playing and creating during their session. They assume that the mysteries of life, and of their own lives, are just enigmas whose solution (or whose decoding key) is known to adults.

The inability to engage in these activities due to gaps in child discourse tends instead to produce boredom, lack of interest, or depression. If this discourse does not allow children to wander through the singular space they inhabit, problems will arise. Some children curb their creativity because they perceive that it may disturb the foundations of the discourse that regulates their link to their parents, and thus diminish the latter's interest in them or even oust them from their place in that discourse. Others discover or assume that their potency will irritate their rival, whom they simultaneously love, and therefore "step aside," as Freud described, to avoid confrontation. These children hide their achievements. Like a leading man who must become obese and coarse to represent a character, they can become mediocre to play the role they assume to have been assigned in their parents' minds. Strictly speaking, children believe that by way of these acts they are protecting their parents' locus in discourse. They fear that if they surpass their parents, the latter will be lost to them.

Other children discover that in order to sustain child discourse and arouse their parents' interest, both essential to their survival, they must be shining stars. As opposed to the group described above, children's remarkable ability to imitate allows members of this group to show off by way of deceit and adjust their performance to the alleged parental demand. For instance, very young children can pretend they are reading by memorizing whole texts. It is an assuaging strategy that fulfills by way of simulacra the wishes they assume or discover their parents have for them. Nonetheless, since these young actors doubt the truth of their performance, they may condemn themselves to a future full of uncertainty about the veracity of their acts.

NOT ONLY AMONG CHILDREN

A remainder of child discourse's strategy to avoid the disturbing effects of creativity is still present in adults, and transforms occasional forays into the unknown into discoveries of something that already existed. There is even a kind of ideology of modesty, accompanied by a theory of creativity, that praises the recognition of parents as the true and only creators.[6] These parents may be "internal" or "external," and in the latter case they are called Gods. Before them, children (humans) can only discover what their Parents have already done; children's voyages will never be original.

Like his Greek predecessors, Descartes assumed that nothing, not even ideas could be human creations. All past and future concepts, philosophies, and discoveries had been "placed" in human brains by God. Learning meant simply revealing information about the laws of the universe that had been previously imprinted in human minds. As a consequence, anything new, as unique, creative, or revolutionary as it might aspire to be, was simply the unfolding of what the father-God had already placed in the minds of his children-humans. Of course, Descartes made use of this argument to assuage the Church—if thoughts are God's work, they cannot be seen as heresies. Even so, the similarities with child discourse are overwhelming.

LYING

The peculiar laxity characteristic of parent-children links, tied to Moore's paradox, becomes more complex as children develop. First, you will have noted that I said that children are not affected by what their parents actually know but by what they assume their parents know. Such distinction has its counterpart in the parental pole of the link. To make their children's assumptions possible, parents cannot expect to really know their children, but neither can they ignore them. They can neither disappoint their children nor strive to confirm the latter's assumptions, an attitude that I defined as partial lack of knowledge. We might say that both children and parents engage in a half-deceit or half-truth.[7]

Parental statements originate in split subjects—split not only between preconscious and unconscious but also between associations and connections. What can only be incorporated through connection is a part of themselves that is alien to them and has been specifically excluded from their psychic counting. The link is hence a crossroads for indeterminacies, and thus the site where the ideal state for the prevalence of connection may develop. For this reason, resulting subjectivities are unpredictable.

The inscription of "p" statements is correlative to trust and dependence. This relationship does not prevent children from mistrusting, an action that is related to the emergence of "I don't believe that p." The ideal of transcription would be the absence of mistrust and of "I don't believe that p" statements. The height of distortion associated with inscription would be the destruction of all certainty by the doubt inherent in these statements. Both extremes are manifested clinically by the restriction of the space for imagination and play, a space that is essential for children's "normal" development.

"Normalcy" in this case means that development consists in the gradual expansion of the paradoxical gap between unquestionable knowledge and challenges to this knowledge (between "p" and "I don't believe that p"), as well as of the range of elements contained in this gap. This expansion reaches a crucial point when children conceive of the possibility that the other may actually lie to them—that parents may not say what they truly think of their children. Children may now think that their assumptions of what their parents know may differ from what their parents *say* they know, and that this difference may even be intentional. A new possible disjunction between "p" and "I don't believe that p" results from this process. Parents may have said "p," but it is possible that they were thinking something else.

The tremendous significance of acknowledging the existence of lies has merited a bold assertion by Piera Aulagnier (1975, 1986). According to this author, this discovery is as essential for children as the discovery of the difference between the sexes, of their own mortality, and of the limits of desire. My respect for this author allows me to misuse her assertion to a certain extent. Her comparison both attaches transcendental value to, and qualifies, the discovery of lies because the difference between the sexes, death, and the boundary of desire are names of impossible things, of inconsistencies that will never cease to be such. In the same way, I suggest that the discovery that the other may not be telling the truth makes way for a new impossible thing, namely, knowing exactly what the other thinks.

As is the case with Epimenides's "I lie,"[8] discovering that the other can lie involves leaving a gap forever open in the link. It is another way of indicating that association alone can never account for what takes place there. Yet at the same time, when children discover the other's lie a new space opens up. Just as others may hide their thoughts, children may hide theirs. There may be secrets, which Aulagnier designates as a condition for thinking. This fact highlights something crucial. The paradox we have been studying acquires new layers, opens up to new depths as children develop. While children both believe and do not believe what they assume their parents have uttered, parents themselves may or may not believe such statements, that is, they may not have spoken the truth. Moreover, now children may know and not know about the origin of their own thoughts—of the emergents of "I don't believe that p." They will partially lack knowledge of an aspect of themselves.

In this way, the notion that the discourse ruling the link may include both truths and falsenesses gives rise to the development of a series of layers that unite and separate, forming a compact, impassable space between the one who attributes knowledge and the one to whom knowledge is attributed. This complex space, which stems from the paradox of both believing and not believing, will prevail in two aspects of child development: a) so-called *childhood sexual theories*, which always differ, sometimes astonishingly so, from theories provided by adults, as clear and transparent as the latter may be; and b) children's faith/lack of faith in their mothers' love for them. The paradox here would read, "She loves me, but I don't believe that she loves me."

This kind of diplopia[9] between being and not being the mother's phallus constitutes an essential step in the evolution of the Oedipus complex. We might think that the latter's end marks the moment when parents are "internalized" or, in terms of Moore's paradox, when "p" terms become part of the unconscious. Yet a remnant of the original child discourse remains active and usually tied to the parents. This is typically evinced by the huge impact the death of our progenitors tends to have, even when we are already adults and have become parents or grandparents. Such a death results in the impresence[10] of those who, according to our assumptions, store a remainder of our being's unknowns.

CHILDREN'S "GRASP"

It is well known that children are especially skilled at grasping essential threads of the linking weft they inhabit. For this reason, they are incredibly shrewd about detecting their parents' state of mind and the status of their link with them. Nevertheless, we should not mystify this ability, which does not imply understanding in causal terms. For example, children cannot explain what they have grasped in a family therapy session, even though their behavior shows how sensitive and precise they are in their answers to circulating latent meanings.

Several factors contribute to children's ability, which is clearly tied to their capacity to develop connections.[11] Children's openness to connection is favored by the fact that their psychic counting's armor is not as solid as that of adults'. Their beliefs, the fixed points in their psychic counting, are still being formed, to a certain extent. Another element that facilitates their openness is the fact that their child discourse protects them from the consequences of their thoughts and imagination—both from the dread of the unknown and from their parents' potential envy. Furthermore, in terms of Moore's paradox, we can add yet another reason. Children do not have to respond to parental "p" statements with verifiable propositions. They need neither say, "I believe that q" or "I believe that r," nor affirm, "I believe that not-p." They simply open the other term of the paradox, "I don't believe that p," without actually having to assert anything else about the "p" statement. In this way, they are in an optimal position to connect indeterminacies or signification gaps that are present in the minds of the utterers of "p." They can grasp in the special way allowed by connection without specifically incorporating its products into their associative world.

PARENTAL ATTITUDES, THOUGHTS, AND BELIEFS THAT AFFECT CHILDREN

Since children are so skilled at detecting subtleties in parental statements, we need to delve further into this topic in order to identify parental attitudes, thoughts, and beliefs that affect children within the link. We can distinguish three levels of meaning that the young can grasp in their parents' utterances in relation to the development of child discourse. The first level is quite explicit. It includes parental yearnings, which may be conscious and comprise the family's social and cultural aspirations. Here we should include first parental ideals transferred to children—not only those that make up parents' ego ideal, but also the remainders of their childhood narcissism. The second level is that of implicit meaning. It is what we usually call latent content, and it speaks of repressed, unconscious aspects of parental statements.

These two levels of meaning, which may be interpreted in Oedipal-narcissistic terms, emerge from, and point to, the contents of parents' psychic counting. The effects of these contents on the link are clear and have been repeatedly discussed in psychoanalytic literature, so I will not dwell on them here. Yet according to my analysis, there is a third level of meaning in the link, somehow tied to parental histories. This level includes those elements of the parents that are alien to them—that were not bound to their psychic counting by the Oedipal-narcissistic interface. For this reason, while they cannot be apprehended through association, meanings produced in this level can connect in the parent-child link and thus acquire determining power. I have called such inconsistencies specific exclusions.

These indeterminacies do not affect the logic of the psychic counting in principle, but if they connect with other indeterminacies by way of the link, they may indeed have an impact. We know that children are uniquely equipped for connection. What is remarkable about this third level is that it enables something that did not exist for mother and father (for it had been specifically excluded from their psychic counting) to become present by way of connection and exist for both parents and children.

Thus, we could say that the first two levels of meaning account for those aspects of parent-child relationships that can be interpreted in Oedipal-narcissistic terms. The third level, however, breaks with interpretive linearity. Even so, since the emergents of this third level lend themselves to be interpreted in terms of the emergents of the first two, we may fall under the illusion that in the parent-child link everything happens in the associative sphere. Doubtlessly, while it is true that like any link, the parent-child link has associative and connective poles, the connective pole is particularly relevant.

We may recognize two levels of meaning, one explicit and one implicit, in any kind of message. Nonetheless, communications theory defines as "noise" anything that has been specifically excluded from the message. For instance, in genetic hereditary transmission there is an explicit level (those elements in the genome that are expressed in the phenotype); an implicit level, which is not expressed in the phenotype but is inscribed in the genome (like recessive genes); and a level of specific exclusions, represented, among other elements, by "redundant" or "junk" DNA.[12] These elements appear to have no function but could be expressed in certain specific situations.

TRANSGENERATIONAL TRANSMISSION

The third level of specific exclusions is related to an enigmatic aspect of transgenerational transmission. It is logical to think that parents transmit the explicit aspects of their narcissistic yearnings and ideals to their children. It is also easy to think that the repressed may be transmitted. Yet there are cases where transgenerational transmission cannot be explained through any of these two levels; effects that are present in one generation respond to causes that can only be found two or three generations earlier. It is as though these effects had skipped one generation, so to speak. For instance, a child (C) may show features of a grandparent (G) that are not present either explicitly or implicitly in that child's parent (P). Instead of the logical transmission sequence $G \rightarrow P \rightarrow C$, we would have an enigmatic sequence $G \rightarrow C$, even if G and C had never met.

We could look at this enigma in the following way. The grandparent $\rightarrow$ parent ($G \rightarrow P$) line serves to transmit not only inclusions tied to the explicit and implicit levels described above, but also specific exclusions tied to the third level. These exclusions are manifested neither explicitly nor implicitly in P because they are not part of P's psychic counting. In fact, we could say that they do not exist in P because they have been specifically excluded. They resemble noise in a message—aspects of P that are alien to himself or herself. Yet in P's link with his or her child (C), these exclusions may manifest themselves as determinations. In other words, those aspects that lack either manifest or latent expression (we could even say, that do not exist) in parents (P) and are related to parents' link with their own parents (G) may be expressed—that is, exist from an associative point of view—by way of connection in the P-C link.

Besides explicit and implicit aspects of parents' psychic counting, parent-child transmission would thus include traits carried by parents that are not part of their associative world. These traits, which would be pure indeterminacy (pure excluded noise), may come to exist as unavoidable facts and marks through their connection with another indeterminacy in the link. They do not appear in children in some magical way. Rather, the link between children and parents affects grandparents' traits that had been pure inconsistency in the parents' psychic counting until then. It is not the reappearance of something that was waiting in the parents' psyche in latent form, like a recessive gene or a portable virus. Not at all. The link transforms what *was not* into something that *is*. It is as though the link founded the grandparent whom the child resembles.

AN EXAMPLE OF TRANSMISSION: OEDIPUS AND POLYNICES

This enigmatic aspect of transgenerational transmission that leads to the appearance in children of elements related to preceding generations may be viewed in two different ways: as the transmission of something hidden (in the model of recessive genes) or as the emergence of something previously non-existent (in the model of specific exclusions). In Sophocles' *Oedipus at Colonus*, Oedipus is confronted with his son Polyneices. Here the parent-child relationship may be read in each of the two ways mentioned above.

Polyneices searches for his old father Oedipus in Colonus. Polyneices' brother Eteocles has snatched the throne of Thebas from him, and according to the oracles Polyneices can only recover it if his father comes with him. Oedipus listens to his son's request and refuses it as follows:

> "*I* may not weep, *I* must put up with it / as long as I live remembering my murderer; [!] (. . .) you drove me out. It is because of you / I am a wanderer begging my daily bread. (. . .) You [Polyneices and Eteocles] are no sons of mine, you are someone else's (. . .) ou will fall yourself, polluted with blood (. . .) Get you gone! I spit you from me. I am no father / of yours, you worst of villains! Pack away / all of these curses that I invoke against you. / You shall not conquer by spear your native land; / you shall not come again to hollow Argos; [where Polyneices would have been saved] you are to die by a brother's hand, and kill him / by whom you were exiled. (Sophocles, 1991, pp. 140–1; author's emphasis)

When he receives this message from his father, Polyneices is forced to serve his sentence. His sister Antigone asks him to give up reconquering Thebes, saying, "Do you see, then, / how right our father's prophecies come out" (Sophocles, ibid., 142). To which Polyneices answers, "Now this must be my care, / this road of mine, ill-omened and terrible, / made so by my father and those Furies of his" (Sophocles, ibid., p. 143). In the link between Oedipus and Polyneices emerge fragments, some of them literal, of a history that is alien to them and seems rather to refer to Laius, grandfather of Polyneices and father of Oedipus, whom they never met.

For instance, Oedipus sentences his son to death by sending him to exile and disowning him, as his own father Laius had done with him. He declares that Polyneices is the son of another and accuses him of parricide. This accusation seems incredible, and we may very well see it as the reverse of Laius's filicide or as a projective accusation directed to Polyneices. We should recall here that Oedipus killed his father at a crossroads without recognizing him. In addition, like his father, Oedipus expects his son to bear the burden of the curse and pay for it, and Polyneices acquiesces.

Apparently, historical data do not justify Oedipus's statement about his son. Neither do they justify the latter's loyalty to these link emergents. Such loyalty is reflected in his willingness to follow the course set by the guardians of the Labdacian debt, the Furies, a course determined by crimes that he did not commit and did not even know had been committed. In Aeschylus's *Seven against Thebes* the role of Oedipus's sons becomes clearer. Their blood is the only thing that will appease the dragon killed by Cadmus. The killing of the dragon marks the origin of the curse flowing through the male line: Cadmus → Labdacus → Laius → Oedipus → Polyneices → Eteocles.

What is the origin of the emergents that outline the backbone of the father-son encounter illustrated by Sophocles? From the perspective of the transmission of concealed information, we ought to think that the curse had already been written but had not manifested itself because it had been repressed in Oedipus. It thus surfaced in the link like an encapsulated spore or recessive gene whose effects become manifest. This version coincides with the Greek's notion of divine inscription, a debt recorded by the Gods, who remember and demand payment. In their reasoning, it does not matter whether or not the record exists in the mind of those who must pay the debt.

Yet our case is more complex, because we aim to explain the facts without resorting to divine intervention. According to the specific exclusion approach, we ought to think that the encounter between Oedipus and Polyneices gave rise to new meanings that had never been inscribed in their minds. The encounter between specific exclusions would produce the "parricide-filicide-fratricide" event. While it may be understood as a repetition of the past, this event would actually be a creation of the link. Oedipus's and

Polyneices' psychic counting would have specifically excluded the elements that connected in the encounter to produce these emergents.

There is no reason to dismiss the possibility that both approaches are valid and that the emergent is the result of a particular interweaving of both. It would be hardly surprising if repressed information and specific exclusions were present in every transgenerational transmission, and if distinguishing them were as hard as it is in this case. It is not easy to set aside the fact that, at least in the case of Oedipus, when the history of Laius surfaces in his link with Polyneices, the repetition of past events that had affected him and been transferred to the relationship with his son may play a role. Even so, if we follow the story narrated in Greek tragedies we find that it is hard to claim that such repetition is the sole determinant. In the history of Oedipus (or in that of Polyneices, of course) retold by Sophocles nothing leads us to surmise the prior, repressed existence of the astonishing emergents that are revealed in this excerpt of the play. Consequently, we can argue that specific exclusions from their psychic counting played a role.

In Oedipus's particular case, we should recall that his psychic counting was built on his strong—if you will excuse the irony—Oedipus complex with Polybus and Merope, his Corinthian parents. In fact, one of the charms of Oedipus's tragedy may be summarized in the same question we posed earlier: How can children be affected by aspects of their parents' history that are unknown to both generations? Perhaps the purpose of the tragedy's avoiding any form of revelation is to increase the discomfort provoked by this question.

NOTES

1. Not until 1915 would he point to the remembering-repetition-working-through triad and to transference neurosis as the keys to psychoanalysis.
2. See Moreno (2010).
3. Children, for their part, wield over their parents the power granted by the fact that they and their development are a testament to their parents' good or poor parenting. Children may expose the deterioration of the parental role in order to demand attention or punish their parents.
4. See chapter 8.
5. Nietzche, F. (1969). *Thus Spoke Zarathustra.* p. 55.
6. Still, it is a complex issue due to the existence of envy, which is so important for Kleinian theory.
7. It is no coincidence that interactions similar to this one are very common in links and are based on dual assumptions. For instance, children pretend they do not know that Santa Claus does not exist, and parents pretend they do not know that their children know.
8. Epimenides the Cretan asserted that all Cretans are liars. This statement is known as "the Epimenides paradox," and was first analyzed by Bertrand Russell. (T.N.)
9. As Lacan (1956) calls it.
10. See chapter 5.
11. See chapters 3 and 4.
12. See chapter 9.

Chapter Eight

Childishness II

The History of Childhood and Toys

CHILDREN AND CHILDHOOD

As I mentioned before,[1] children can grasp the major threads of their family weft and respond to them. For this reason, the initial stitches in children's subjectivity will be conditioned by family expectations. These expectations, in turn, are constrained by the social discourses that establish what *child* means in each historical period. Saying that children are configured according to their society's definition of childhood is, therefore, a valid simplification. You probably know the phrase "children resemble their times more than their parents." This saying is particularly suitable in relation to general characteristics. Yet in terms of singularity, which is what interests me here (without dismissing the relevance of epochal marks), up to now children emerge from their parents' link. It is this link that is clearly regulated by current discourse.

Children's subjectivity stems from a complex interaction between biology and upbringing, and upbringing is regulated by the discourse prevalent in the family's environment. Note that I am distinguishing *childhood* from *children*. I define childhood as the set of institutional interventions that act upon the physical child (whom we could also call infant) and its family to produce what each society calls "a child." Thus, if we overlooked case-specific singularities (contradicting in part what I said in the previous paragraph), *child* is the product of the effects of the institution of childhood on biological materiality. That is why children who are produced in historical periods with differing notions of childhood are different, as we shall see.

127

Variations in the concept of childhood and in the children produced by this concept have always existed. Yet until recently, modifications developed relatively slowly; it took several generations for them to become evident. For this reason, a generation's beliefs regarding childhood could be seen as invariant. Today, instead, there is evidence that practices related to children are changing at an unprecedented speed. Ours might be the first generation traversed by more than one notion of childhood. It is hence hard to distinguish *symptomatic forms* from *social variations*. The speed of these changes, moreover, bears significant consequences on child psychoanalytic practice. It is obvious, then, that considering childhood as an invariant is inappropriate and anachronistic. The difficulties and challenges posed by shifts in this concept led to my interest in this topic.

HYSTERIA AND CHILDHOOD

I pointed out elsewhere[2] that hysteria changes according to the expectations it anticipates in that other to whom its actions are directed in each historical period. This is how I put it: "The hysteric and her other (or the master who represents him) create a deep bond. She entices his desire by unmasking him as castrated, and he provides her with a place where completion may be imagined as possible thanks to the magnificent and desirable object into which she is transformed (. . .) Because it inhabits the void it generates in the other, it is to be expected that hysteria will change along with the other's attire, which, in turn, adapts to the times" (Moreno, 1994, p. 359).

That is why the presentation of hysteria varies across history depending on the figure it recognizes as its master, which it challenges and whose recognition it simultaneously seeks. At some point it was the Church, before which hysteria presented itself as a saint or a heretic; at other times it was the medical sciences, before which it appeared as an exception; and later psychoanalysis, before which it presented itself as an indispensable ally.

Something very similar happens with childhood. The reason for this similarity is that discourses regulating links where children and hysterics participate operate in a similar way. Both children and hysterics dwell in the space between being desired as an object and being actually taken for that object. In other words, in order to be, both children and hysterics must arouse and sustain a desire referring to them in that other they are addressing, and then prevent this desire from being fulfilled with them as objects. How can I induce interest, how can I become desirable for that other without literally satisfying the demand I inspired? This enigma may very well characterize the spaces inhabited by children and hysterics, a correspondence that explains the remarkable similarities between them. For instance, both are often subject to abuse, and when this happens they often become suspect based on this particular relationship of dependency toward the other. They are supposed to have somehow "offered themselves" to abuse.

Nevertheless, not everything about children and hysterics is similar. I would like to highlight one difference related to the origin of the desire they arouse. Typically, to be desired the hysteric must create a gap in her current "master" to make him see that, despite his alleged completion, he still needs her. What happens with children is different. At birth they find that the threads with which the weft of their story will be woven have already been laid. Infants arrive in a world that has already created expectations about their fate. Even if they can introduce crucial variables later, the game will start with the cards they have been dealt. Consequently, children's major goal, their point of departure (already mentioned in the previous chapter), is to incite their parents' interest.

To do so, they can resort to two surprising skills. They can trace the outline of their parents' desire with regard to themselves, and they can also pretend they are their parents' object. In reality, they do not have enough detachment to develop an extrinsic view of the facts that would allow them to devise a strategy. "Trace" and "pretend" are hence not the most suitable terms. We could say that at the beginning children are this tracing and this pretense, or rather that they are little more than that. As a consequence, they are strongly affected by their assumption of what is expected from them. As we shall see, such sensitivity is pivotal to the continuity of a society's way of life over time.

IMMUTABLE AND MUTABLE PHENOMENA

If we are to study historical changes in the notion of childhood, we should clarify some points. First, there are immutable phenomena about which we may easily pose the following question: How was this phenomenon interpreted across history? Such ease, which stems from assuming that the phenomenon does not change over time and is not affected by our interpretation of it, does not characterize the study of the history of childhood.

For instance, let us look at the sun, that bright sphere that has risen in the east every morning and set in the west every evening since long before a mind existed that might ponder it. It is true that this sight was interpreted in different ways: as a God that traverses the sky every day; as part of a rigid sphere enveloping the universe; as a body that turns around us; as the fixed center of a universe that turns around it; or, nowadays, as a young little star lost in the infinite around which our planet turns. Nonetheless, without fear of making too big a blunder, we can say that from the point of view of an observer standing on our planet, the sun and its trajectory are invariable. Our interpretations have not affected it. Those who study the history of beliefs about the sun need not worry about the effects of these beliefs on the object "sun."

This may seem like an obvious generalization. Still, it is not so in the case of the topic we are discussing here because a) childhood is not an immutable phenomenon, and b) it is different for each culture. Furthermore, the answer a society gives to the question, "What is a child?" affects children. They respond to the ways in which they are conceived of and, since their responses tend to confirm current beliefs, the latter are reaffirmed as a blind spot. Consequently, those who are experiencing this situation logically see their notion of childhood as an invariant of humanity. In this sense, then, childhood is not like the sun.

CHILDREN'S PLASTICITY: CONFIGURATION

What is responsible for children's remarkable plasticity? What is the role of childrearing practices? So far we have dealt with the issue of transgenerational transmission in relation to transmitted contents. As I mentioned earlier, transmissions from parents to children may include manifest and latent contents, and even specific exclusions from their psychic counting. Now, however, we are dealing with a different type of transmission. This type—which perhaps ought to be called *configuration*—is much more significant than content transmission with regard to the cultural variation of the species, and involves both infant plasticity and the practice of childrearing.

In our species configuration is favored by the fact that unlike other vertebrates, humans are born with a nervous system that is not fully developed. For this reason, *Homo sapiens* cubs are particularly vulnerable and are configured (that is, they complete the development of their nervous system) during the childrearing period.[3] This developmental feature, which might have posed a huge obstacle to the survival of our species, may have actually constituted one of the keys to its success. It enabled humans who lived in a certain time and society to tailor childrearing practices to the subjects who would make up that society in the next generation. In this way, the subjects produced can function properly in their society. What is more, variations can be transmitted as if through a chain.

"Proper subjects" means subjects who have been especially configured to process each society's beliefs and practices and, at the same time, are capable of managing their children's upbringing and thus produce the subjects of the next generation. This entire process must be somehow regulated by the notion of childhood that prevails in a certain time and culture. There must hence exist some kind of articulation between the idea of childhood, childrearing practices, and the subjects needed for the future. Such articulation, which is certainly a very complex phenomenon, could be essential to the cultural transmission and transformation typical of human beings. Not just contents, information, and rules are transmitted through culture, but also subjectivities and modes of production of subjectivities. The medium for this transmission is necessarily the practice of childrearing.

The following sections review beliefs about childhood and childhood as an institution in three periods of western history, namely, the Middle Ages, modernity, and the current era. I will first offer an overall description of childhood in each period. Then I will attempt a more ambitious analysis of some of the reasons behind its features. Finally, I will venture into the history of games and toys. Needless to say, in this journey I will abandon the approach I had chosen for the previous chapters, which focused on the particular and the singular.

BRIEF DESCRIPTION OF CHILDHOOD IN THE MIDDLE AGES

One of the most significant facts about medieval children is that there are neither written records of their way of life or their upbringing,[4] nor images of them in paintings or sculptures. Generally speaking, children were not represented save when religion demanded their representation, as is the case with the baby Jesus and his mother. In these images, however, Christ appeared as a miniature adult that did not respond to our current view of children, except (sometimes) for his size. Paintings from that period show a small God with majestic demeanor who is being presented to the world by his mother, but he neither looks at her nor touches her.

The absence of representation was not due to artists' clumsiness or ignorance; the Greeks' realistic representations were well known, as were Augustine's fourth-century homilies on the importance of children. This absence is simply the consequence of the rejection of childhood's specific traits. In the Middle Ages childhood reality did not deserve attention. Childhood was but an inconsequential passage, a somewhat shameful period that people did not need to engrave in their memory, a state that must be tolerated in order to reach the only valued age—that of mature adults. Medieval biographies tend to skip this bothersome phase. Bernard of Clairvaux highlights the courage and humbleness of Christ in accepting to come to the world in the humiliating guise of a baby, unlike Adam, who came as an adult, thus escaping such degradation (Ariès, 1962).

Many historians relate medieval children's irrelevance to the extremely high infant mortality rate (50 percent in Imperial Russia). Children's lives, states Ariès (1962), were looked at with the same ambiguity as fetuses are today; infanticide was the equivalent of today's abortion. People believed that children had no soul, and it was not uncommon to bury them in the backyard, as we would do with a pet. The parent-child link was dramatically more distant than the modern one. For instance, according to Ross (1974), in fourteenth- to sixteenth-century Italy, after being baptized middle-class new-borns were handed to their *balia* or nurse (who usually lived in the country-side) for two years. Families rarely visited them during those years. When boys turned seven they started work as apprentices and lived with their master (who was not necessarily their father), while girls entered a convent at age nine or ten.

This custom was not limited to Italy. Wickes (1953) states that out of 21,000 children born in Paris in 1780, only 700 (3 percent) were raised by their parents. There were no schools, and people did not think that children possessed unique qualities (associated with gradual development) that war-ranted a special kind of training or education. Young people learned by living with and helping adults. Change over time was ignored, as was the separation between the adult and child worlds. Children were the immature form of adults. Genre art, of which Brueghel's paintings are an example, shows chil-dren and adults mingling at work and at play, as was the case in everyday life. The entire medieval community played. There were no games, toys, or clothing especially designed for children. Neither was there a division be-tween harmful and appropriate games or toys,[5] because children were not viewed as indifferent rather than innocent in relation to sexuality.

In the Middle Ages, therefore, children were considered immature beings that were not very interesting and did not deserve exceptional treatment. Their passage through the state of childhood must be endured until they matured, just as we wait for early fruits to ripen. Consequently, they were not represented, educated, dressed, or treated in any special way.

BRIEF DESCRIPTION OF MODERN CHILDHOOD

Many reasons have been offered to explain the shift in the notion of child-hood that occurred in the sixteenth and seventeenth centuries.[6] The truth is that if we look at any point in time between the nineteenth century and the first decades of the twentieth, we will find that the concept of childhood *and* children had considerably changed since the Middle Ages. Moreover, these were the children encountered by Freud. Modern children were conceived of as innocent—as free of evil, sin, and sexuality.[7] Being fragile and helpless, they must be sheltered from potential deviations caused by adult influence. Based on this notion, they were cared for and trained so that they would be well educated. There was a kind of obsessive focus on this endeavor. As opposed to their medieval counterparts, modern children excited the greatest interest in an environment that ceaselessly represented and wrote about them.

Now, the fact that modern children received so much "care" does not mean that they were considered important in and of themselves. Rather than a present-day reality, they were a promise for the future. For this reason, if a conflict emerged at any point between favoring these beings as they were in the present and favoring their potential, modern pedagogical, psychological, and childrearing ideology would not hesitate for a moment to prioritize the future. While they were not told so explicitly, children were viewed only as a promise. Such view configures the typical mode of modern child discipline. Children were subject to (sometimes extremely severe) punishment in order to rear them properly for the days to come.

In this way, everything in young people's lives and environment was organized around what was truly important, that is, future progress. Being a good breastfeeding baby, a good toddler, a good student, a good teenager, a good parent, a good grandparent, and even a good aunt or uncle, brother or sister was tied to the production of beneficial effects for children's future development. If these goals resulted in their current happiness, such benefit would constitute an added value.

Modern children responded docilely and malleably to these demands. The adult world, in turn, rewarded their docility, which was tinged here and there with cute mischievousness. We find this dynamic portrayed in stories and films with a modern ideology. They portray young heroes whose innocent nature allows them to show the deviant adults who have caused their suffering the true moral meaning of life, which the young heroes have learned from "good" adults.

Like literature, toys were especially designed to contribute to the "proper training" of children. Modern children were docile in the sense that they accepted to embody this potential ideal. They played games chosen by parents-educators and "learned" within set molds. Their most common toys stimulated the creativity typical of associative games, where fantasies expressed did not interfere with the reality sanctioned by adult beliefs. These games were highly favored over connective games.[8]

The strict division between different ages is evident in all modern practices; the separation between children and adults, which did not exist in the Middle Ages and will gradually disappear in our times, was categorical. There were schools, learning systems, clothing, toys, and literature appropriate for each age. Educating children may have been modern families' most important mission and the reason for their staying together. Families were assisted, or rather controlled, in their performance of this role by public, private, and religious bodies that "protected children" so that the "men of the future" would reach the finish line at whatever cost. Seen as a kind of depository to be molded and filled with knowledge, children occupied a privileged place in the ideal of "progress," of a "guaranteed future" so dear to modernity.

The paradigm of the modern child may have been the Renaissance baby Jesus. The latter is no longer depicted as a little man-King but as a sensuous child who tenderly gazes at and touches his mother. Such tenderness may also be observed in the virgin, a modern mother who is devoted and loving and who inevitably eroticizes her son. There is a chapter in Jesus's history that is particularly congruent with the status of modern children. The Son of God, who deserved so much devotion, actually had a mission. One might argue that it was for this reason that he was the object of so much care. As we all know, his mission was to sacrifice himself in order to redeem the sins of those who venerated him. Correlatively, we might say that modern children were cared for and venerated due to the mission they must accomplish, namely, relaying the torch of progress to the next generation. As psychoanalysts know, this torch often represented other missions, no longer conscious or explicit, which tended to be grouped under the category of "debts."

BRIEF DESCRIPTION OF PRESENT-DAY CHILDREN

It is hard for me to talk about contemporary children for several reasons. One is the lack of perspective. Another is the ideological content that inevitably surfaces when we discuss these issues. Yet another is that we live in a transitional stage characterized by unprecedented speed that does not seem to produce a stable form of childhood or family. As a result, the most outstanding aspect of today's children is the way in which they are gradually distancing themselves from modern cultural expectations. This process is congruent with what is taking place in parents' minds. Adults brought up under modern ideology oscillate between thinking that their children change because the childhood paradigm has changed, and thinking that they are dealing with aberrations of the ideology in which they were reared.

The truth is that the features of modern children discussed above are contradicted one by one by the features of present-day children. I will therefore be brief. Our times are marked by the so-called information revolution and the decline of the ideal of progress. Since this modern ideal was focused on children, contemporary families are being affected by the loss of one of their key incentives and are proving to be ineffective at producing and sustaining children in the modern manner. Today's children constantly show that they are not adequately represented by images generated by the modern notion of childhood.

To begin with, these children are not innocent, or at least do not respond to the modern ideal of innocence. Psychoanalysis showed the inaccuracy of this image, and so do both daily news reports that inform us of the existence of young criminals and the popularity of videogames and TV series whose violent scenes would have been considered inadmissible twenty years ago. At the same time, both the traditional categorization of children as fragile and defenseless and their unpunishable nature are now being revised. At times, the idea of sheltering the young from adult influence seems to have been reversed. Children are neither docile nor malleable. Rather, they increasingly show signs of resisting their image as a "gap to be filled with adult content." In this sense, child heroes typical of contemporary films are no longer obedient children who espouse the ideals abandoned by evil adults. Rather, they free themselves from the restraints imposed on them by that "traditional" society.

Regardless of adult directives, current children's favorite games are not associative but connective.[9] When the young play these games they elude through a bypass, as it were, the framework imposed by the signifiers provided by their family and connect directly with the framework imposed by the media. Child discourse, which, as I pointed out earlier,[10] is based on the assumption that adult minds can provide answers to its questions, does not seem to hold, at least in its earlier guise. Strictly speaking, since they are more familiar with information innovations than their progenitors, children often teach them "how things actually are."

The modern ideal of striving to learn and receive an education has lost its power. The erstwhile categorical division by ages does not seem to hold either. There is one life stage, adolescence, which both children and adults seek to emulate. The permanent presence of "metamorphoses" in childhood games and the passion for plastic surgery among adults seem to be attempts to achieve this goal. Moreover, rather than producing enlightened "citizens of the future," schools are becoming providers of technological tools for connection in the information world.

The obsolescence of modern educational methods (which are still valid in the school system) is a cause for general concern. Children are bored because the discourse they are used to (instantly changing media flashes) is not the prevailing one at school, whose narratives they often find unbearable. To address the profound crisis of the institution, several countries (Argentina among them) are designing an educational method that includes the mediation of a computer network in the classroom. Each child will have a computer on his or her desk (a project called OLPC, one laptop per child). In short, practically every modern institution seems incapable of analyzing or producing present-day children.

THE APPROPRIATENESS OF CHILDHOOD
AS A "SUBJECT FACTORY"

As we were saying, any form of childhood might seem ludicrous or, at least, inappropriate if examined from a different historical time. Yet there is a remarkable match between the predominant notion of childhood in a certain society at a certain time, and the type of subject "required" by this society to function. Rather than saying that the childhood constructed by a certain time and culture is a mistake or the product of ignorance, we may see it as a specific practice that was carefully designed to produce subjects that are suitable for future society. This approach allows us to acquire a clearer view than the mere judgment of prevalent rearing styles in different periods. Let us consider each of the three periods analyzed here from this perspective.

For medieval thinkers, the Sacred World had already been created. It was not even conceivable to expect any form of innovation from humans, its transitory inhabitants. Viewed as a "non-place" where immature humans resided, childhood was perfectly appropriate for the production of subjects able to preserve this immobility. In this way, the transmission diagram during this period would be as follows:

$$\text{ADULT-adult} \rightarrow \text{ADULT-adult,}$$

Where "adult" is a child, and "ADULT," is an adult. Children entered the chain as little adults who needed only to preserve the persistence of the same. Childhood did not exist as a stage in and of itself; it was only a period that had to be endured until maturity. *To be* meant *to be an adult*.

Modern childhood, by contrast, generated children who were "trained" by adults and, in this sense, constituted superb receptacles for adults' projections. "Childhood purity" made it possible for the ideal of perfection to develop. This ideal, however, was no longer divine, as in the Middle Ages; it was the ideal of a manmade world. Children could progress and accomplish in the future what adults had not been able to achieve in the present. The transmission diagram would be as follows:

$$\text{Adult} \rightarrow \text{child}$$

Enlightened adults thought they knew the best "configurations" for future men and women, and properly reared children must realize this ambitious project.

Currently, children have become the favored vehicle for the transmission of the whirlwind substitutions of an information network that bears an impact on all human beings. To achieve this transmission, childhood needs to free itself from the modern rule dictating that children must be guided by adults. This shift certainly gives rise to new concerns. In fact, hardly any institution controls children today. Nonetheless, the latter evince a particular ability to transmit lightning substitutions due to their remarkable plasticity and to the fact that they do not need to understand something by means of association in order to transmit it—they can just connect it. The need to understand as a condition for transmission is a modern requirement.

The transmission diagram for this stage would be as follows:

Media → child → Adult/child

Thanks to a technology that expands at remarkable speed, the media increase their power day by day. This power, moreover, is not based on the content they transmit but on their ability to propagate it. To achieve this purpose, they are constantly optimizing the process of simultaneously and instantly entering and transferring information across the human universe. The information world aims to penetrate every nook and cranny of culture, a process that has transformed power strategies. The expansion model of information technology is quite similar to that of computer and biological viruses. To endure, information must be transmitted. As a consequence, the emphasis is not on its effects or on the quality of its content but on its dissemination. In addition, it is as though preserving information did not make much sense. Everything is marked by the certainty of a swift obsolescence.

To transmit and propagate (the main goal of Web 2.0), the use of effective vehicles is essential. In this sense children are irreplaceable. They are the ones who more quickly and efficiently grasp and transmit the information of the world they inhabit. For this reason, the typical image of our time is the opposite of modernity's—children are "instructing" adults on current innovations. Modern institutions have made great efforts to exert some control over the flood of information in the media, which, thanks to technological progress, permeate society in an increasingly rapid and invasive way.

At the peak of modernity, everything that was not considered proper for children was carefully kept away from them. Books, toys, shows, movies, conversations, and jokes were conscientiously classified as only suitable for a certain age. Today the absolute failure of these screens has become evident. Neither the TV, nor the Internet, nor written media are able to handle this categorization. The "mature audience" label on TV is ineffective and has disappeared in many countries. "Parental control" devices on the Internet are useless. In short, all efforts made to this end have been futile. The media succeed in breaking these barriers and the screen reaches us all, irrespective of age.

Still, I think that children are the favored receptors of this information. The alliance between computers and children is much more efficient than the alliance between computers and adults. The aim is for adults-to-be, who are today's children, to come to view networked computers as an extension of themselves that is as natural to them as the watch to contemporary adults. Rational inertia typical of modern adults—that is, the attempt to "understand" rationally why or how facts are related—has become a hindrance. Connection, so well developed among present-day children, does not require us to make this attempt.

THE HISTORY OF GAMES AND TOYS

Few doubt that play and human-ness have been related from the start, whether because play has been part of human life from the beginning or, as Tattersall (2001, 2002) suggests, because language (which is seen by many as the attribute that distinguishes us from the other hominids) was invented by primitive children based on games. Many of the games we know stem from sacred ceremonies, divination practices, dances, or ritual fights. Ball games evoked a divine struggle to possess the sun; teetotums, tops, and dice seem to derive from divination practices; and circles, from ancient matrimonial rites. Play is thus tied to ritual.

Still, rite and play are opposed in relation to the sacred. Instead of preserving the substance that originated them, as rites do, games cancel their content and only preserve something of the form of sacred drama. Lévi-Strauss condensed this opposition between play and rite in the following formula: while rite transforms events into structures, thus fixing historical points on the calendar, play transforms structures into events, that is, dissolves the milestones evoked and chronological time (Agamben, 1975).

THE MINIATURIZATION OF THE PAST

Nonetheless, regardless of their connection to the sacred, it has been insistently pointed out that toys and games have a special relationship with the context in which they emerged. They "make appear" something of the past in the playful present. That is why Lévi-Strauss and Agamben state that toys are, in a way, the very essence of history; they miniaturize old objects that belonged to an earlier socioeconomic period. "The toy is what belonged—once, no longer—to the realm of the sacred or of the practical economic" (Agamben, 1975, p. 80). That is why toys would be something like history in its pure state, a historical essence, in the sense that we may grasp an entire temporality contained in the object. (This is very similar to the role of clothing in earlier times.)

Modern parents and educators perceived that toys could become a significant ally in the implementation of the project of "childhood" that suited that particular time. New games and toys, so-called educational toys, were especially designed to "mold" children's minds properly. In this sense, almost all modern toys have a key motivation. Children "pretend play" to be like grown-ups, in fact, like the grown-ups of the past: "the young doctor," "the young chemist," "the young nurse," and so on and so forth. Objects recreate elements from an age that preceded them.

I remember that in my childhood, in the 1950s, we played Cowboys and Indians, Pirates. . . . Like the toys we used, those cowboys, Indians, and pirates were evocations of past times. One of my favorite toys was my "curved saber of San Martín," a toy made of painted tin that evoked the Argentine hero for whom, I must confess, I felt scant admiration.[11] Amazingly, even though World War II had recently ended and Perón had come to power, we did not play soldiers, or planes, or Nazis and Allies, or Perón and Evita, or anything related to current events. The contention that toys are a miniaturization of the past was thus amply proved.

The second element that transformed toys during modernity (and still does today) was technology. It became possible to reproduce objects in small sizes (miniaturize them) more precisely and in large scale.[12] Dolls, which used to be made by craftsmen, were now mass-produced. "Pretending to be grown-ups" became little more than a kind of educational training. One of the first toys to facilitate such training was the famous Meccano, a constructional toy invented by Frank Hornby in early-twentieth-century England. Bronze pieces with holes in them could be joined with screws to "build" true engineering mockups. All this, I will say it again, does not alter the allegation that, above all, toys "miniaturize the past."

TOYS AS COMMODITIES

In the mid-1950s mass media began venturing into the world of toys. Until then toy publicity had been insignificant. For instance, during 1955 in the United States, Marx's, a leading toy brand sold USD 50 million and spent only USD 312 in ads. While these figures have not been reversed, the amount spent by toy manufacturers on publicity nowadays is far greater than the amount spent in manufacturing. Toys have become above all an object that children yearn to have. Ads (directed to children rather than to their parents) clearly aim to promote them as emblematic consumer objects.

During modernity play was seen as the natural expression of the spirit of childhood. It was not experienced as an act of object possession. The focus was on social interaction. Now toys are acquiring value as property. This shift is particularly evident in card games. Like chess, checkers, or backgammon, traditional decks of cards (French or Spanish) may have different commercial values, but that does not alter the value or the moves of the cards or pieces. A cheap chess knight can move in the same way as an expensive one. The ace of spades has the same value in a cardboard deck or a Kent deck.

Yet the Magic, Pokémon, or Yu-Gi-Oh cards collected by children today are different. They have varying commercial values, and their "skills" and "powers" change with their price. As is the case with stock exchange shares, there are catalogues with up-to-date "quotations" of the cards, which children know and download from the Internet. Based on such knowledge, they set the "commercial" value of their deck and plan their trades or purchases. In this way, a player with a deck worth, let us say, 40 dollars will hardly be able to beat the owner of a 400-dollar deck. "Special," more powerful cards are more valuable than "regular" ones (for instance, the Yu-Gi-Oh card Elemental HERO Air Neos is being offered on the Internet for USD 7 to 35). It may seem awful, but (and this may make it even more horrendous) this development is absolutely consistent with changes in the adult world, and perhaps even more so with the features of the world to come.

THE MINIATURIZATION OF THE FUTURE

Presently I would like to highlight another feature of present-day toys where, as I understand it, the entire history of toys is being reverted. For a while now toys favored by children have ceased to evoke the past. Rather, they seem to have been designed by a futurologist.[13] Robots and space ships cross space faster than light speed, laser beams pierce everything, cloned beings transmute, and warriors have unheard-of skills such as cloning, mutating, sex-changing, and sucking the energy from their dead victims. [14] The miniaturization of the past, if it still exists, is of interest only to collectors young and old, who see their possessions as valuable objects with which one does not usually play.

We need to determine the precise dimension of this change. Nonetheless, as I stated earlier, in my experience the value of historical preservation through toys has decreased, and a new value has appeared in its place—anticipation. Toys incorporate innovations tied to their anticipation of the future. *Today's toys miniaturize the future.* What happened to the view of toys as the essence of history? Has their evocative power simply reverted? The notion of childhood underlying current childrearing practices may not require individuals to preserve the past through toys. Today the expectation is rather that future subjects should get ahead of the breathless times to come thanks to an anticipatory practice reflected in current play.

This reversal from past to future may be related to the shift in the transmission paradigm. The Adult → child chain of transmission typical of modernity has broken. Toys no longer narrate or bring back the past but tend to forestall the future, a role for which present-day children are essential, as I already mentioned. Consequently, the educational role of toys has also been reversed in relation to time, as we shall see.

TOY MAKERS' PUBLICITY STRATEGIES

Assuredly, this was not a sudden occurrence. An important factor in this shift must have been the appearance of comics first, and TV series and video-games later. Their advent brought about a vital change tied to consumption and the entry of toys into the market. In this sense, examining the shift in toy manufacturers' sales strategy may be enlightening. During modernity their strategy seemed to be as follows: parents were explained the "educational and beneficial" properties of toys. They consequently bought the toys and somehow imposed them on children, who played with them and produced their own meaning. This meaning originated in the adult world and did not modify the Adult → child direction of the parent-child link.

Present-day children are valuable consumers, and media transformations have enabled toy ads to reach them directly. Not only is publicity directed to children; toy design and ads seem to be specifically devised to bypass parents. Adults do not understand these toys, let alone the slogans used to promote them. The current approach is hence the opposite of the modern approach. Untrained adults cannot understand the drawings and codes of Pokémon, Magic, Yu-Gi-Oh, or Sakura cards. If they tried to play one of the latest Gameboy, Play Station, or Wii games, they would find themselves in a bind unless a young one "coached them" (while the workings of these games would be obvious to any child). Furthermore, there are no instructions.

Of course, whether or not these games are "educational" does not seem to be at all relevant to their marketing; toys catch on regardless of this consideration. In reality, games are educational but not in the sense parents expect them to be, and even less in the sense of molding children to be "like their parents." They are educational only in a figurative sense, more because of their role in ongoing renovation, evolution, and change than because of their content. Today's object-toys serve as training devices for a high-tech informational future, which requires children to be configured and instructed to carry out new practices and to be very different from adults.

NOTES

1. See chapter 7.
2. Moreno (1994).
3. As we know today, while its development is much more critical during the early years, the human central nervous system continues to evolve throughout our whole lives. In this sense, results obtained by cognitivists and neurobiologists, who distinguish between "explicit" (or declarative) and "implicit" (or non-declarative) memory, are relevant here. The first kind of memory is accessible to consciousness and refers to the recognition of objects, people, and situations. Implicit memory, by contrast, is not accessible to consciousness and alludes to the ways in which we react to different situations. At the same time, depending on the endurance time of a memory, we may distinguish short-lasting from long-lasting memory. For long-lasting memory to occur, neuronal anatomic changes must take place that involve the activation of RNA and the change in the number and distribution of synapses. It is tempting to think that explicit memory is tied to what I call here transgenerational transmission of information, while implicit memory (especially the long-lasting type) is tied to what I call transgenerational configuration (Kandel, 1998, 1999; Ansermet and Magistretti, 2004).
4. There is one exception, namely, the diary of Héroard, Louis XIII's physician, who took detailed notes on the life of the Dauphin since his birth in 1601. Yet its value is limited because

it is full of obvious exaggerations that may have been aimed at extolling the figure of the young prince (deMause, 1974).

5. According to Héroard, courtiers amused themselves by teaching one-year-old Louis XII to offer his penis to be kissed instead of his hand (E. W. Marwick, 1974).

6. Reasons stated are cultural (the Renaissance as a kind of return to Hellenic art and culture); political (Church and state as enemies of the patriarchal system whereby children were the property of their parents); economic (emerging industries and technologies that required numerous skilled workers); and sociological (changes associated with the constitution of the bourgeois family, more closely knit and focused on children). Besides taxing my knowledge, expanding on these reasons would change the direction of this discussion.

7. Corea and Lewkowicz (1999) point out that psychoanalysis greatly contributed to erasing this notion. Very little has been said about this process, but Freud's (1896) well known "seduction theory" was a clear attempt to defend childhood innocence, and his rejection of it meant also the rejection of the idea of innocent children.

8. See chapter 3.

9. See chapter 3.

10. See chapter 7.

11. San Martín was a major hero of Argentina's War of Independence. (T.N.)

12. As Benjamin (1936) pointed out with regard to the artwork, large-scale production affects "the aura" and the value of originality.

13. See chapter 3.

14. There is indeed a particular combination between magical thinking (which has always been present) and the technology of the future.

Chapter Nine

The Emergence of Human-ness

HUMANS

Only one species, ours, dominated by a kind of compulsion, seems to be obsessed by change. Evidence shows that this constantly accelerating race to incorporate development after development and innovation after innovation, each more complex than the last, started only some 40,000 years ago—when we came to Europe. Since then, Cro-Magnon groups residing in different places and/or at different times evolved differently, as evidenced by their remainders. It is as though from the Upper Paleolithic on, Homo sapiens had been characterized by variation. The shape and complexity of utensils, the number and disposition of tombs, the types of animals hunted, the ornaments used, and group customs, all differ.

As we saw in chapter 1, it is this ability to change that categorically distinguishes humans from all existing hominids and from the rest of the animal world. Yet even if it seems that the search for human origin, like the search for the origin of any species, should focus on the appearance of one or several physical attributes that are decisive for the species, I believe that this mystery should be tackled from a different perspective. Humans' distinctive feature, in my view, is the use of an extrasomatic channel of cultural transmission that breaks with the primacy of genetic command, which had determined evolutionary changes in the Earth's living beings for billions of years. As I stated before,[1] humans are the only animals capable of effecting radical variations in their contact with their environment without changing their genome. This quality undoubtedly represents a monumental difference between us and every other existing species—a leap and, why not, a creation.

So if we consider that what is strictly human is the ability to produce, record, and transmit events accumulating in culture in a complex way, thus leading to ceaselessly changing customs and an evolution independent of genes, the "origin of man" does not coincide with the appearance of the species 200,000 years ago. Rather, it should be situated in the puzzling times of the beginning of the extinction of the Neanderthals 40,000 years ago. Today scientists believe that the first Homo sapiens (our species) appeared just 200,000 years ago.[2] It was genetically identical to us but behaved like any other hominid until the Upper Paleolithic, about 40,000 years ago. Then a stunning event took place, which has been called "the great leap forward" (Diamond, 1992) or "the creative explosion" (Pfeiffer, 1982). Homo sapiens "turned" human and started appropriating the planet.

Nowadays everything seems to be human property. Every existing species that comes to our notice has to submit to our power to avoid a significant risk of dying. Yet it was not always like that. During the 3.5 billion years prior to the great leap our planet knew of no event resembling human overflow. Individuals of *Homo* genus' species have swarmed the world for about 3 million years. Descending from *Homo antecessor* (which emerged as a species approximately 1 million years ago), Homo sapiens appeared 200,000 years ago in Africa. We must have started migrating from this continent [where, according to Stringer and McKie (1997), we were close to extinction] some 100,000 years ago, and arrived in Europe 50,000 years later. Back then Europe was Neanderthal territory, and Neanderthals also descended from *Homo antecessor*. We coexisted with our cousins for nearly 20,000 years (and for some time and in certain places, with *Homo erectus* as well). Approximately 25,000 years ago, however, we were the only hominids on the planet.

THE ENIGMATIC NEANDERTHAL

Since more than 200,000 and until about 25,000 years ago,[3] an hominid apparently very well adjusted to its environment dwelled in almost all of Europe, the Middle East, Afghanistan, and up to Siberia—*Homo neanderthalis*, or simply Neanderthal. The name stems from the Neander valley (*Thal* in German), where its remains were first found in 1856. Even though scientists believe that Neanderthal is not a human ancestor, it had more "human" traits than current primates or than any known hominid except the recently discovered *Homo antecessor*. Its physical build and upright posture resembled those of humans, and it buried its dead. The oldest tomb that has been found is Neanderthal and it is around 100,000 years old (Fleming, 1996).

Ralph Solecki found a great amount of pollen from colorful flowers in a Neanderthal tomb in Shanidar, and therefore he and others concluded that Neanderthals paid tribute to their dead with flowers (Solecki's 1971 book was titled *The First Flower People*).[4] Currently, however, scholars believe that perhaps they buried their dead only to prevent them from being eaten by scavengers. One of the Shamidar tombs contained an older Neanderthal who was partially blind and an invalid and had lost an arm when still alive. Such a finding suggests that a community had taken care of him. Some believe that the fact that children were buried is a sign that they received special treatment.

Like their ancestor *Homo erectus*, Neanderthals had mastered the use of fire and seem to have cared for their sick, elderly, and children. They were extremely brawny and strong. Abundant fractures and contusions found in their remains make one suspect that their lives were very hard. Scientists believe that Neanderthals did not live beyond forty. While the average male height was slightly less than 5'7", they were about twenty-two pounds heavier than modern men of that height due to their powerful muscles and their stoutness. Judging by the volume of the skull, their brain was slightly larger than both the human brain (88.5 to 82.4 in^3) and the brain of every other known hominid.[5] Neanderthals may have resembled modern humans quite a bit in looks. Johanson and Edey (1981) illustrate this resemblance very eloquently: "I consider Neanderthal conspecific with Homo sapiens, with myself. One hears talk about putting him in a business suit and turning him loose in the subway. It is true; one could do it and he would never be noticed" (Johanson and Edey, 1981, p. 20).

Nonetheless, there is an issue that does not seem to be in dispute— the differences that divide the first cultures called human from Neanderthal culture. The most interesting conjectures about these differences stem from studying the tools built by Neanderthals. These consist mainly of stone blades known as "handaxes," made from one piece and free of ornaments. While they are somewhat more sophisticated than the ones used by *Homo habilis* and *Homo erectus* for 2,000,000 years, these tools scarcely varied over time and across Neanderthal territory. Remains separated by tens of thousands of years or thousands of miles present the same tools. Evidence allows us to conjecture that Neanderthal habits followed the same trend; they remained the same across thousands of years and miles.

This striking monotony is not exclusive to our Neanderthal cousins; it is typical of all non-human hominids. It seems that once a technological innovation occurred, such as the *Homo erectus*'s stone handaxe, it was incorporated and could persist with no significant variation for millions of years. Something similar may have happened with the appearance of a sixth phalanx in the hand or with any other genetically determined biological acquisition. We ought to add that the number of these "innovations" is small. The general landscape is boring, as boring as that of every other animal species, which tediously maintains its habits.[6]

THE GREAT LEAP

Paleoarcheologists can distinguish quite precisely a Cro-Magnon skeleton from the skeleton of a different hominid by its physical aspect. Today they can even examine remains' DNA to confirm their findings. Yet cultural traces are the ones that make it possible to differentiate these skeletons unequivocally. At first, Cro-Magnon hominids used the same tool for everything. Their technique has hence been called Swiss Army Knife. Since 40,000 years ago, however, quite suddenly Cro-Magnon cultural productions became much more sophisticated and varied than those of *Homo neandertalis* or *erectus*. Tools were made not only of stone but also of bone, ivory, and antlers. They consisted of two or more pieces embedded in each other that varied according to use. There were needles to sew, fishing hooks, bows, arrows, ropes.

These tools exhibited a singular feature: they varied over time and across space. Furthermore, some of them possessed only an ornamental, representational function, which shows that Cro-Magnons developed a taste for art and for recording experiences. Another purpose may have been to represent social difference, which also distinguishes Cro-Magnons from all other animals. Cave paintings such as those of Lascaux, Altamira, and Puente Vesgo illustrate this feature, which has surprised more than one socio-biologist, as ornamentation is a kind of excess with no apparent adaptive purpose.

From the animal remains accumulated in their caves we may deduce that Cro-Magnons had a refined knowledge of animal behavior and remarkably organized hunting practices. They must have developed some form of calendar early on, because they built camps in suitable areas during the right period of time to wait for the great herds of migrating mammals (Calvin, 1991; Diamond, 1992; Rothschild, 1993; Stringer and Andrews, 2005). Some species hunted by Cro-Magnon, such as giant buffalos, bison, and entire herds of deer would be hard to catch even with today's automatic rifles. Moreover, along with hunting skills we may find another major Homo sapiens trait, that is, the extermination of other species that shared their dwelling places. Apparently, neither the much less progressive Neanderthal nor any of the earlier hominids did that. Their population growth, dissemination, and ability to progress and exterminate seem to have been negligible in comparison to ours.

The truth is that despite Neanderthals' adjustment to their environment and their having a larger brain and stronger muscles than Cro-Magnon, they disappeared with relative suddenness, concomitantly with our meteoric expansion. Today scientists think that there is a connection between the extermination of Neanderthals and the striking development of humans during the Upper Paleolithic. It would not have been an open war, as it is usually depicted in fiction, but more likely a competition for resources. Evidence has appeared relatively recently of a potential peaceful coexistence between Cro-Magnon and Neanderthal. Based on the discovery of Cro-Magnon objects in some of the last Neanderthal strongholds in Burgos and Châtelperrorian, scholars speculate about either bartering or the potential imitation by Neanderthals of some of primitive humans' accomplishments (Gee, 1996; Tattersall, 2002). Nevertheless, recent DNA evidence seems to rule out the (also fictionalized) possibility of some sort of hybridization between the species, unless the children born from these couplings were barren.[7] The collapse of Neanderthals may have simply heralded a sequence of events characteristic of Homo sapiens history, namely, the extinction of the species that share its habitat.[8]

WHAT KIND OF CHANGE IS IT?

The key question is, what promoted the change that made Cro-Magnon so much better? This question is appealing because it seems congruent with another one: How was human-ness born? "Human" may very well be the name of the gap separating us from the rest of our relatives, especially Neanderthals, who are similar to us in so many ways.

From a Darwinist perspective, we should relate the change directly to the emergence of a physical attribute commanded by the genome. Nonetheless, somatic evidence fails to account for this gap. Besides the great overall resemblance, the Neanderthal brain was larger than ours, and genetic differences between us must have been negligible.

Discrepancies between Neanderthal and human nuclear DNAs are likely much smaller than discrepancies between the nuclear DNAs of humans and chimpanzees. This makes sense because the branch that connected us with chimpanzees broke off about 6 million years ago, while the ancestors we share with Neanderthals lived only 600,000 years ago. Now, modern humans share 98 percent of our genetic code with chimpanzees. A detailed study (Pearson, 2001) concluded that the base sequences of chimpanzee DNA show a difference of only 1.3 percent with ours. Yet the active and determining DNA fraction shared would actually be much larger due to the presence of redundant or junk DNA.[9]

All these calculations allow us to estimate that the difference between active Neanderthal DNA and active human DNA would be less than 0.1%. Until recently, those searching for the causes of this discrepancy argued that despite brain volume and a remarkable development of areas linked to speech and lateralization, Neanderthals had not been able to speak because of the shape of the base of their skull. In 1989, however, a fairly complete 60,000-year-old Neanderthal skeleton (Moshe) that was discovered in Israeli caves provided evidence that destroyed this thesis—a hyoid bone. The conclusion was that Neanderthals were as able to articulate words as we are. Due to the shape of their skull base, instead of "Bye, gorgeous" they might have said, "Wuy, nohnouh." Nevertheless, in terms of the configuration of their throat, they would have been able to say it.

Obviously, a little over 40,000 years ago a true event, a click, *something* determined the surprisingly rapid expansion of Cro-Magnons' domain over that of their cousins, who were so similar to them in some ways. Available physical evidence fails to explain this change. The genome may have determined a necessary but not sufficient condition. Strictly speaking, this may have been the first radical change in the biological world that was not commanded by genes.

The most convincing evidence that physical differences cannot explain human development is that according to paleoarcheological findings, the behavior characteristic of humans—their ability to come into contact with inconsistencies—appeared much later than the species itself.[10] In Israel, where Neanderthals lived for more than 200,000 years, Homo sapiens started dwelling alongside them approximately 100,000 years ago. What is most striking is that tools and places that Neanderthals and Homo sapiens left behind are essentially identical. Despite their genetic differences, existing evidence suggests that both species behaved in the same way (Stringer and McKie, 1996; Tattersall, 2000).

Yet in the Upper Paleolithic everything changed. Around 40,000 years ago, when *Homo sapiens* had existed for 160,000 years, the creative explosion occurred. After 2,500,000 years of slightly noticeable changes in the manufacturing of stone tools that resulted in fairly monotonous archeological evidence, in a few thousand years sapiens cultures flourished that were distinct enough to receive their own name— Chatelperronian/Aurignacian, Gravettian, Solutrean, Magdalenian. In Richard Klein's view, these variations point to "the most fundamental change in human behavior that the archeological record may ever reveal" (Klein, 1999, p. 524).

Some thirty years ago, when scholars believed that the human species had been born in Europe 50,000 years earlier, they explained this creative explosion as follows: enter Homo sapiens, a new species whose genome determines a new brain, behavior, and language. This species displaces all its ancestors and exterminates Neanderthals. Human attributes emerged directly and simply from a biological change, just as it had been happening among living beings for billions of years.

Data, however, suggest that the human species originated 150,000 years before its arrival in Europe and 160,000 years before the emergence of the Cro-Magnon culture. Unlike the origin of any other species, the mysterious origin of humans can no longer be reduced to a change in the genome. What, then, facilitated this leap that did not separate the Upper Paleolithic Homo sapiens from other hominids but from the earlier Homo sapiens? The most incredible step in the history of human culture still lacks a cause. The enigma of the origin of man is now twofold—that of the origin of the species, and that of the origin of human-ness within the species.

MATERIALITY AS A CAUSE OF CHANGE

An explanation of this mystery by means of biological materiality did not take long to appear. Any significant variation in animal species is considered to derive from a physical change that started in the genome. The dramatic leap made by Homo sapiens was viewed as a second biological event, the first one being the origin of the species. Something caused the leap but left no marks on skeletons. It is in this sense that Klein (1989) states that around fifty thousand years ago, a breakthrough in the African lineage took place, a "neurological change" that made it possible for Cro-Magnons to develop new cultural behaviors. This change might very well have happened to Neander-thals, but it did not.

The problem is that since we emerged as a species 200,000 years ago, no paleoanthropological or genetic evidence has been discovered to support the theory of a biological change. What is more, if, as Klein suggests, a genetic mutation had happened 50,000 years ago, this mutation would have propagated radially from a focal point, likely giving rise to population diversity or to two species. Contrariwise, cultural changes that followed the Upper Paleolithic creative explosion appeared in a complicated mosaic of mini-explosions that spread with striking speed. Art innovations, new tools, ornaments, weapons expanded like wildfire wherever somatically identical humans already dwelled. Such development would not be expected of a genetic change affecting a population whose generations are separated by approximately twenty-five years.

What characterizes humans is not that first leap, but the fact that we have not stopped taking leaps. Where there are humans, there are changes. These changes involve a series of consecutive supplementations that configure the most characteristic human trait, that is, progress outside the genome. If the arguments offered by Klein and the supporters of a biological cause of change were valid, there ought to have been repeated lineage breakthroughs that generated neurological changes, and these, in turn, would have determined ongoing cultural explosions.

Nonetheless, Klein may be right about one thing. *There was* a lineage breakthrough. It was not, however a break in a genetic lineage, and it was not due to neurological effects (even though, according to current knowledge, it may have had neurological consequences). It was actually a much more radical rupture. From genetic information and command, we have shifted to an information system and command based on *extrasomatic transmission*

and accumulation of information (in culture) by way of the practice I defined
as the *third childrearing strategy.*[11]

COULD THE DIFFERENCE STEM FROM
OUR ABILITY TO SPEAK?

Nobody seems to doubt these days that the tiny change responsible for such
huge consequences was tied to the mechanical and brain capacities that made
it possible for Cro-Magnons to use articulated language. In my opinion,
however, this answer does not exhaust the matter by any means. It is true that
the great leap and language mastery are connected. Nonetheless, the creative
explosion was not due to the fact that we "suddenly" started speaking. It is
true that language allowed Cro-Magnons to communicate relatively complex
issues to each other, which would have perhaps been impossible for Neanderthals—issues related to social life, survival, and resource use, among
others. Still, while the hypothetical acquisition of language may have led to a
better adjustment and improved hunting and defense skills, it does not seem
that these arguments suffice to explain the explosive transformation that
occurred in the Upper Paleolithic.

After all, there are animals that can communicate fairly complex messages tailored to their kin, but they did not produce an outburst comparable to
the great leap. In fact, dolphins can communicate with each other by way of a
complex language that we do not understand. *Homo habilis,* who inhabited
the Earth more than 2,000,000 years ago, already displayed both a bulge in
Broca's area and lateralization (they were primarily right-handed). We may,
therefore, assume that they mastered a rudimentary form of language, or at
least a complex system of sound communication (Foley, 1996). *Homo erectus* shows greater development of one hemisphere, a feature that is also
related to speech, and some claim that only a talking species could have
controlled fire the way they did.

In 1969 Gardner and Gardner were able to teach chimpanzees a great
number of symbols by way of manual gestures, symbols that the apes used to
communicate in a way that the authors considered almost human. Still, they
admitted that the chimpanzees did not develop a grammar and syntax like
ours (see also Calvin, 1994 and Savage-Rumbaugh, Shanker, and Taylor,
1998). Chimpanzees have a very complex social system that includes politics; they implement elaborate Machiavellian strategies that must require
manifold "communicational" exchanges (de Waall, 1982). Furthermore,
there is no evidence that Neanderthals were mute or that they did not communicate (Salomon, 1992). Rather, the significant level of social organization they must have possessed makes one suspect that they had at least some
kind of gestural or sound communication. Moreover, the finding of a hyoid

bone, as we mentioned earlier, utterly refutes the contention that they were not mechanically capable of speaking (Holden, 1998).

It is true that we cannot separate human intelligence from syntax. Still, I do not think that we can reduce the cause of the great leap to language acquisition. Moreover, if we claimed that the cause was indeed that Homo sapiens could speak, we would generate a new problem. Why did they not take this leap during the previous 160,000 years? Should we argue that they had a brain, vocal chords, and the anatomical disposition for speech but they needed to develop culturally first? If we did so we would fall into a circular argument. They evolved culturally due to language, and they developed language thanks to their cultural evolution. It might be so; circular arguments often make it possible to understand an event, and the great leap was an event. All this evidence only increases our curiosity regarding this question: What made Homo sapiens produce the creative explosion that split their history and separated them from the rest of the animal world for good?

THE HYPOTHESIS

What separates us from the rest of living beings is, above all, that we are affected by events that transcend the logic whereby we understand the world in each situation.[12] In addition, we are capable of recording the supplementations resulting from these events and storing them in a kind of informational pool called culture, where accumulation is selective. Furthermore, this informational pool evolves and may be transmitted to future generations outside the genetic code. Radical innovations (such as an invention in the cultural world or the emergence of a new species in the biological world) only occur under certain conditions. The cart cannot be invented before the wheel. Nonetheless, this does not mean that innovations are simply the consequence of the conditions under which they emerged. In the same way, for the great leap to happen the right conditions must have previously developed among our hominid ancestors.

There are several research lines that point in this direction. Judging by a large amount of evidence, scholars believe that language had made significant progress in hominids, even though it is hard to identify specific steps. The bipedal position freed the front limbs, making it possible to use them as tools. Brain volume had been growing for more than 5 million years. We had been using tools for 2 or 3 million years, and these tools were gradually becoming more sophisticated. And let us not forget fire, conquered by *Homo erectus* a couple of million years ago. To this list, William Calvin (1987, 1990, 1994) adds the ability to coordinate successive movements needed to throw something with precision. This skill would have also developed slowly in the hominid series. According to Calvin, it is an essential precursor of the ability to connect thoughts, words, or actions. Chimpanzees, for instance, are quite good at "hammering" a nut with a stone to break it, but their throw is much clumsier than little children's.

In reality, whatever our ancestral anthropomorphism might lead us to think, events giving rise to the evolution from monkey to man are not evolutionary benefits in themselves. Having a big brain is very costly (a large brain uses a lot of energy, more than 20 percent of our nutritious resources) and poses a high risk at birth. Its development must have required sacrifices, for instance, abandoning a vegetarian diet. Monkeys' protruding abdomen is due to the intestinal development needed to extract energy from leaves. Favoring brain development involved abandoning this easy diet and working to incorporate nutritional elements rich in calories and more easily digested, such as meat or termites (Wong, 2000b). "Belly or brain" may have been the alternative that started 6 million years ago with *Ramapithecus*. Bipedality, furthermore, may have reduced the ability of *Australopithecus* (like the famous Lucy) to spend time on trees. Throwing with precision would not have been very useful for lions, for instance.

In other words, nothing suggests that the course followed by these changes was the best. If we focus on the physical aspect—height, skull shape, brain capacity, verticalness, or mandibular protrusion—we may easily create a sequence of gradual and increasing progress in the evolution from *Australopithecus* to *Homo habilis*, from *Homo habilis* to *Homo erectus*, through *Homo antecessor* and finally to us. These individuals are increasingly taller and erect. Their brain becomes larger and larger, and their jaw more prominent. Like a bud that slowly unfolds to become flower, crawling monkeys have become humans.

This process was illustrated by a drawing, as well known as McDonald's logo, which stirred many thoughts in my child mind. To the left lies a poor primate with a stupid face, dragging its body and long arms with difficulty. Step by step, inch by inch, degree by degree this primate elongates until it becomes an elegant, erect human who moves forward toward the right margin of the page, where the drawing not only ends but gives the reassuring feeling of having reached a final substantiality. We know now that our species was born in Africa, but the man in question was always a blond, smiling Anglo-Saxon. The implication was that the path from monkey to man went from an inferior to a superior species.

From a biological perspective, however, humans are not the fulfilled goal of a design. Darwin's dangerous idea (Dennett, 1995) is that evolution is the result of the combination of several factors, among which chance prevails. Consequently, there is neither a predetermined direction nor a preceding design. The evolutionary picture that shows hominids slowly changing each of their features to become "human" certainly distorts the facts (Tattersall,

2000) and tends to obscure the great leap's revolutionary, foundational nature (Lorentz, 1974).

Like any event, this one is above all a leap—a break in the chain of causality that made the hitherto impossible possible. We cannot, therefore, talk of a determining cause. We can speculate, perhaps, on the conditions for the production of this change and on its effects. Besides granting humans the ability to transcend the domain of their logic, the great leap led to the development and implementation of the ability to record, selectively accumulate, and transmit data to the next generation through an extrasomatic channel, that is, a channel that travels outside of and parallel to the genetic code.

RECORDS

Humans have a passion for recording experiences. We record everything that happens to us. "He that has eyes to see and ears to hear," states Freud "may convince himself that no mortal can keep a secret" (Freud, 1905, pp. 77–8). Then we cannot help but transmit it, tell it, or show it in some way. There must be a reason why we spend most of our time exchanging information, recording and transmitting all kinds of events. Most interestingly, and nobody knows more about this than psychoanalysts, we record and transmit much more than we believe we do. This feature is essential to understand both humans' everyday life and their history. Records of experiences and events are so important to humans that their history is traversed by so-called "information revolutions" (Rotschild, 1993, Devlin, 1999). This term designates the discovery and implementation of a new recording method that, in turn, affects the accumulation and distribution of the data it manages. Each of these information revolutions implemented new practices and brought about profound changes in humanity.

The first recording system used by humans was probably each community's collective memory, and must have been associated with the presence of elderly people in social groups. Humans' remarkable longevity and postmenopausal survival among females, both costly from a biological point of view and exclusive to our species, seem to have been specifically designed to favor the operation of the recording and transmission system (tradition), which is supported by myths, legends, and anecdotes typical of each region and period.[13]

To what extent did the development of this recording system favor the great leap? I cannot answer this question, but evidence found on primitive humans' family life, so different from Neanderthals (Binford, 1989), point in that direction. The next "information revolutions" would have consisted of the appearance of inscription systems suitable to record and predict events, of the use of such systems to mediate exchanges, and finally of their use for writing, which facilitated the autonomy of recording systems from personal memory. Each of these steps has had tremendous consequences for humanity.

In 1452 Johannes Gutenberg invented the printing press. This invention constituted another crucial milestone in the path toward making the information pool more and more accessible and independent from social controls. The next decisive move was the launch of the first electronic microprocessor in 1971. The latter marked the beginning of what is probably the most recent information revolution, which is now at the height of its development and whose consequences are still hard to assess. Perhaps the Internet medium, the so-called Web 2.0,[14] with its promotion of social networks, is the new information revolution. It is important to point out that each recording system is linked to a transmission practice with important effects on subjectivity. Today, for instance, the Internet grants immediate access to an information pool that is, in principle, available to all and to which we all contribute, whether we want to or not, with information that has no source (such as the information that appears on the web).

SELECTIVE DATA ACCUMULATION

Thanks to our ability to record data, casual findings, haphazard discoveries, the suffering of a natural calamity by a group, or the knowledge of how to use a new resource may be transmitted to the information pool we call *culture*. Once the evoked event is recorded, it becomes autonomous from the memory of the person who experienced it and is incorporated into the non-genetic heritage. At first, the environment where recording occurred must have been the family and social spaces where transgenerational transmission was inscribed. Today the cultural pool is becoming increasingly independent of any type of social or institutional contact. Such independence is, in my view, the most radical meaning of the word *globalization*.

Culture, the pool of supplementations resulting from events, is a living, interactive, and shifting deposit constantly being created, where experiences are recorded extra-somatically. It thus operates in parallel with the recording system that is common to all living beings—the genetic code. Both systems are similar in many ways. In both of them, novelty is supported by a platform grounded on the species' entire history, which it supplements and whose meaning it reformulates *après-coup*. As a result, we can reconstruct a history of supplementations. In both genetic and cultural transmission each step marks a point of irreversibility of occurrences. As time goes by, both systems tend toward increasing complexity, and we therefore say that they progress. Predictions about the future of an evolutionary line can only be conjectural because change plays an inevitable, pivotal role in both systems.

The great difference between these systems is that while the genetic system has no other way of recording than the materiality of the four DNA bases, which grants it a fixed inertia tied to the amount of time needed for genetic transmission (generational change), the cultural system has become independent of the materiality of records, or rather, it only depends on the materiality of the information carrier. The latter can be the spoken word, signs, rites, the written word, an image, a magnetic tape, a millimetric chip, an electromagnetic wave, or a set of organized atoms. [15]

This difference, in turn, gives rise to another whose consequences are even more remarkable. While the implementation of genetic changes necessarily takes several generations, the inertia of the cultural information system may be as short as technology allows it to be. Furthermore, this is also the case with the time that elapses between "changes." A long time ago, a significant cultural variation may have taken centuries to be effected. In today's "information era" (Devlin, 1999; Cobo y Pardo, 2007) changes, which should actually be called whirlwind substitutions, may be almost instantaneous, and are marked from the start by the necessary and preannounced obsolescence of new devices.

So just as every species "carries" a genetic heritage that is in itself a record of the history of successful biological events, each modifying and being supported by the previous ones, humans have a cultural heritage that operates in a similar way. The history of successful cultural events is recorded. Each event is actually the last one in a series where each term modifies the previous ones, and they all accumulate to make up the platform for any future change. Every human achievement refers to a long history that may have started back in the Cro-Magnon era.

It is hard to hypothesize about the intelligence of humans who have been utterly isolated from their culture. If they were able to survive, which is unlikely, they would probably be quite similar to chimpanzees. "Discoveries" by potential non-human "geniuses" are doomed to die with their inventor or, in the best-case scenario, to endure locally for a while thanks to imitation. These acquisitions neither survive nor serve as platforms for future improvements precisely because they can only be transmitted through imitation. [16] If this had not been not the case (and this is the most convincing proof of my argument) chimpanzee culture would have shown a different kind of "progress" over the last 6 million years. [17]

Our extrasomatic knowledge can be transmitted and tends toward increasing complexity. Resulting accumulation, in turn, renders selection necessary. Old information is gradually set aside—with a certain degree of inertia and the help of the in-built obsolescence of novelties—to be replaced by new information. In other words, "selection" favors those ideas that have a greater ability to propagate and endure, which are not necessarily the "best" ones.

An interesting philosophical and ethical problem is posed—the information that propagates is not necessarily true or the best (Blackmore, 2000).

TRANSGENERATIONAL TRANSMISSION: THE THIRD CHILDREARING STRATEGY

The third childrearing strategy[18] requires both the transgenerational transmission of information and configuration.[19] In the case of primitive humans this transmission was likely focused on family and social life. Nowadays we see the technological transmission and recording of information as a "natural" phenomenon. Yet a few tens of thousands of years ago there was no means of transmission other than orality. A culture's knowledge must travel through generations by way of personal communication. Back then, transgenerational transmission was entirely dependant on the parent-child link and childrearing practices.

It is well known that humans are not the only ones who remain in contact with their parents for a long period of time. Elephants, whales, and gorillas, among others, do so as well. Nevertheless, human offspring's interaction and dependence are unique. To begin with, they are born in a state of greater neurological immaturity and spend much more time in a dependent link with their progenitors than any other mammal cub. The evolutionary advantage of having already reached maturity at birth is obvious. Immaturity increases the risk of death, imposes a cost on the parents (who cannot procreate other babies during that time), exposes babies to attack by predators, and limits the number of cubs per litter.

Nonetheless, with regard to the learning process during early contact and the configuration of the species' young according to variable cultural parameters,[20] immaturity grants an enormous advantage. Human offspring's early contact with their parents takes place while brain connections are being created. This feature is essential for extrasomatic transmission. There is a theory (the neotenic theory) that maintains that humans differ from chimpanzees mainly in that they keep their babies in a state of immaturity for a longer period of time. For babies to be educated, they must be born immature *and* develop in a suitable family environment; it is precisely during childrearing that the essential information-configuration that produces subjects of a certain culture is transmitted.

Some indirect evidence allows us to surmise significant differences between human and Neanderthal families with regard to this issue. Having studied the French cave of Combe Grenal, L. Binford (1989) asserts that Neanderthal men and women lived separately—the males by themselves, and the females with their children in different dwellings. The males did not bring food home; they ate where they hunted. The females were the ones who had to bring up the children and provide nourishment for them. This type of social and childrearing contact is not unusual. This is how lions and orangutans live. Such a way of life would explain the peculiar stoutness of Neanderthal females, which contrasts with the gracefulness of Cro-Magnon women. Bindford's conjectures led him to state that, like most females, Neanderthal females' signs of being in heat could be seen or smelled. Males and females, therefore, did not form couples. Rather, they copulated during heat and continued their lives without sexual contact. This behavior would explain the state of relative malnutrition of many Neanderthal children and women. [21] From a strictly Darwinian point of view, the males had no reason to care for the offspring when they did not know if those babies carried their genes.

This would not have happened in the families of primitive humans, which gathered in communities to perform childrearing tasks. During their long period of immaturity and dependence, human babies probably received education and care in a linking interaction assisted by the community. Two other features of *Homo sapiens* that differentiate them from most animals and, as far as we know, from the other hominids should be included in this discussion. One is longevity; the fact that females survive about thirty years after menopause is an utterly unheard-of characteristic among superior animals. This trait may be understood as a way of favoring the development of transgenerational information transmission through the extrasomatic channel, a resource that reaches full development in the context of the third childrearing strategy.

Unlike the other hominids, whose life expectancy apparently was under forty years, humans are genetically programmed to live longer. Cro-Magnon skeletons have been found that belonged to individuals older than sixty, which is congruent with modern humans' life expectancy. At the same time, the fact that human females lose their ability to procreate when they still have a third of their lives to live is truly intriguing. The logical thing (and what happens with the other superior animals) is for a female to preserve her ability to procreate until the end of her life, because having barren individuals competing for resources is extremely expensive for the survival of a species. That is why it is natural for an individual to die as soon as it is unable to reproduce. Still, there must be a reason why genes have prevailed among humans that determine the survival of the elderly and of postmenopausal women.

According to evolution scholars like Jared Diamond (1992), the reason is that these features were essential for successful transgenerational transmission. Successful transmission requires the presence of grandparents—of a family where three generations overlap. Today we can just read a book, turn on the TV, or go on line to learn what happened half an hour, thirty years or ten centuries ago, or how to think about something or do something according to *already produced knowledge*. I can find out what Dr. Sigmund Freud thought in 1914 without having had the pleasure of meeting him because I can read one of his articles. I can also find out when to plant gladioli bulbs by reading a gardening book or by using a search engine on the Internet. If I live in Florida, I can check when a tornado will strike and hear or read what to do to protect myself without asking anybody.

In other words, I can access our cultural heritage without having to talk to or interact face-to-face with anyone. I certainly do not need to ask my grandmother or my parents. Nonetheless, before the appearance of recording methods rendered personal contact irrelevant, the presence of elderly people must have been critical. They played the role of true living books, deposits of knowledge that could be transmitted from one generation to the other.

NOTES

1. See chapter 1.
2. There are actually two theories. The multi-regionalist theory, pioneered by M. Wolpoff (1997), claims that we are the product of independent evolutions that started with *Homo erectus*. The "Out of Africa" theory, spearheaded by R. Stringer (Stringer and McKie, 1996), maintains that our species originated in Africa 200,000 years ago and expanded from there to the rest of the planet. Although the debate continues, the second theory (which I follow here) has provided more evidence and is more generally accepted (see Tattersall, 2002; Templeton, 2002; Pääbo, 2010).
3. The most recent Neanderthal fossil ever found dates back some 30,000 years (Hublin et al., 1995), but even more recent remains have appeared in Spain and Portugal (Delson and Harvati, 2006).
4. See also Leroi-Gurhan (1975), Shreeve (1995), and Tattersall (2002).
5. From the alleged size of the fetus and the diameter of the pelvic canal, Trinkaus (1989a) deducted that gestation time for Neanderthal offspring was one year. This fact suggests that they would have reached greater development than human babies at birth and would have been less moldable. Yet the validity of Trinkaus's conjecture has been challenged (Shreeve, 1995).
6. That is why Binford (1989) called these developments "biological technology." Nonetheless, Zilhao and d'Errico (2000) detect some variations in Neanderthal "culture." Such variations, however, are in no way comparable to Cro-Magnon's and are likely imitations of its Homo sapiens neighbor.
7. This is also being debated. The multi-regionalist theory maintains that it is not so. Moreover, in 1999 the remains of a young person were found in Portugal that might belong to a hybrid (Wong, 1998, 1999, 2000a; Trinkaus and Duarte, 2000). Yet Tattersall (2001, 2002) claims that this idea is not well grounded.
8. According to R. M. May, president of the Royal Society, species extinction provoked by humans has accelerated in the past 100 years. Extinction is now 1,000 times greater than it was before our appearance. We are dealing with a larger cataclysm than the one that decimated dinosaurs 65 million years ago (M. Gibbs, 2001).
9. The reason for this deduction is that there are plenty of places in the genome called pseudogenes or "dead genes." These are copies of inactive genes that do not manifest phenotypically. For this reason, they are not selected or eliminated from the genetic pool, and therefore change at a much greater pace than non-silent genes. That is why the percentages of difference mentioned above have been clearly overestimated. The similarity between the active genes of humans and those of Neanderthals would have been greater than 99.9 percent (Colby, 1996; Li and Graur, 1991; Moxon and Wills, 2000).
10. Consider, however, the excellent article by Heather Pringe (2013).
11. See chapter 10.

12. See chapter 1.

13. Myths and legends contain information that can generally be shown to be of great use to the community where they circulate. They deal with discoveries concerning natural and social laws or provide rules that create a necessary social order, an order that in the other animals operates through instinctive commands. As Lévy-Strauss (1963) points out, mythical stories are particularly stable and immune to individual distortions or interpretations.

14. See chapter 2.

15. Even by way of specific exclusions that connect, as we saw in chapter 7.

16. See chapter 10.

17. At a certain moment there may be a few chimpanzees that may know how to carry out the procedure because they copied it. Some even talk about "chimpanzee cultures" that show some variation in their features depending on the region. For example, all chimpanzees kill the parasites they find when grooming each other. Nevertheless, in Taï they crush them with a finger against their forearm, in Gombe they crush them against leaves, and in Budongo they put them on a leaf to examine them before eating them or throwing them away (Whiten and Boesch, 2001).

18. Chapter 10 discusses the first and second strategies.

19. See chapter 8.

20. See chapter 8.

21. What is the reason for human females' showing no visible physical signs of their ovulation and always being biologically receptive, features that are unique in the animal world? This question has given rise to more than one clever theory. The most accurate one considers that these traits are critical for women to keep their partners and be assisted by them during pregnancy and childrearing. The male must remain with the female to make sure that another male will not impregnate her (Diamond, 1997).

Chapter Ten

The Biological History of the Parent-Child Link

Childrearing Strategies

The previous chapters assessed the significant role of the parent-child link in determining human difference. Transgenerational transmission, I stated, travels through an exclusive extrasomatic channel parallel to the genetic transmission channel we share with every living being. This exclusive channel has a system for recording events and selectively accumulating data whose most sensitive, crucial link is the parent-child relationship. I have called the childrearing system that develops in this link the *third childrearing strategy*. Besides inaugurating extrasomatic transmission, this strategy can configure subjects that will maintain and continue the chain in the next generation. I call it "third strategy" because there are two other childrearing methods in the biological world that have preceded this one from an evolutionary perspective. What follows is a description of the three methods.

THE SIGNIFICANCE OF CHILDCARE AND GENETIC TRANSMISSION

From the viewpoint of biological evolution, the only significant thing about individuals is their ability to preserve their genes. In this sense, a good gene is one that is transmitted, that is, that generates the traits that will ensure its transmission. Now, for a species to survive, individuals' genes must be transmitted to the only possible carriers, namely, their offspring. Furthermore, the chain will only endure if these offspring-carriers are suitable specimens, capable of surviving and procreating and of efficiently transmitting their genes. That is why caring for one's young means caring for their genes. According to evolutionary biologists, this is the main reason for the relevance of the parent-child link in the animal world.

Of course, natural selection must have affected childrearing methods. It is logical to think that a) in average, babies that have been poorly equipped for life by their parents will live less than babies that have been well equipped; b) equipping one's offspring has a cost; and c) as a result, the parent-child link will have evolved, that is, will have been the object of the Darwinian machine.[1] At the same time, natural selection acts upon the young with particular harshness and effectiveness for three reasons: babies are inexperienced and immature; by acting before the cubs procreate, natural selection nips in the bud the transmission of the genes involved; and the number of offspring born generally exceeds (sometimes by far) the number that can live with existing resources.

I would like to illustrate this process with a case where the difference between newborns and survivors is relatively small. A polar bear gives birth to approximately two cubs a year, and to twenty during her entire life. Out of this total, only two survive in average. It is hence easy to envision that in a niche where many female polar bears and their cubs coexist, cubs' survival will depend not only on their strength and on chance but also, and perhaps primarily, on the quality of the mother-child link. The Darwinian machine will necessarily operate by optimizing the efficiency of this link in every circumstance.

What I stated above may lead us to think that the evolutionary trend of the link should be homogenous; the line that provides increasingly effective care for its offspring will be favored by selection. Here we are faced with an intriguing situation. While in many species parents take "personal" care of their offspring with varying degrees of devotion and during varying periods of time, in many other species (most) they never make contact with their brood. Among invertebrates, for instance, most parents have no direct connection with their children. Parents and children do not even know nor could, apparently, recognize each other. Furthermore, we are not dealing with primitive, neglected species on the one hand, and more developed, caring species on the other. There are two clearly different strategies to protect the genes contained in the next generation, that is, two childrearing strategies. We are not, therefore, discussing two different evolutionary stages but two different approaches to gene preservation.

CHILDREARING STRATEGIES

The first childrearing strategy is not based on contact. Offspring (generally large in numbers) are provided with an instinctive information package that allows them to survive with no direct care of any sort. Strictly speaking, however, while the babies have no link to their progenitors,[2] it would not be right to say that parents do not take care of their brood. Guided by their instinctive knowledge, they deposit the eggs (which may contain enough nutrients for the first stages of the embryo's life) in an environment that is suitable for the babies' birth and development, and genetically transmit knowledge to them in the guise of instinctive commands. Activated by proper environmental stimuli, these commands will allow babies to survive with no parental care and to procreate suitable descendents whom they will not meet and to whom they will transmit the same genetic commands.

There are examples that show how even without being in direct contact with them during childrearing, parents can anticipate and meet their offspring's needs. Eumeninae wasps, for instance, deposit their eggs in the perforated pith of plant stalks. They line up the eggs inside the trunk so that the first egg is in the bottom and the last one, closer to the surface. After placing the eggs the mother wasp leaves the nest forever. Like most species that use the first childrearing strategy, Eumeninae wasps have no personal link to their offspring.

Yet, how do the babies know on which side of the stalk they must come out? A mistake might be fatal. K. W. Cooper (1957) proved that the mother wasp indicates the right side through the shape (concave or convex) of the mud stopper that separates the eggs from each other. Baby wasps instinctively "read" this sign and go toward the right end. In this case we can identify a sign left by the mother to her young, but most species that use this childrearing strategy leave no message (or at least we have not found any). Newborns only need "natural" environmental stimuli to activate their development in the right direction.

Another strategy used by parents to tend to the fate of the genes contained in their brood, which we might call second childrearing strategy, is closer to ours and less widespread in nature than the first one. It consists in devoting individualized care to one's offspring for a variable period of time. Babies in these species are usually born in a relatively smaller number and with longer intervals between parturitions than first-strategy users. The second strategy prioritizes giving cubs food and protection during the life stage when they are most helpless and vulnerable, and prolongs their maturation and growth under their parents' care. While it is not exclusive to mammals, this strategy enables breastfeeding, and it gave rise to the parent-child link in the biological world. Furthermore, the third strategy, which is circumscribed to humans, doubtlessly emerged from it.

There are, of course, intermediate modalities that I am not including here. Many species do not personally take care of their babies but protect their eggs. In addition, there are different categories of "caregivers." Among some mammals, such as orangutans, whales, or elephants, parent-child interaction is deep and lasts several years, whereas among some insects that use the second strategy the relationship is apparently reduced to protecting the brood from predators for a short time (Clutton-Brock, 1991; Tallamy, 1999).

Is one strategy better than the other? It is impossible to tell. Both have been successful, as attested by the survival of the species. While we might think that the second one is better or more advanced than the first in terms of offspring preservation and potential development, this is not necessarily true if we take into account that the main goal of biological history is to improve gene preservation and transmission. The second strategy requires huge energy expenditure during adult life, energy that will not be employed to increase reproduction, for instance. Moreover, this strategy demands less frequent parturitions and the reduction in the number of babies per litter, which, in turn, notoriously constrains the effectiveness of the Darwinian machine, as we shall see next. Some mothers of species that use the first strategy literally explode at the birth of billions of babies. They thus provide a dramatic demonstration of this strategy's primary goal—to make the most of parents' energy so as to engender the largest number of children.

WHAT IS THE USE OF SWITCHING STRATEGIES?

An evolutionary shift must have occurred at some point that separated the branches of species using each of these strategies. It is likely that this change did not happen in an identifiable single instant. In some cases it may have involved a reversal—animals that were using the second strategy "evolved" toward the use of the first one. In addition, even though it is true that higher vertebrates tend to employ the second strategy and invertebrates the first one, we cannot claim that this is always the case. While most insects pay some attention to their eggs but none to their brood, some do care for their young. Several beetle species in the genus Gargaphia "herd" and protect their offspring as a couple during the first days of their young's lives (Tallamy, 1999). At the same time, there are vertebrates that display complex behaviors. For instance, most fish and tortoises do not care for their babies personally. We cannot, therefore, talk about "primitive" and "advanced" species.

In the realm of evolution we cannot even assert that a strategy is better or worse than the other in general terms. Everything depends on the circumstances. Sociobiologist E. O. Wilson believes that the choice of childrearing strategy could be the species' response to unusually unfavorable or favorable environments (Tallamy, 1999). In the first case the offspring are in too much danger; in the second, competition becomes too intense. We could indeed claim that the shift from one strategy to another involves an increase in complexity. This affirmation is true partly because each new strategy "adds" a new behavior to childrearing and introduces greater restrictions to the system without eliminating the conditions that prevailed in the previous strategy. These changes, however, do not allow us to identify evolutionary "lines."

In the first strategy the parent-child "link" is confined to genetic transmission and to the instinctive creation of proper conditions for egg development. In the second one we may add personal care for the cubs, which, as we shall see, opens the way for some teaching and tune-up of babies' instinctual heritage within the link with their parents. In the third strategy a new feature is incorporated—the parent-child link becomes the backbone of extrasomatic, cultural, or non-genetic evolution.[3]

Yet each addition has a cost, and from an evolutionary viewpoint success hinges on the quality of genetic transmission. Furthermore, increased complexity does not cancel previous achievements. In any case, looking at things in perspective, we cannot deny that the second strategy must have stemmed from the first one. What could be the reasons for the success of this step?

THE DISADVANTAGES OF CHILDCARE

Pondering the advantages of caring for one's offspring is important because this activity has obvious disadvantages. Childcare requires time and energy, confines the area occupied by adults to the surroundings of the nest, and adds countless dangers posed by predators. Yet as I mentioned earlier, the main drawbacks of the second strategy are the greater distance between litters and their reduced number, which hinder the effectiveness of the Darwinian machine.

Specialists in infectious diseases and farmers know how useless it is to combat insects and germs with the same antibiotic or pesticide during long periods of time. Germs and insects "learn" to survive surprisingly quickly. Laboratories do not lag behind in this race and soon launch a new, effective product. They know, however, that the fate of this product will eventually be the same as that of the old ones. As we described in the case of information innovations, the "progress" of both pests and pesticides is marked by their future obsolescence.

This trait creates a kind of parallel evolution of germicides and germs and pesticides and pests whose ending seems unpredictable. I still remember the astonishment my fellow students and I experienced more than thirty years ago when we saw a bedbug emerge (joyfully, we thought) from the huge cloud of DDT we had sadistically poured on it in our infested boarding house room. In little more than ten years bedbugs had "learned" to be as vulnerable to the erstwhile deadly DDT as to talcum powder.

Something totally different happens with animals that use the second strategy. The other day someone was telling me how wolves had been eliminated in Russia until twenty years ago. Hunters would simply spread meat laced with strychnine in their territory. To trap the wolves, they would stretch out ropes forming a fence around them and tie colored rags to the ropes. Apparently, wolves would be scared by the rags billowing in the wind and would retreat into a narrow area fenced by ropes and rags, where they could be easily shot. In the last hundred years steppe wolves have learned neither to curb their fear nor to produce immunity to strychnine despite the fact that this inability, along with other factors, might lead to their inevitable extinction.

Where does this remarkable difference between the learning methods of bedbugs and wolves lie? In a way, it is tied to the use of different childrearing strategies, more specifically, to the major disadvantage of the second strategy—the limited number of potential offspring. Animals that use the first strategy can (and tend to) lay vast quantities of eggs in clutches separated by relatively short periods of time.

I would like to take a look at an insect that is familiar to all and whose habits regarding the number of eggs laid by reproductive cycle, and the frequency with which they are laid, is not exceptional. I am referring to mosquitoes. A female mosquito lays about 500 eggs and lives about thirty days. Let us suppose that the females (which are the ones that bite) are able to lay eggs only once in their lives and that all the eggs develop into procreating adults. After a year of giving birth, about 2 x 1,026 mosquitoes would be born. To get an idea of the magnitude of this number, if these mosquitoes were lined up they would form a column of approximately 6.21^{20} miles—a column that could wrap around the world 200 quintillion times.

Luckily for us, this does not happen; most eggs do not become adults. Nonetheless, it is interesting to note that in the same one-year period a fortunate couple of eagles, which practice the second childrearing strategy, would have engendered two pigeons that would be just about to leave the nest without being able to procreate yet. Even so, two would exceed the average number of surviving chicks. In other words, among users of the first childrearing strategy the [developed babies]/[laid eggs] ratio is far smaller than among users of the second strategy.

We might think that this exuberant exaggeration of births is a way of compensating for the remarkable helplessness of mosquito larvae, which lack parental care. Perhaps this is true, but even if it may seem cruel, this huge "infant mortality" rate is the cornerstone of the species' survival insurance; it is precisely what gives pesticide manufacturers a headache. So large a brood ensures the efficiency of the Darwinian machine, for it multiplies the variation of genetic combinations and the probability of mutations, thus increasing the variability of the genome on which the machine operates by way of selection.

In this way, when an unfavorable circumstance occurs, the species that can afford having an ultra-large litter thanks to the use of the first strategy see an increase in their ability to face a potential calamity. They can resort either to a mutating gene or to the genetic recombination that offers the best response to the situation. The new carriers of the gene in question will propagate much quicker, for those who do not carry it will die and leave them an open field. In a short period of time, therefore, the resistant gene will be part of the genome of all or most of the population. The bedbug that flew around smugly among the DDT clouds in my student boarding house represents the triumph of the Darwinian machine over DDT. Contrariwise, like most species exterminated by the disproportionate progress of our civilization, steppe wolves attest to the failure of the machine to counteract the effects of the most implacable predator that has ever lived on this planet.

Beyond relative differences in direct parent-offspring contact, both childrearing strategies share a common trait. The fact that a species has learned a certain behavior implies that its individuals have been endowed by evolution with a genomic capacity that facilitates this response. The second strategy entails the cubs' ability to "learn to use" this potentiality of their genome more adequately thanks to their contact with their parents, which is not possible in the first strategy. The latter, as we have seen, offers greater speed for this "learning process" (a way of referring to natural selection over a great variation), which biologists prefer to call "adaptation." In other words, users of the second strategy may develop their potential with greater plasticity, whereas users of the first strategy show a greater ability to expand the range of that potential. Yet "learning" cannot exceed the scope of the genomic potential of each species. The capacity to do so is exclusive to the third childrearing strategy.

Strictly speaking, then, the second strategy does not involve relinquishing the selection mechanism in any way. Species using this strategy do, however, give up the ability to procreate a great number of babies in a short period of time, an ability that speeds up the operation of the Darwinian machine. Consequently, the second strategy appears as a commitment to a certain excellence in the finished product at the expense of the effectiveness of natural selection. The complex adjustments needed to switch from the flying, feeding, and childrearing techniques of the mosquito to those of the eagle may demand such excellence.

In both species these features depend on the potentiality of their genome, which is the end product of a long evolutionary process that differs for each species. Yet for the eagle's potential to be realized, an adjustment and a maturity level are needed that inevitably require experiencing a parent-child link. This is not the case with mosquitoes; the only contribution of the parents is the genome.

WHAT IS THE USE OF CHILDREARING?

Events take place in the context of the parent-child relationship typical of the second strategy that are very important for the development and survival of the cubs. These are, for instance, recognition among species members and recognition between parents and children. The second form of recognition is particularly significant for large colonies with intense social behavior. The second strategy also involves providing food (either captured or predigested food, or secretions like milk) and protecting the young from danger while they are defenseless.

Yet besides these obvious and well-known facts, "personal" parent-child interaction facilitates two essential phenomena that tend to be interrelated. These phenomena give rise to new events that are inaccessible to species that do not favor parent-child contact, and involve the possibility of a particular form of learning within the link. Learning is based on imitation, on the one hand, and on the tune-up of the young's instinctive machine, on the other.

Since it is on the basis of this interaction that the third childrearing strategy will unfold and this strategy is one of the keys to the emergence of humans, it is important to trace the boundary between the two rearing modes as best as possible. As I discussed earlier,[4] the existence of an extrasomatic channel for event transmission, recording and selective accumulation of data, as well as the configuration of the young based on established cultural beliefs, was pivotal to humans' great leap. All this took place in the realm of the third childrearing strategy, which undoubtedly emerged as a supplement to the second strategy. The latter's achievements, therefore, are not necessarily absent in the former.

The question repeatedly posed in relation to this issue is, how present are these achievements? Can we compare the contributions of the parent-child link in humans to the contributions of this link among other animals? The loving care for their offspring evinced by orangutan or whale mothers clearly shows that childrearing attributes that have always been considered "human" are also typical of other animals. Is there a qualitative difference between both strategies with regard to the childrearing link?

My answer is decidedly affirmative. Nevertheless, how can we explain similarities between, say, the link between a gorilla mom or a bitch and her babies, and the human childrearing link? Are they simply analogous? Or is there a non-analogical similarity due to the persistence of something animal-instinctive in the human link? Was the animal instinct, which, we might say, commands the entire childrearing linking among gorillas and dogs, utterly eliminated in humans and replaced by the history of development recounted earlier?[5] Or was it simply "overlaid" by cultural aspects that make us think that these similarities are only due to human "development"?

I would not know how to answer these questions. Nevertheless, I think that just as purely instinctivist explanations of the human mother-child link fail to account for it in full, so does considering this link as a simple consequence of the Oedipal complex or desire. Not everybody claims, as I did, that there are qualitative differences between human and other animals' childrearing. Many scientists categorically affirm that there is "no qualitative difference." Bonner (1980), an advocate of this position, states already in the title of his excellent *The Evolution of Culture in Animals* that human culture is but a step in an evolutionary continuum encompassing the entire animal kingdom. Contrariwise, others (and I among them) consider that the emergence of humans entailed a break; it opened an extrasomatic transmission channel that can record and selectively accumulate overlapping and increasingly complex events in human culture.

This channel did not exist prior to the great leap, even though the two mechanisms mentioned (imitation and instinctive tune-up) are certainly its precursors. Still, it does not seem possible to think that the great leap completely eliminated instinctive human behavior. It may have disabled this behavior, deactivated part of its power—even denaturalized its essence by redirecting its tendencies toward cultural parameters. Yet we cannot say that instinctive behavior disappeared. Human history begins with our animal past. It is important, then, not to confuse mechanisms typical of the second childrearing strategy with those of the third, nor to forget that the latter could not have done away with the achievements of the other two strategies.

Perhaps we should address this issue in two different ways. One is taking the path suggested by the following question: To what extent can we explain human childrearing solely from a cultural perspective and set aside what we might crudely call maternal instinct? Many psychoanalysts would probably be angered by the very fact that I am posing this question. They take for granted that instincts (*Instinkte*) pertain to animals, and drives (*Triebe*), to humans. Nonetheless, it is my contention that we should at least wonder if this is actually the case. To what extent has *Trieb* cancelled *Instinkt*'s commands?

The second option follows the path indicated by another, perhaps polemic question: To what extent are non-human animals capable of using the extrasomatic intergenerational communication channel that characterizes the human phenomenon? In other words, is there in the animal world a culture, a tradition, a teaching that is transmitted from parents to children outside the genetic realm? How the controversy created by this question unfolds will certainly depend to a large extent on the definition of the terms used, especially *culture* and *transmission*.[6] It is undeniable that in the world of the second strategy parents can teach their children skills. Nonetheless, while they can reach great complexity, these teachings only include two basic chapters, namely, imitation and the modulation of instincts during interaction. Let us look at these two elements separately.

IMITATION

There is no doubt that learning through imitation, particularly cubs' imitation of adults is very important in the world of the second strategy. Experiences with animals irrefutably prove that in some non-human species, consistent learning is possible by way of imitation or emulation (usually by young animals) of behaviors of more expert animals. This practice does not exist or is almost irrelevant among users of the first childrearing strategy.

In any case, information transmission by imitation clearly differs from the transmission typical of the third strategy. Without exception, imitation acts are dependent on the presence of the object originating them (to learn how to do "something" we must be in the presence of that "something"). They neither leave transmissible records (there is no way of communicating a finding other than by showing it), nor accumulate or progress significantly (each discovery must start and end in itself). So-called mirror neurons are likely to play a key role in this process. These neurons were found by Rizzolatti (Rizzolatti and Sinigaglia, 2008) and others in the premotor cortex (in the frontal lobe of higher mammals) and are highly specialized. They are activated both when a subject sees somebody make a certain movement and when this subject performs that movement, and are involved in imitation.

Lorenz (1973) discovered imitative behavior among his grackles and geese, and so did Kawamura (1963) in his well-known work with Japanese macaques. Experienced macaques and grackles are able to inform inexperienced ones of their findings in the presence of the act to be imitated. When she was about two years old, Imo, a genius female macaque of a troop in semi-captivity observed by Kawamura, discovered a technique to wash food that also salted it. It consisted in throwing sweet potatoes (provided by the scientists) to the sea, picking them up, scrubbing them, and eating them. Slowly (more so the older than the younger members), the whole troop imitated her procedure. Some even succeeded in applying this method to separate wheat from sand. They threw a fistful of sand mixed with wheat (also provided by the scientists) to the sea. Since the wheat floated while the sand sank, they could separate the grain, which they retrieved with some effort.

We would be mistaken, however, if we thought that imitation only occurs among captive animals. Goodall (1965) observed chimpanzees cover twigs with saliva to make them sticky and then introduce them in termite nests to take out the termites, which they sucked. This behavior was transmitted to the whole group by way of imitation. Yet macaques and chimpanzees lack a recording system that would allow them to transmit this innovation without the act, and they are obviously unable to progressively accumulate supra-individual knowledge. In other words, they cannot narrate or leave a "written record" of what they did. The only means of transmission they possess is direct imitation of what they see, and so transmitted knowledge hardly goes beyond one generation.

The great difference between them and humans does not seem to lie in the cleverness needed to discover, invent, or imitate, but in the ability to record and transmit. What was learned may survive with the species only as long as animals live in contact with the object that provoked the experience. What endures, however, is a knowledge acquired through imitation, not a proce-dure that is added to the species' heritage. How many genius macaques like Imo and outstanding chimpanzees like Kenzi were there in millions of gener-ations? Yet none of their discoveries is recorded in ape or primate "culture," whatever that is.

The ability to record events, which makes them transmissible and capable of advancement, is characteristic of only two types of transmission, namely, extrasomatic and genetic. The first one is exclusive to humans. In this sense, the difference between imitated knowledge and knowledge acquired by way of genetic evolution is remarkable. Genetic evolution, which develops slow-ly, is incorporated into genetic heritage by way of natural selection. Once it is inscribed in the genome it becomes part of the species' heritage and is trans-mitted from one generation to the next, even if the conditions that favored its appearance have vanished. Contrariwise, the transmission of knowledge ac-quired through imitation that is observed in non-human animals is produced relatively quickly, depends on the material presence of the experience to be imitated, and does not become part of the species' heritage. That is why, unlike knowledge inscribed in DNA (and the knowledge typical of the third childrearing strategy), it rarely progresses or becomes more complex.

This inability to transmit via genes behaviors that were acquired in life concerned and puzzled Darwin himself, but was actually solved by A. Weis-mann in 1880 (Churchill, 1968). In *Descent of Man* Darwin writes that Du-reau de la Malle "gives an account of a dog reared by a cat, who learnt to imitate the well-known action of a cat licking her paws, and thus washing her ears and face (. . .) which he ever afterwards practised during his life of thirteen years" (Darwin, 1874, p. 88). Would the dog culture have incorporat-ed so hygienic and practical a habit? Would de la Malle's dog at least have taught this behavior to its descendents? These are the questions posed by Darwin.

The answer, we now know, must have been negative. Otherwise we would have certainly found out. Dogs continue to be dogs with dog habits unless their genetic code tells them differently. Dog trainers are not inter-ested in the puppies' breed and pedigree because of what parents may teach or transmit to these puppies in life. Rather, trainers know that the genome may have features inscribed in it that are of interest to them, such as docility, fierceness, and hunting or guarding skills.

In any case, the significance of learning by imitation in the animal world is undeniable. Hinde and Fisher (1951) noted how titmice found out how to open the milk and cream bottles that milkmen used to leave by the door. By pecking at the aluminum lids, the birds had access to a delicious dairy breakfast during the time left between the milkman's arrival and the homeowners' withdrawal of the bottles. It seems that the acquisition of this knowledge stemmed from the discovery of the technique by a clever and lucky titmouse in a British town. Soon other birds in the species imitated it, and a few years later all England titmice knew how to open bottles.

This ability to incorporate new behaviors by imitation may be very important for the survival of a species, especially when sudden changes, such as those produced by humans, are taking place in their environment. Yet, has this knowledge endured? Do present-day titmice know how to open bottles in an era when milkmen have disappeared and bottles have been replaced by carton containers? In the absence of the experience, will macaques or titmice be able to teach their children what they once learned? They will probably not—not because they lack the intelligence to solve these problems but because they cannot record them to facilitate transmission. While the very significant ability to imitate an individual's discovery still exists as a potential, imitation's capacity to generate lasting change is limited. We need to take this limitation into account so that we can precisely assess the scope of the difference that, according to my hypothesis, determined the emergence of human-ness.

TUNING UP INSTINCTIVE RESPONSE

The existence of the parent-child link makes it possible for interactions produced in it to determine the development of one among several innate dispositions. Cubs may have a series of different instinctive dispositions that are ready to be launched toward development. Which one will be launched depends on which among several possible parental stimuli they receive. Parents may thus favor one disposition in their children, and their "choice" may be the result of a "choice" among several of their own dispositions. Their pick, in turn, may be tied to their life experiences, to what cubs' development evokes in them, or to environmental changes. In the parent-child relationship, then, progenitors trigger and modulate the unfolding of their children's dispositions. Adults can thus stimulate a certain genetically predisposed development in their babies, and the latter's behavior, in turn, stimulate certain actions in their parents. This process (which was probably the precursor of the human parent-child link) may therefore operate like a machine with two articulated poles and promote a remarkable flexibility in the system.

There is an example of this type of parent-child interaction that is particularly clear because it is a hyper-simplified version of a potentially complex phenomenon. Coastal oystercatchers have two methods of opening the mussels they catch. They may take the mollusks out of the water, place them on hard sand, and break the shell with strong pecks (hammerers), or they may plunge their thin bill between the valves to sever the mussel's adductor muscle so that the shell will open (stabbers). Both techniques require great skill; young birds must spend months training with their parents to develop it. Now, despite the fact that both methods belong in the same species, coastal oystercatchers use only one throughout their lives—the one their parents used.

What is going on here? Is this a case of pure genetic inscription or of learning by imitation? Experiments carried out by Norton Griffiths (1967) show that the behavior chosen depends both on genetic information and on contact with the parents. To prove this, he exchanged the eggs of "hammerer" and "stabber" oystercatcher populations and found that in both cases the babies developed the technique favored by their adoptive rather than their genetic parents. The situation, then, seems to be like this: oystercatchers have a dual innate disposition inscribed in their genome; they can develop both techniques. Which one will prevail depends on the chicks' interaction with their parents during the first three or four months of coexistence.

While in this example there are two dispositions that may unfold, the number of dispositions in this or any other species can be much larger. Furthermore, parental stimuli may trigger one or several of the n responses (or sequences of responses) stored in the information packet of the children's genome. While n cannot be infinite, it can be very high. At the same time, parents may possess genetically inscribed information to carry out one of several "educational" acts directed to their children. Which acts they will eventually perform may depend on hormonal changes, the state of the ecosystem, their own life experience, their personal link with a certain baby, and the behaviors that are prepared or presented in the link during its development. This process constitutes a kind of development machine. I am referring to the Aristotelian machine discussed in chapter 1, which is flexible and complex.

J. Goodall (1965), for example, showed that when a baby chimpanzee climbs a branch that is too thin, its mother gently rocks the trunk to make the baby climb down. The child's descent stops the mother's stimulus. "Rocking the trunk" might be one of the manifold options available to the mother to respond to the complex stimulus "baby on too thin a branch." "Climbing down" is an innate response to this specific stimulus and will, in turn, halt the mother's behavior. Learning is the concatenation of these behaviors. For this reason, the link interaction between non-human parents and children is extremely significant, as it increases the potential for environmental changes to modify animal response. In other words, it renders the system much more flexible, which seems to be one of the great advantages enjoyed by users of the second strategy compared to users of the first one. The second strategy results in greater flexibility due to the young's imitative skills and their ability to develop one among several innate behaviors, a "choice" triggered by the link with adults during the childrearing process.

SIR MEDAWAR AND THE JUKEBOX

While I was writing this chapter I came across a brilliant lecture titled "The Future of Man," given by Sir Peter Medawar in 1959. In this lecture Medawar compares the situation I just described (genetic inscriptions in animals that use the second childrearing strategy) with the jukebox, which was so popular back then in bars and clubs. Jukeboxes have a limited, predetermined, and identical number of records and buttons. Pressing a button activates a mechanism that plays one and only one of the records contained in the machine.

In this way, once the coin has been inserted, pushing a certain button is tantamount to choosing which record the jukebox will play among all the ones it contains. "Press button 4" is the stimulus that instructs the jukebox to carry out the routine of playing the music in record number 4, which was already recorded. Even though the stimulus is coming from the outside, the jukebox does not need to receive any musical contribution. What it plays is something that is already inscribed in it as potency and is "waiting" for a request. The "push button 4" stimulus is elective rather than instructive. As such, it does not produce anything new but enables the development of what was already inscribed in the machine.

Perhaps a more appropriate, current example that speaks of the vast complexity of responses allowed by this mechanism is the execution of a software application in a computer. Let us recall that jukeboxes, like computers, can only reproduce what is already "inside" them as potency, which can be a huge number of intricately linked inscriptions such as a large software application. Yet in this type of system there is no room for radical innovation; the answers have always already been written. This situation is analogous to our example of the oystercatchers. There are two options inscribed, like records in a jukebox—"hammerer" and "stabber." Which one will be activated depends on the "button" or stimulus. Hammerer parents stimulate the appearance of the "hammerer" record or sequence of commands. Stabber parents, the appearance of the "stabber" sequence.

A case that perhaps fits even better with the jukebox example is the development of bird song, both the song that distinguishes each species and the song that enables parents and children to recognize each other. Undoubtedly, the disposition to sing in a certain way is genetically inscribed as potency, as is birds' ability to recognize each other through song. Nonetheless, in many species the external elective stimulus of parental song is necessary for chicks to develop their own ability to sing.[7] A thrush will never be able to reproduce the goldfinch's melody, but it needs to listen to its parents' thrush song in order to produce its own. There are hence regional differences among the songs sung by the same species.

The juiciest aspect of Medawar's jukebox metaphor is certainly the comparison he makes between this machine and a tape-recorder. The jukebox, says Medawar, is not a tape-recorder. The latter does not have inscriptions of recorded songs, but can receive a sequence of sounds from the outside and *record* it. This sequence constitutes a different type of stimulus, namely, the music or set of sounds that is inscribed in the tape, which leaves marks in it and can be played in other tape-recorders. This type of stimulus is not elective but *instructive*. For Medawar, the tape-recorder is the model that may be applied to humans, for we are capable of recording and eventually perpetuating information as culture. I believe this would be a rudiment of one (just one) component of the third childrearing strategy.

HOW DID HUMAN-NESS EMERGE?

Evolutionary development tends to follow specialization lines. As soon as a new acquisition appears, if it progresses, new development lines will emerge based on it. Flying, which started with reptiles, may reach a specialization as subtle as that of the humming bird or the albatross.[8] It is likely that something similar happened with the jukebox mechanism, along with the ability to imitate. It is obvious that the "jukebox strategy" involves a growing brain volume to accommodate more wiring. The more wiring we have, the more potential responses.

At a certain moment about 5 million years ago, which many believe to be pivotal to our history (Stanley, 1996), the ability to inscribe a growing number of potential responses in the brain was favored over other skills, such as Australopithecus' tree climbing or apes' leaf eating. This new "specialty" of having a larger number of potential responses inscribed in the neuronal system required an increase in cerebral mass, which accompanied the whole *Homo* genus and culminated with Neanderthals. The latter were probably capable of accumulating in their voluminous brain (larger even than ours) the highest number and complexity of responses inscribed in a species, which is the basis for great jukebox potential.

Now, human difference must not have consisted in the addition of a larger number of "potentialities," that is, of neurons or wiring to that system—a larger number of responses inscribed in the brain jukebox-style. The emergence of human-ness is not likely to have depended on the addition of anything that was homogenous with what was already there. Rather, it had to do with a different use of this vast potential. In reality, such a change would not be unusual. The emergence of radical innovation in the biological world is often based on elements that had "been there" for a long time without being immediately "used" in a revolutionary way, as they would be later.

For instance, let us look at feathers and flying, or lungs and breathing. The emergence of flying reptiles, birds, did not coincide with the appearance of feathers. Neither did the emergence of fish that breathed air and conquered land coincide with the appearance of lungs. Feathers and lungs had been present for millions of years in reptiles and fish before birds flew or animals with lungs used air to breathe. Until then, feathers had been an odd method to protect reptiles' skin, and lungs, a flotation system for fish. Both flying and breathing air, then, were events that made use of a disposition that had not been designed for that purpose but "was there," available. The event in these cases is the use—the "invention" of the use—rather than the object used.

Something analogous may have happened with hominids' brain, which grew steadily at a rate of about 6 ounces per million years during 6 million years. Perhaps it meant the development of a successful specialization, that is, taking maximum advantage of the use of imitation and the jukebox method in the hominid series. This was an "expensive" specialization because the development of a relatively large brain involves considerable energy expenditure and poses obstacles to giving birth. Perhaps such comprehensive exploitation of the possibilities of the second strategy reached its peak with *Homo antecessor* and Neanderthals. It is assumed that tools and ornaments found in Neanderthal camps dating back 30,000 years, which are similar to the ones used by Cro-Magnon, were the product of Neanderthals' imitation of their human neighbors (Gee, 1996; Tattersall, 2002; Stringer and Andrews, 2005).[9]

Just as flying and air-breathing techniques "used" feathers and lungs that had existed for millions of years (we might say that birds' invention of flying "found" feathers and air-breathing vertebrates' invention of breathing, lungs), the third (human) childrearing strategy "used" that very well developed Aristotelian machine, a huge jukebox brain, to take the great leap. We might say that humans' creative explosion found a big jukebox-brain ready to "explode." Yet the human difference responsible for the great leap—the ability to come into contact with inconsistencies, produce events, and record and selectively accumulate achievements and transmit them through an extrasomatic channel to children configured in specific childrearing practices—transcends any type of jukebox.

NOTES

1. See chapter 1.

2. There may even be an extreme case where parents are predators of their own offspring. It is obvious that among these species evolution has opted for a highly economic strategy; it has even eliminated the expenditure involved in providing a mark that prevents filicide. What is more, filicide may very well function as a suitable mechanism for so-called negative selection, that is, favoring the disappearance of the least apt.

3. See chapter 9.

4. See chapter 9.

5. See chapters 5, 7, and 8.

6. Bonner defines "culture" as "the transfer of information by behavioral means, most particularly by the process of teaching and learning. It is used in a sense that contrasts with the transmission of genetic information passed by the direct inheritance of genes from one generation to the next" (Bonner, 1980, p. 9). Information is accumulated as knowledge. In this definition the enigma is shifted to the words "accumulated" and "knowledge."

7. Birds' migrating behavior is also essential (Bonner, 1980; Lorentz, 1974).

8. This does not mean that evolution always favors the more specialized line. Rheas, for example, are the result of an evolutionary line or strategy that started with flying birds and favored not flying.

9. See chapter 9.

References

Aczel, A. D. (1997). *Fermat's Last Theorem*. New York: Delta Books.

Aeschylus (467 BC). *The Seven Against Thebes*. Translated by Robert Emmet Meagher. New York: Dover Publications, 2000. [*Los siete contra Tebas*. In *Tragedias* Madrid: Editorial Gredos].

Agamben, G. (1978). *Infancy and History: The Destruction of Experience*. London: Verso, 2007. [*Infancia e historia*. Buenos Aires: Adriana Hidalgo, 2003].

———. (2002). *The Open: Man and Animal*. Translated by Kevin Attell. Stanford, CA: Stanford University Press, 2010. [*Lo abierto. El hombre y el animal*. Buenos Aires: Adriana Hidalgo, 2006].

Akazawa, T., Aoki, K., and Kimura, T., eds. (1989). *The Evolution and Dispersal of Modern Humans in Asia*. Tokyo: Hokusen Sha.

Ansermet, F. and Magistretti, P. (2004). *Biology of Freedom: Neural Plasticity, Experience, and the Unconscious*. Translated by Susan Fairfield. New York: Other Press, 2007. [*A cada cual su cerebro, plasticidad neuronal e inconsciente*. Buenos Aires: Katz Ediciones, 2006].

Ariès, Philippe (1960). *Centuries of Childhood: A Social History of Family Life*. Translated by Robert Baldick. New York: Vintage, 1962. [*El niño y la vida familiar en el Antiguo Régimen*. Madrid: Editorial Taurus, 1987].

Arthur, W. B. (1993). "Why Do Things Become More Complex?" *Scientific American* 268 (5): 92.

Ascott, R. (1999). *Reframing Consciousness: Art, Mind and Technology*. Oregon: Intellect Books.

Aulagnier, P. (1975). *The Violence of Interpretation: From Pictogram to Statement*. Translated by Alan Sheridan. Hove, UK, and Philadelphia: Brunner–Routledge, 2001 [*La violence de l'interprétation*. Paris: Presses Universitaires de France].

———. (1986). *Un intérprete en busca de sentido* [An Interpreter in Search of Meaning]. Mexico: Siglo XXI, 1994.

Badiou, A. (1988). *Being and Event*. Translated by Oliver Feltham. New York: Continuum, 2005. [*L'être et l'événement*. Paris: Ed. du Seuil].

Baudrillard, J. (1995). *The Perfect Crime*. Translated by Chris Turner. London: Verso Books, 1996. [*El crimen perfecto*. Barcelona: Editorial Anagrama, 1996].

Bauman, Z. (2000). *Liquid Modernity*. Cambridge, UK/Malden, MA: Polity Press. [*Modernidad líquida*. Mexico: Fondo de Cultura Económica, 2003].

Benjamin, Walter (1936). "The Work of Art in the Age of Mechanical Reproduction." In *Illuminations: Essays and Reflections*. Translated by H. Zohn. New York: Schocken Books, 1968, pp. 217–51.

179

Berenstein, I. (1986). "Acerca de las convicciones" [On Convictions]. Proceedings of the VIII Simposium and Internal Conference, APdeBA.

———. (1997). "Vínculo familiar. Hechos, sucesos y acontecimientos" [The Family Link: Facts, Occurrences, and Events] *Revista de la Asociación Argentina de Psicología y Psicoterapia de Grupo* 20:11–24.

———., ed. (2000). *Clínica familiar psicoanalítica. Estructura y acontecimiento* [Family Psychoanalysis: Structure and Event]. Buenos Aires: Paidós.

———. (2001). *El sujeto y el otro* [The Subject and the Other]. Buenos Aires: Paidós.

———. (2007). *Del ser al hacer* [From Being to Doing]. Buenos Aires: Paidós.

———. and Puget, J. (1997). *Lo Vincular* [On Links]. Buenos Aires: Paidós.

Berners Lee, T., with Mark Fischetti (2000). *Weaving the Web: The Original Design and Ultimate Destiny of the World Wide Web*. New York: HarperCollins.

Binford, L. R. (1989). "Isolating the Transition to Cultural Adaptations: An Organizational Approach." In E. Trinkaus, ed: *The Emergence of Modern Humans. Biocultural Adaptations in the Later Pleistocene*. Cambridge, UK: Cambridge University Press, pp. 18–41.

Blackmore, S. (2000). "The power of memes." *Scientific American* 283 (4): 52–61.

Bokanowski, T. and Lewkowicz, S., eds. (2009). *On Freud's Splitting of the Ego in The Process of Defence*. London: Karnac.

Bonner, J. T. (1980). *The Evolution of Culture in Animals*. Princeton, NJ: Princeton Sc. Library.

Borges, J. L. (1941a). "The Library of Babel." Translated by James E. Irby. In *Labyrinths: Selected Stories and Other Writings*. New York: New Directions, 1964, pp. 59–66. ["La biblioteca de Babel." In *Ficciones*. Buenos Aires: Sur, 1944].

———. (1941b). "The Garden of Forking Paths." Translated by Donald A. Yates. In *Labyrinths*, op. cit., pp. 19–29. ["El jardín de los senderos que se bifurcan." In *Ficciones*, op. cit].

———. (1944). "Funes the Memorious." Translated by James E. Irby. In *Labyrinths*, op. cit., pp. 59–66. ["Funes el memorioso." In *Ficciones*, op. cit].

———. (1944). "A New Refutation of Time." In *Other Inquisitions*. Translated by Ruth L. C. Simms. Austin: University of Texas Press, 1964, pp. 171–87. ["Nueva refutación del tiempo." In *Otras inquisiciones* Buenos Aires: Emecé, 1960, pp. 235–257].

———. (1960). "Ars poetica." In *Dreamtigers*. Translated by Harold Morland and Mildred Boyer. Austin: University of Texas Press, 1964, p. 89. ["Arte poética." In *El hacedor*. Madrid: Alianza Editorial, 1972].

Brunet, M. et al. (2002). "A New Hominid from the Upper Miocene of Chad, Central Africa." *Nature* 418 : 145–151.

Buber, M. (1942). "What Is Man?" In Between Man and Man. Translated by R. G. Smith. London: Kegan Paul, 1947, pp. 1–39. [¿*Qué es el hombre?* Mexico: Fondo de Cultura Económica, 1949].

Calvin, W. H. (1987). "The Brain as a Darwin Machine." *Nature* 330: 33–34.

———. (1991). *The Ascent of Mind: Ice Age Climates and the Evolution of Intelligence*. New York: Bantam.

———. (1994). "The Emergence of Intelligence." *Scientific American* 271 (4): 100–107.

Churchill, F. B. (1968). "August Weismann and a break from tradition." *J. Hist. Biol.* 1: 91–112.

Clark, A. (2009). "La mente extendida: entrevista a Andy Clark" [The Extended Mind: Interview with Andy Clark]. Available at http://www.desdeelexilio.com/2009/07/27/la–mente–extendida–entrevista–a–andy–clark/

———. and Chalmers, D. J. (1998). "The Extended Mind." *Analysis* 58:10–23.

Clutton–Brock, T. H. (1991). *The Evolution of Parental Care*. Princeton, NJ: Princeton University Press.

Cobo Romaní, C and Pardo Kulinski, H. (2007). *Planeta Web 2.0, inteligencia colectiva o medios fast food* [Planet Web 2.0, Collective Intelligence or Fast–Food Media]. Barcelona: Grup de Recerca d'Interaccions Digitals, Universitat de Vic.

Colby, C. (1996). "Introduction to Evolutionary Biology." Available at http://earth.ics.uci.edu. 8080/faqs/faq–intro–to–biology.html.

Cooper, K. W. (1957). "Biology of Eumenine Wasps: V Digital Communications in Wasps." *J. Exper. Zool.* 134: 469–509.

Corea, C. (2001). Personal communication.

———. and Lewkowicz, I. (1999). *¿Se acabó la infancia? Ensayo sobre la destitución de la niñez* [Is Infancy Over? Essay on the Destitution of Childhood]. Buenos Aires: Editorial Lumen.

Darwin, C. (1859). *The Origin of Species.* New York: Bantam Classics, 1999.

———. (1874). *The Descent of Man (Second Edition).* London: J. Murray.

Dawson, Jr. J. W. (1999). "Gödel and the Limits of Logic." *Scientific American* 280 (6): 76–81.

———. (1999). "The End of Nature versus Nurture." *Scientific American* 281 (6): 94–99.

Deacon, T. W. (1997). *The Symbolic Species: The Co–Evolution of Language and the Brain.* New York: W. W. Norton & Company.

Deleuze, G. (1962). *Nietzsche and Philosophy.* Translated by Hugh Tomlinson. New York: Columbia University Press, 1983. [*Nietzche y la Filosofía.* Buenos Aires: Anagrama, 1971].

———. (1988). *The Fold: Leibniz and the Baroque.* Translated by Tom Conley. Minneapolis: University of Minnesota Press, 1992. [*El pliegue: Leibniz y el barroco.* Barcelona: Paidós, 1989].

Delson, E. and Harvati, K. (2006). "Palaeoanthropology: Return of the Last Neanderthal." *Nature* 443: 772–3.

deMause, L., ed. (1974). *The History of Childhood.* New York: Harper and Row. [*Historia de la infancia.* Madrid: Editorial Alianza, 1982].

———. (1974). "The Evolution of Childhood." In L. deMause, ed. op. cit., pp. 1–73. ["La evolución de la infancia." In deMause, L, ed. op. cit., pp 15–92].

Dennet, D. (1995). *Darwin's Dangerous Idea: Evolution and the Meaning of Life.* New York: Simon and Schuster.

Devlin, K. J. (1999). *Infosense: Turning Information into Knowledge.* New York: W. H. Freeman & Co.

de Vore, I., ed. (1965). *Primate Behaviour: Studies of Monkeys and Apes.* New York: Holt, Rinehart and Winston.

de Waall, F. (1982). *Chimpanzee Politics: Power and Sex among Apes.* New York: Harper and Row. [*La política del chimpancé.* Madrid: Alianza Editorial, 1993].

Diamond, J. M. (1992). *The Third Chimpanzee: The Evolution and Future of the Human Animal.* New York: Harper Collins.

———. (1997). *Why Is Sex Fun? The Evolution of Human Sexuality.* New York: Basic Books.

Ducrot, O. and Todorov, T. (1972). *Encyclopedic Dictionary of the Sciences of Language.* Translated by Catherine Porter. Baltimore: Johns Hopkins University Press, 1979. [*Diccionario enciclopédico de las ciencias del lenguaje.* Buenos Aires: Siglo XXI].

Eco, U. (1973). *Travels in Hyperreality.* Translated by William Weaver. New York: Harcourt Brace Jovanovich, 1986.

Edelman, G. M. (1992). *Bright Air, Brilliant Fire: On the Matter of the Mind.* New York, Basic Books.

Ferrater Mora, J. (1979). *Diccionario de Filosofía* [Dictionary of Philosophy]. Sixth Edition. Madrid: Alianza Editorial.

Fleming, P. (1996). "Neanderthals." Available at http://www.proam.com/origins/research/neand3.htm.

Fodor, J. and Piatelli–Palmarini, M. (2010). *What Darwin Got Wrong.* New York: Farrar, Straus and Giroux.

Foley, J. (1996). "Fossil Hominids." Available at http://earth.ics.edu:8080/faqs/fossil_hominids.html/ramidus.

Fox, D. and Smolka, J. (2002). "The Inner Savant." *Discover* 23 (2): 44–9. ["El genio interior." In *Discover en español* 6:4, April 2002].

Frege, G. (1892). "On Sense and Reference." Translated by M. Black. In *Translations from the Philosophical Writings of Gottlob Frege*, P. Geach and M. Black (eds. and trans.), Oxford: Blackwell, third edition, 1980.

Freud, S. (1893). "On the Psychical Mechanism of Hysterical Phenomena: Preliminary Communication." SE 2:1–17.

————. (1895). "Project for a Scientific Psychology." SE 1:281–391.

————. (1896). "Further Remarks on the Neuro–Psychoses of Defence." SE 3:157–185.

————. (1900). *The Interpretation of Dreams*. SE 5.

————. (1905). "Fragment of an Analysis of a Case of Hysteria." SE 7:1–122.

————. (1908). "Creative Writers and Day–Dreaming." SE 9:141–154.

————. (1909a). "Analysis of a Phobia in a Five–Year–Old Boy." SE 10:3–152.

————. (1909b). "Notes upon a Case of Obsessional Neurosis." SE 10:153–318.

————. (1912a). "The Dynamics of Transference." SE 12:97–108.

————. (1914a). "Remembering, Repeating and Working–Through." SE 12:145–156.

————. (1914b). "On Narcissism: An Introduction." SE 14:67–102.

————. (1915). "Instincts and Their Vicissitudes." SE 14:109–140.

————. (1915b). "The Unconscious." SE 14:159–215.

————. (1916). "Introductory Lectures on Psycho–Analysis." SE 16:241–463.

————. (1917). "Mourning and Melancholia." SE 14:237–258.

————. (1918). "From the History of an Infantile Neurosis." SE 17:1–124.

————. (1920). "Beyond the Pleasure Principle." SE 18:1–64.

————. (1923). "The Infantile Genital Organization." SE 19:139–146.

————. (1924). "The Dissolution of the Oedipus Complex." SE 19:171–180.

————. (1932). "New Introductory Lectures on Psycho–Analysis." SE 22:1–182.

————. (1937). "Analysis Terminable and Interminable." SE 23:209–254.

————. and Breuer, J. (1893–95) *Studies on Hysteria*. SE 2.

Gardner, R. A. and Gardner, B. T. (1969). "Teaching Sign Language to a Chimpanzee." *Science* 165 (3894): 664–672.

Gee, H. (1996). "Neanderthal Winter Collection." Available at http://www.nature.com/nature7.html.

Gibbs, W. (2001). "On the Termination of Species." *Scientific American* 285 (5): 40–9.

Glanville, R. (1999). "Acts Between and Between Acts." In Ascott, R., ed., op. cit., pp. 11–16.

Gleick, J. (1987). *Chaos: Making a New Science*. New York: Penguin Books.

————. (1999). *Faster: The Acceleration of Just About Everything*. New York: Pantheon Books.

Glocer Fiorini, L., ed. (2008). *El cuerpo. Lenguajes y silencios* [The Body: Languages and Silences]. Buenos Aires: Lugar Editorial and APA Editorial, Buenos Aires.

Goodall, J. (1965). "Chimpanzees on the Gombe Streem Reserve." In de Vore, I., ed., op. cit., pp. 425–473.

Gosse, P. H. (1857). *Omphalos: An Attempt to Unite the Geological Knot*. London: John Van Voors; Paternoster Row.

Green, M. S. (1999). "Moore's Many Paradoxes." *Philosophical Papers* 28 (2): 97–109.

Griffiths, A. P. (1963). "On Belief." In Griffiths, A. P., ed. *Knowledge and Belief*. Oxford: Oxford University Press, 1967, pp. 127–143. ["Creencia." In Griffiths, A. P., ed. *Conocimiento y creencia*. Mexico: Fondo de Cultura Económica, 1974].

————., ed. (1967). *Knowledge and Belief*, op cit. [*Conocimiento y Creencia*, op. cit.].

Guth, A. (1997). *The Inflationary Universe: The Quest for a New Theory of Cosmic Origins*. New York: Penguin.

Hawking, S. and Mlodinow, L. (2005). *A Briefer History of Time*. New York: Bantam.

Hinde, R. A. and Fisher, J. (1951). "Further Observations on the Opening of Milk Bottles by Birds." *British Birds* 44 (12): 393–396.

Hintikka, J. (1962). *Knowledge and Belief: An Introduction to the Logic of the Two Notions*. Ithaca, NY: Cornell University Press.

Hofstadter, D. (1979). *Gödel, Escher, Bach: An Eternal Golden Braid*. New York: Penguin.

————. (2007). *I Am a Strange Loop*. New York: Basic Books.

Holden, C. (1998). "No Last Word on Language Origins." *Science* 282 (5393): 1455–58.

Hublin, J–J. et al. (1995). "The Mousterian Site of Zafarraya (Andalusia, Spain): Dating and Implications of the Paleolithic Peopling Process in Western Europe." *Paléontologie humaine / Human paleontology*. Comptes–Rendus de l'Acádemmie des Sciences de Paris. (321) 2a: 931–7.

Johanson, D. C. and Edey, M. (1981). *Lucy: The Beginnings of Humankind*. London: Penguin, p. 20.

Kandel, E. (1998). "A New Intellectual Framework for Psychiatry." *Am J Psychiatry* 155 (4): 457–469.

———. (1999). "Biology and the Future of Psychoanalysis: A New Intellectual Framework for Psychiatry Revisited." *Am J Psychiatry* 156 (4): 505–524.

Kawamura, S. (1963). "The Process of Sub–Cultural Propagation Among Japanese Macaques." In Southwick, C. S., ed. *Primate Social Behavior*. Princeton, NJ: Van Nostrand, pp. 82–99.

Klein, M. (1955). "The Psychoanalytic Play Technique, Its History and Significance." In *The Writings of Melanie Klein*, Vol. 3. London: Hogarth Press, pp. 122–140.

Klein, R. (1989). *The Human Career: Human, Biological and Cultural Origins*. Chicago: University of Chicago Press, 1999.

Lacan, J. (1949). "The Mirror Stage as Formative of the Function of the I." In *Écrits: A Selection*. Translated by Alan Sheridan. New York: W. W. Norton, 1977, pp. 1–7. ["El estadio del espejo como formador de la función del yo." In *Escritos*, Vol. 1. Buenos Aires: Siglo XXI Editores Argentina].

———. (1956). *Seminario 4. "La relación de objeto"* [Seminar 4. Object Relations]. Buenos Aires: Paidós, 1994.

———. (1964). *The Four Fundamental Concepts of Psycho–Analysis*. Translated by Alan Sheridan. London: Hogarth, 1977. [*Los cuatro conceptos fundamentales del psicoanálisis* Barcelona: Barral, 1977].

———. (1967/1968). *L'Acte Psychanalytique* [The Psychoanalytic Act]. (Unpublished transcription of Seminar XV).

LaHaye, R. (1999). "The ICR and Lucy: Bearing False Witness against Thy Neighbor." Available at http://www.eskimo.com/~pierres/lucy.html.

Laplace, P. S. (1814). *A Philosophical Essay on Probabilities*. Translated by F. W. Truscott and F.L. Emory. New York: Dover, 1951.

Laplanche, J. (1992). "The Unfinished Copernican Revolution." Translated by Luke Thurston. In *Essays on Otherness*. London: Routledge, 1999, pp. 53–85. ["La revolución copernicana inacabada." In *La prioridad del otro en psicoanálisis*. Buenos Aires: Amorrortu Editores].

——— and Pontalis, J. D. (1959). *The Language of Psycho–Analysis*. Translated by Donald Nicholson–Smith. London: The Hogarth Press, 1973. [*Diccionario de psicoanálisis*. Buenos Aires: Editorial Labor, 1967].

Lemley, B. (2002). "Guth's Grand Guess." *Discover* 23 (4): 32–39. ["La gran adivinanza de Guth." *Discover en español* 6: 5, May].

Leroi–Gourhan, A. (1975). "The Flowers Found with Shanidar IV, a Neanderthal Burial in Iraq." *Science* 190: 562–564.

Levín, R. (1995). "El psicoanálisis y su relación con la historia de la infancia" [Psychoanalysis and its Relationship with the History of Childhood]. *Psicoanálisis* 17 (3): 613–33.

Lévi–Strauss, C. (1958). *Structural Anthropology*. Translated by Claire Jacobson and Brooke Grundfest Schoepf. New York: Basic Books, 1963. [*Antropología Estructural*. Buenos Aires: EUDEBA, 1968].

———. (1962). *The Savage Mind*. Translated by John and Doreen Weightman. Chicago: The University of Chicago Press. [*La pensée sauvage*. Paris: Librairie Plon].

Lévy, P. (1997). *Collective Intelligence: Mankind's Emerging World in Cyberspace*. New York: Basic Books.

Lewkowicz, I. (1990). "Cultura, inconsistencia, consistencias, dialéctica" [Culture, Inconsistency, Dialectic] (Unpublished).

———. (1997). "La irrupción del acontecimiento: Badiou, Deleuze, Castoriadis" [The Bursting–In of the Event: Badiou, Deleuze, Castoriadis]. Seminar taught at AAPPG, Buenos Aires.

———. (2000). Personal communication.

———. (2004). *Pensar sin Estado* [Thinking without the State]. Buenos Aires: Paidós.

Lewin, R. (1987). *Bones of Contention: Controversies in the Search for Human Origins*. New York: Simon and Schuster.

184   *References*

Linnaeus, C. (1735). *Sistema Naturae*. Edited by Maria Sara Johanna Engel–Ledeboer and Hendrik Engel. Amsterdam: B. de Graff, 1964.

Li, W. H. and Graur, D. (1991). *Fundamentals of Molecular Biology*. Sunderland, MA: Sinauer Associates.

Lorenz, K. (1973). *Behind the Mirror, a Search for A Natural History of Human Knowledge*. Translated by Ronald Taylor. Boston: Houghton Mifflin Harcourt, 1974. [*La otra cara del espejo*. Barcelona: Plaza & Janes, 1983].

Marwick, E. W. (1974). "Nature versus Nurture: Patterns and Trends in Seventeenth–Century Child–Rearing." In deMause, L., ed. *History of Childhood*, op. cit., 259–301. ["Naturaleza y Educación: Pautas y tendencias de la crianza de niños en la Francia del siglo XVII." In deMause, L., ed., op. cit., pp 286–332].

Maynard Smyth, J. (1986). "Contemplating Life without Sex." *Nature* 324: 300–301

Medawar, P. (1954). "The Future of Man." In *The Future of Man: The BBC Lectures*. New York: Basic Books, 1960.

Meltzer, D. et al. (1975). *Explorations in Autism: A Psycho–analytical Study*. Perth: Clunie Press.

Miller, B. et al. (1998). "Emergence of Artistic Talent in Frontotemporal Dementia." *Neurology* 51 (4): 978–982.

Milner, J. C. (1988). "El material del olvido" [The Material of Forgetting]. In Yosef Yerushalmi, ed. *Usos del olvido* [Uses of Forgetting]. Buenos Aires: Nueva Visión, 1989, pp. 67–78.

Moguillansky, R. (1999). *Vínculo y relación de objeto*. Buenos Aires: Polemos.

Moore, G. E. (1925). *Principia Ethica*. Cambridge, UK: Cambridge University Press.

Moreno, J. (1993). "Lo traumático y el vínculo parento–filial" [The Traumatic and the Parent–Child Link]. *Diarios Clínicos* 6: 33–38.

———. (1994). "La histeria hoy, la sexualidad hoy" [Hysteria Today, Sexuality Today]. *Psicoanálisis* 16 (2): 357–369.

———. (1997). "Freud, la castración, la feminidad" [Freud, Castration, Femininity]. Presented at the 40 International Psychoanalytic Congress, Barcelona, July.

———. (1998). "Pubertad" [Puberty]. *Cuadernos de APdeBA* 1: 11–37.

———. (1999). "Realidade Virtual e Psicanálise" [Virtual Reality and Psychoanalysis]. *Revista de Psicanálise* 4 (3): 535–545.

———. (2000a). "¿Hay lugar para lo indeterminado en psicoanálisis?" [Is There Room for the Undertermined in Psychoanalysis?] In Berenstein, I., ed., op. cit., pp. 76–115.

———. (2000b). "Conexión, asociación, realidad virtual y psicoanálisis" [Connection, Association, Virtual Reality, and Psychoanalysis]. Presented at the Scientific Colloquium, APdeBA, November.

———. (2000c). "La interfase Edipo Narciso" [The Oedipus–Narcissus Interface]. Presented at the XXIII Fepal Conference, Gramado, Brazil, September.

———. (2009a). "The Splitting of the Ego and Virtual Reality." In Bokanowski, T. and Lewkowicz, S., eds., op. cit., pp. 84–95.

———. (2009b). "Cuerpo y realidad virtual" [The Body and Virtual Reality]. In Glocer Fiorini, L., ed., op. cit., pp. 201–216.

———. (2010). *Tiempo y trauma. Continuidades rotas* [Time and Trauma: Broken Continuities]. Buenos Aires: Lugar editorial.

Moxon, R. and Wills, C. (2000). "DNA Microsatellites: Agents of Evolution?" *Scientific American* 280 (1): 94–99.

Nietzsche, F. (1885). *Thus Spoke Zarathustra: A Book for All and None*. Translated by Walter Kaufmann. New York: Penguin, 1969.

Norton–Griffiths, M. (1967). "Some Ecological Aspects of the Feeding Behaviour of the Oystercatcher *Haematopus ostralegus* on the Edible Mussel *Mytilus edulis*." *Ibis* 109: 412–424.

———. (1969). "The Organization, Control and Development of Parental Feeding in the Oystercatcher (Haematopus ostralegus)." *Behaviour* 34: 55–114.

O'Reilly, T. (2005). "What Is Web 2.0? Design Patterns and Business Models for the Next Generation of Software." Available at http://www.oreillynet.com/pub/a/oreilly/tim/news/2005/09/30/what–is–web–20.html.

Old Testament, The King James Version. Available at http://www.kingjamesbibleonline.org/ Genesis–Chapter–1/

Ortega y Gasset, J. (1940). *Ideas y creencias* [Ideas and Beliefs]. Madrid: Alianza Editorial, 2001. [The essay "Ideas and Beliefs" was included as an appendix in *What Is Knowledge*. Translated and edited by Jorge García–Gómez. Albany: SUNY Press, 2001].

Orwell, G. (1949). *1984*. London: Secker and Warburg.

Pääbo, S. (2010). "A Draft Sequence of the Neanderthal Genome." *Science* 328 (5979): 710–722.

Pearson, H. (2001). "Humanity: It's All in the Mind." *Nature Science Updates*. Available at http://www.nature.com/news/2001/010424/full/news010426–8.html.

Peirce, C. S. *The Essential Peirce. Selected Philosophical Writings. Volume 2 (1893–1913)*. Edited by The Peirce Edition Project. Bloomington, IN: Indiana University Press, 1998.

Pfeiffer, J. (1982). *The Creative Explosion: An Inquiry into the Origins of Art and Religion*. New York: Harper and Row.

Prensky, M. (2004). "The Emerging Online Life of the Digital Native: What They Do Differently because of Technology, and How They Do It." Available at http://www.marcprensky. com/writing/Prensky–The_Emerging_Online_Life_of_the_Digital_Native–03.pdf.

Price, H. H. (1934). "Some Considerations about Belief." In Griffiths, A. P., ed., op. cit., pp. 41–59. ["Algunas consideraciones sobre la creencia." In Griffiths, A. P., ed., op. cit.].

Pringe, Heather (2013). "The Origins of Creativity." *Scientific American* 308 (3): 24–29.

Puget, J. (2000). Personal communication.

———. and Berenstein, I. (1989). *Psicoanálisis de la pareja matrimonial* [Psychoanalysis of the Matrimonial Couple]. Buenos Aires: Paidós.

Rheingold, H. (1991). *Virtual Reality: The Revolutionary Technology of Computer–Generated Artificial Worlds—And How It Promises to Transform Society*. New York: Summit Books.

———. (2002). *Smart Mobs: The Next Social Revolution*. Cambridge, MA: Perseus Books Group.

Ridley, M. (1993). *The Red Queen: Sex and Evolution of Human Nature*. New York: Penguin Books.

Rizzolatti, G. and Sinigaglia, C. (2006). *Mirrors In The Brain: How Our Minds Share Actions and Emotions*. Translated by Frances Anderson. New York: Oxford University Press, 2008. [*Las neuronas espejo. Los mecanismos de la empatía emocional*. Barcelona: Paidós].

Ross, J. B. (1974). "The Middle–Class Child in Urban Italy, Fourteenth to Early Sixteenth Century." In deMause, L., ed. op.cit., pp. 183–228 ["El niño de clase media en la Italia urbana del siglo XIV a principios del XVI." In deMause, L., ed, op. cit, pp. 206–254].

Rothschild, M.: (1993). "Cro–Magnon's Secret Weapon". *Forbes ASAP Magazine* (9/1993). Available at http://www.bionomics.org/text/resource/articles/ar_020.html.

Sacks, Oliver (1995). *An Anthropologist on Mars: Seven Paradoxical Tales*. New York: Knopf. [*Un antropólogo en Marte*. Barcelona: Anagrama, 1997].

Salomon, J. C. (1992). "Thus Spoke Neanderthal." *The Cancer Journal*. 5 (3). Editorial.

Sarlo, B. (2000). *Siete ensayos sobre Benjamin* [Seven Essays on Benjamin]. Buenos Aires: Fondo de Cultura Económica.

Savage–Rumbaugh, S., Shanker, S. G. and Taylor. T. J. (1998). *Apes, Language, and the Human Mind*. Oxford: Oxford University Press.

Sebeok, T., ed. (1977). *A Perfusion of Signs*. Bloomington, IN: Indiana University Press.

Seife, C. (2000). *Zero: The Biography of a Dangerous Idea*. New York: Viking Penguin.

Shreeve, J. (1995). *The Neanderthal Enigma: Solving the Mystery of Modern Human Origins*. New York: Viking Penguin.

Sibilia, P. (2005). *El Hombre Postorgánico: cuerpo, subjetividad y tecnologías digitales* [Post–organic Man: Body, Subjectivity, and Digital Technologies]. Buenos Aires: Fondo de Cultura Económica, 2005.

Siegfried, T. (2000). *The Bit and the Pendulum: From Quantum Computing to M Theory—The New Physics of Information*. New York: John Wiley & Sons, Incorporated.

Silberman, S. (2001). "The Geek Syndrome." *Wired* 9.12. Available at http://www.wired.com/ wired/archive/9.12/aspergers.html

Sophocles I: Oedipus The King, Oedipus at Colonus, Antigone. Translated by David Grene. New York: Penguin, 1991. ["Edipo Rey" and "Edipo en Colona." In *Esquilo, Sófocles, Eurípides. Obras completas.* Madrid: Cátedra, 2012].

Solecki, R. (1971). *Shanidar: The First Flower People.* New York: Knopf.

Stanley, S. M. (1996). *Children of the Ice Age: How a Global Catastrophe Allowed Humans to Evolve.* New York: W. H. Freeman and Company.

Steuer J. (1992). "Defining Virtual Reality: Dimensions Determining Telepresence." *Journal of Communication* 42 (4): 73–93.

Stewart, I. and Cohen, J. (1997). *Figments of Reality: The Evolution of the Curious Mind.* Cambridge, UK: Cambridge University Press.

Stringer, C. B. and McKie, R. (1996). *African Exodus: The Origin of Modern Humanity.* London: Jonathan Cape.

Stringer, C. and Andrews, P. (2005). *The Complete World of Human Evolution.* London and New York: Thames and Hudson.

Stringer, C. and Grün, R. (1991). "Time For the Last Neanderthals." *Nature* 351:701–2.

Strohemeier, J. and Wesbrook, P. (1999). *Divine Harmony: The Life and Teachings of Pythagoras.* Berkeley, CA: Berkeley Hills Books.

Surowiecki, J. (2004). *The Wisdom of Crowds.* [*Cien mejor que uno. La sabiduría de la multitud o por qué la mayoría siempre es más inteligente que la minoría.* Barcelona: Urano].

Tallamy, D. W. (1999). "Child Care among the Insects. Why Do Some Insect Parents Risk their Lives to Care for their Young?" *Scientific American* 280 (1): 72–77.

Tattersall, I. (2000). "Once We Were Not Alone." *Scientific American* 282 (1): 56–62.

———. (2001). "How We Came to Be Human." *Scientific American* 285 (6): 56–63.

———. (2002). *The Monkey in the Mirror: Essays on the Science of What Makes Us Human.* New York: Harcourt Inc.

Templeton, A. R. (2002). "Out of Africa Again and Again." *Nature* 416:45–51.

Treffert, D. A. (1989). *Extraordinary People: Understanding Savant Syndrome.* New York: Ballantine Books.

Treffert, D. A. and Wallace, G. L. (2002). "Islands of Genius." *Scientific American* 286 (6): 76–85.

Trinkaus, E. (1989a). "Morphological Contrasts between the Near Eastern Qafzeh–Skhul and Late Archaic Human Samples: Grounds for a Behavioral Difference?" In Akazawa, T., Aoki, K., and Kimura, T., eds., op. cit., pp. 277–294.

———., ed. (1989b): *The Emergence of Modern Humans. Biocultural Adaptations in the Later Pleistocene,* op. cit.

———. and Duarte, C. (2000). "The Hybrid Child from Portugal." *Scientific American* 282 (4): 102–3.

———. and Shipman, P. (1993). *The Neanderthals: Changing the Image of the Mankind.* New York: Knopf.

Tucker, M. S. (1974). "The Child as Beginning and End: Fifteenth and Sixteenth Century English Childhood." In deMause, L., ed., op. cit., pp. 229–57 ["El niño como principio y fin: la infancia en Inglaterra de los siglos XV y XVI." In deMause, L., ed., op. cit, pp 255–285].

Voltaire (1764). *Philosophical Dictionary Part 4.* In *The Works of Voltaire.* Vol. VI. Translated by William F. Fleming. Akron, OH: The Werner Company, 1904.

von Uexküll, Jakob (1934). "A Stroll through the World of Animals and Men." In *Instinctive Behavior: The Development of a Modern Concept.* Translated and edited by Claire H. Schiller. New York: International Universities Press, pp. 5–81.

Whiten, A. and Boesch, C. (2001). "The Culture of Chimpanzees." *Scientific American* 284 (1): 61–7.

Wickes, I. G. (1953). "A History of Infant Feeding. Part II. Seventeenth and Eighteenth Centuries." *Archives of Disease in Childhood* 28: 232–240.

Winnicott, D. (1971). *Playing and Reality.* London: Tavistock. [*Realidad y juego.* Buenos Aires: Galerna, 1972].

Wittgenstein, L. (1921). Tractatus Logico–Philosophicus. Translated by D.F. Pears and B.F. McGuinness. New York: Humanities Press, 1961.

————. (1953). *Philosophical Investigations*. Translated by G.E.M. Anscombe. Oxford: Blackwell.

Wolpoff, Milford (1997). " No 'Homo erectus' at Ngandong." Human Origins News, January 4.

Wong, K. (1998). "Ancestral Quandary: Neanderthals Not Our Ancestors? Not So Fast." *Scientific American* 278 (1): 30–2.

————. (1999). "Is Out of Africa Going out the Door?" *Scientific American* 281 (2): 13–14 .

————. (2000a). "Who Were the Neanderthals?" *Scientific American*, Special Edition 13 (2): 28–37.

————. (2000b). "Early Humans Ate Termites." Available at http://www.sciam.com/ news/ 011601/2.html.

Zeilinger, A. (2000). "Quantum Teleportation." *Scientific American* 282 (4): 32–41.

Zeman, J. (1977). "Peirce's Theory of Signs." In Sebeok, T., ed., op. cit., pp. 22–39.

Zilhao, J. and d'Errico, F. (2000). "A Case for Neanderthal Culture." *Scientific American* 13 (2): 34–5.

Index

About the Author

Julio Moreno received an MD (with honors) in 1968 and a PhD in Medical Sciences from Buenos Aires University in 1975. After working in basic science research at UCLA's Medical Center, he relocated to Buenos Aires, where he trained as a psychiatrist and psychoanalyst. He is currently a full member and training analyst of the Buenos Aires Psychoanalytic Association (APDEBA), as well as a specialist in child and adolescent psychoanalysis and in couple and family therapy. In addition, he is a faculty member in APdeBA's Psychoanalytic Institute, the Master's Program in Family and Couples at APdeBA's University Institute (of which he is co-director), the School of Psychology at Buenos Aires University, and the University of Hospital Italiano.

Moreno has published numerous journal articles and book chapters on physiology and psychoanalysis, as well as three books: *Ser humano. La inconsistencia, los vínculos, la crianza* [Being Human: Inconsistency, Links, Upbringing]; *Tiempo y trauma. Continuidades rotas* [Time and Trauma: Shattered Continuities]; and *La infancia y sus bordes. Desafíos para el psicoanálisis* [The Edges of Infancy: Challenges to Psychoanalysis].

Judith Filc, PhD, MD, is a translator, editor, and published poet. She has translated and edited articles and books for numerous presses and journals, including *The International Journal of Psychoanalysis* and *Psychoanalytic Dialogues*.